MILES MORALES

STRAIGHT OUT OF BROOKLYN

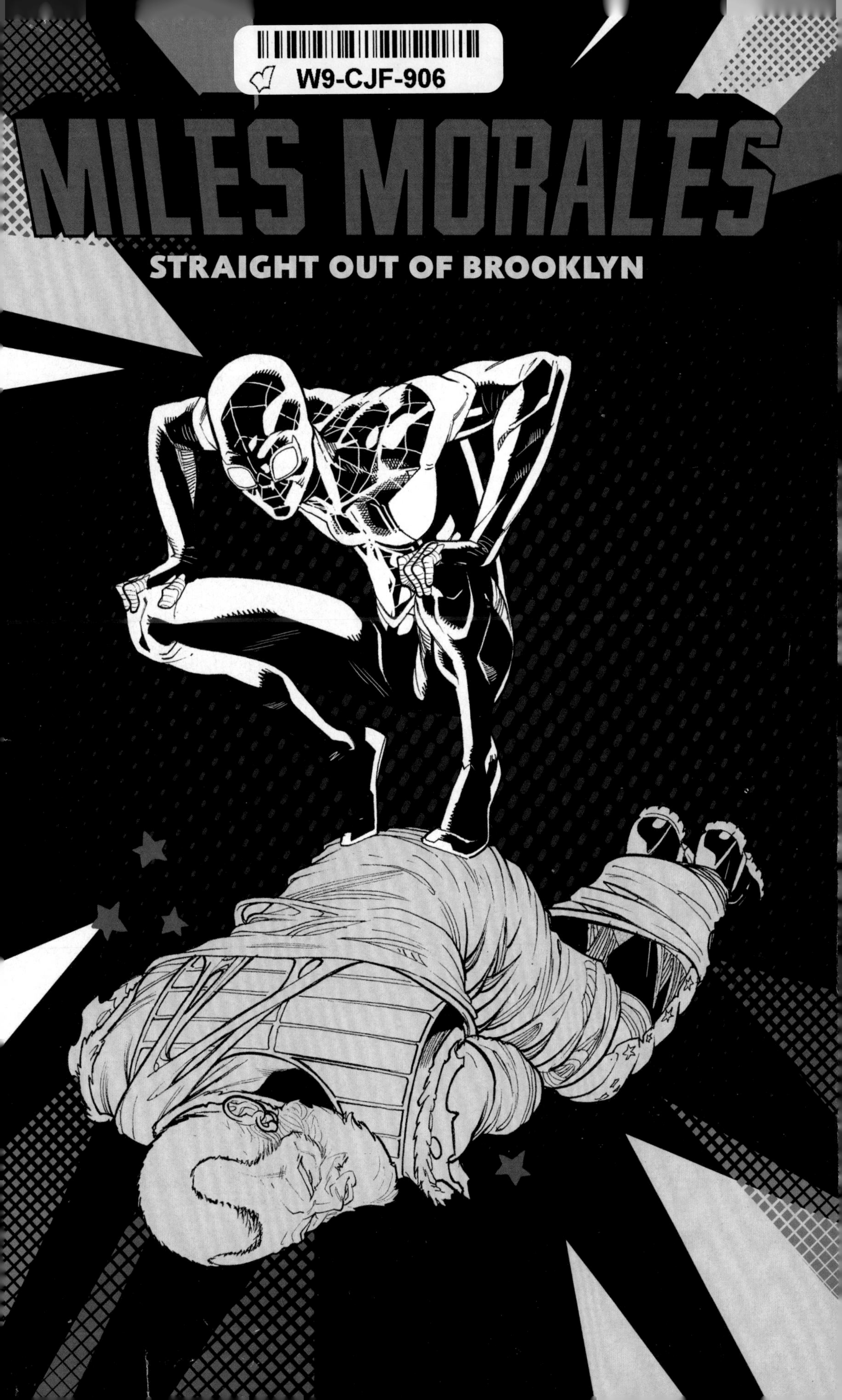

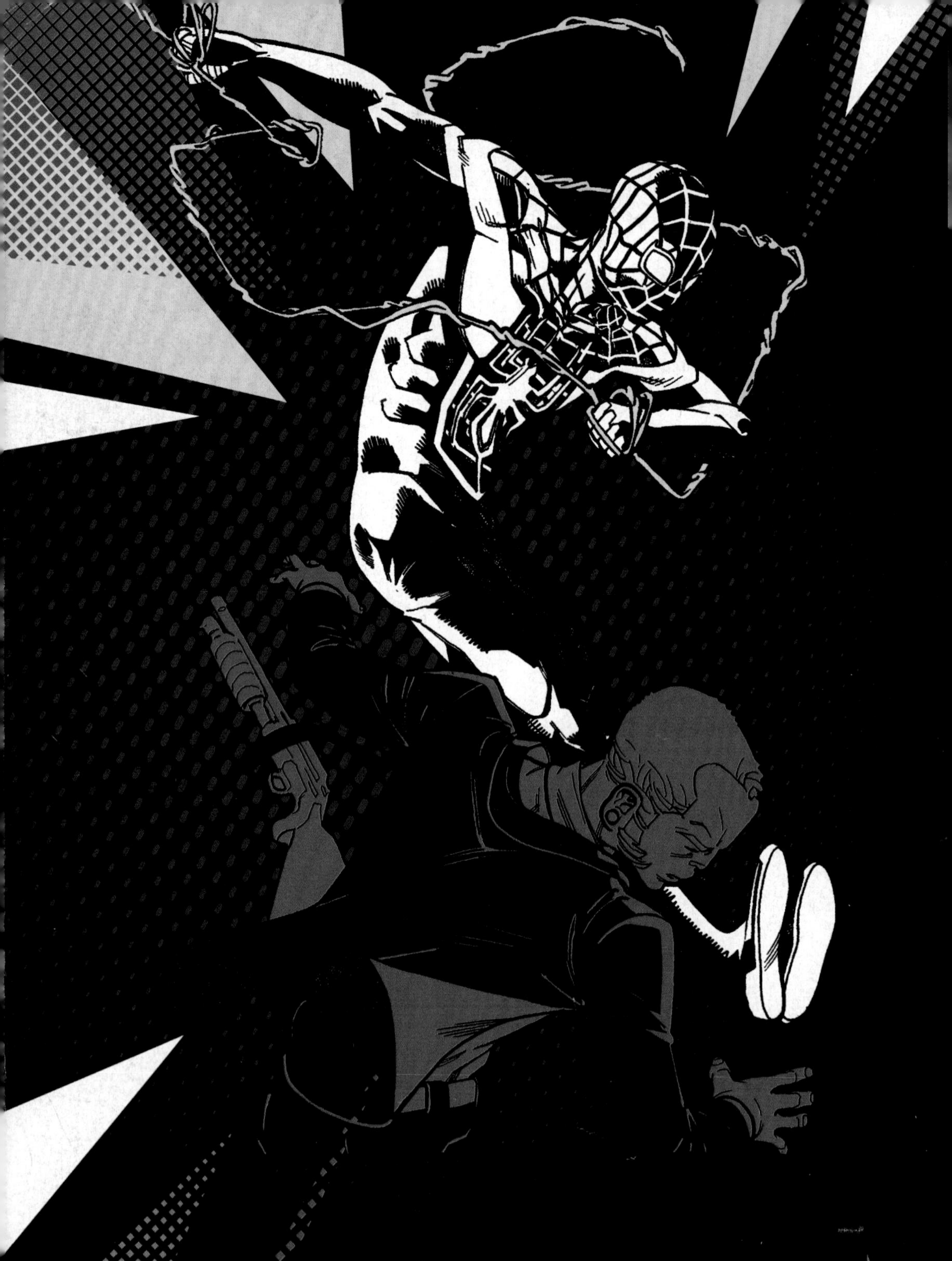

COLLECTION EDITOR **JENNIFER GRÜNWALD** + ASSISTANT EDITOR **CAITLIN O'CONNELL**
ASSOCIATE MANAGING EDITOR **KATERI WOODY** + EDITOR, SPECIAL PROJECTS **MARK D. BEAZLEY**
VP PRODUCTION & SPECIAL PROJECTS **JEFF YOUNGQUIST** + BOOK DESIGNER **JAY BOWEN**

SVP PRINT, SALES & MARKETING **DAVID GABRIEL** + DIRECTOR, LICENSED PUBLISHING **SVEN LARSEN**
EDITOR IN CHIEF **C.B. CEBULSKI** + CHIEF CREATIVE OFFICER **JOE QUESADA**
PRESIDENT **DAN BUCKLEY** + EXECUTIVE PRODUCER **ALAN FINE**

MILES MORALES VOL. 1: STRAIGHT OUT OF BROOKLYN. Contains material originally published in magazine form as MILES MORALES: SPIDER-MAN #1-6. First printing 2019. ISBN 978-1-302-91478-3. Published by MARVEL WORLDWIDE, INC., a subsidiary of MARVEL ENTERTAINMENT, LLC. OFFICE OF PUBLICATION: 135 West 50th Street, New York, NY 10020. **Printed in Canada.** DAN BUCKLEY, President, Marvel Entertainment; JOHN NEE, Publisher; JOE QUESADA, Chief Creative Officer; TOM BREVOORT, SVP of Publishing; DAVID BOGART, Associate Publisher & SVP of Talent Affairs; DAVID GABRIEL, SVP of Sales & Marketing, Publishing; JEFF YOUNGQUIST, VP of Production & Special Projects; DAN CARR, Executive Director of Publishing Technology; ALEX MORALES, Director of Publishing Operations; DAN EDINGTON, Managing Editor; SUSAN CRESPI, Production Manager; STAN LEE, Chairman Emeritus. For information regarding advertising in Marvel Comics or on Marvel.com, please contact Vit DeBellis, Custom Solutions & Integrated Advertising Manager, at vdebellis@marvel.com. For Marvel subscription inquiries, please call 888-511-5480. **Manufactured between 5/24/2019 and 6/25/2019 by SOLISCO PRINTERS, SCOTT, QC, CANADA.**

MILES MORALES

STRAIGHT OUT OF BROOKLYN

Saladin Ahmed
WRITER

Javier Garrón
ARTIST

David Curiel
COLOR ARTIST

VC's Cory Petit
LETTERER

Brian Stelfreeze (#1) &
Marco D'Alfonso (#2-6)
COVER ART

Kathleen Wisneski
ASSISTANT EDITOR

Nick Lowe
EDITOR

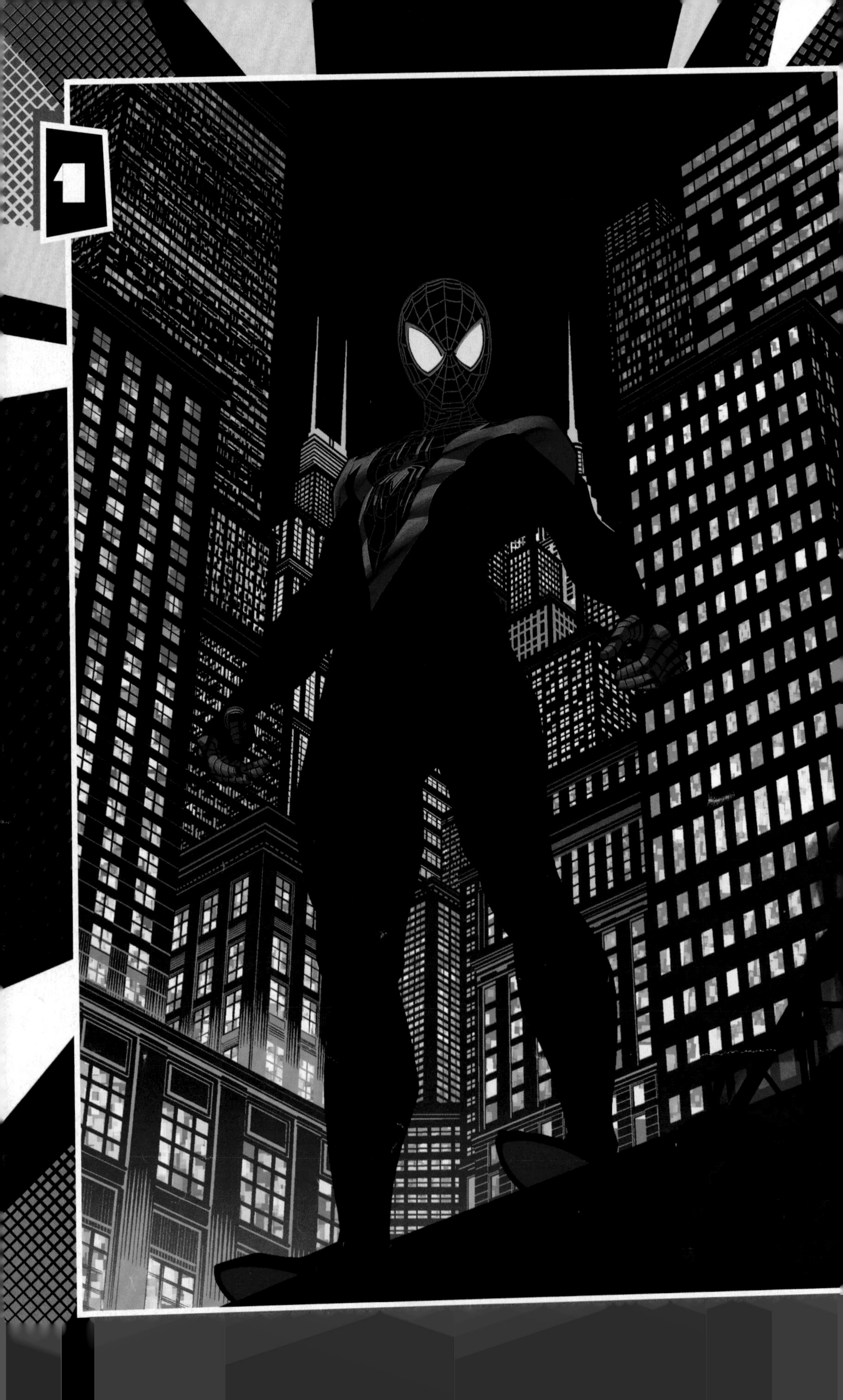
1

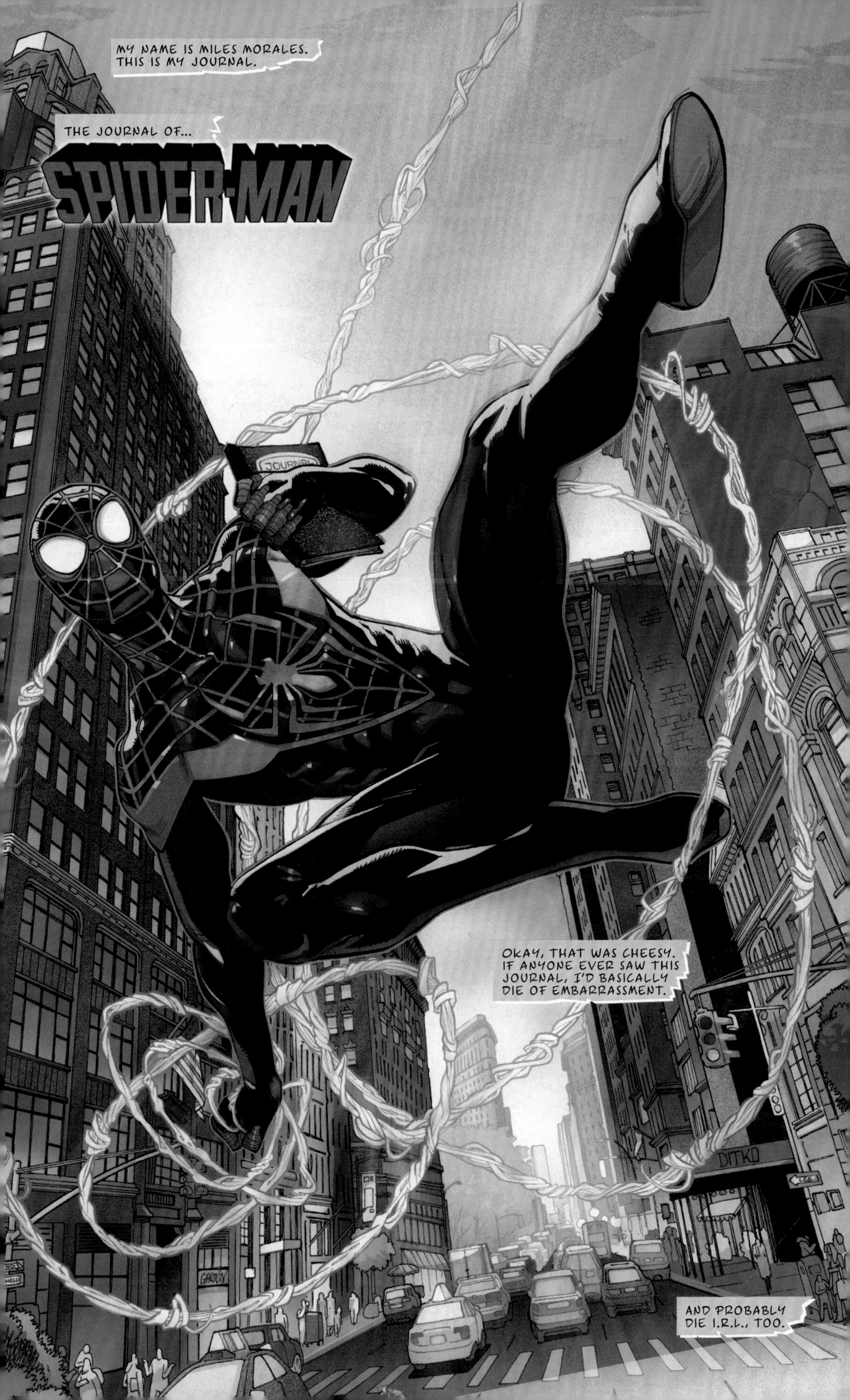
MY NAME IS MILES MORALES. THIS IS MY JOURNAL.
THE JOURNAL OF...
SPIDER-MAN
JOURNAL
OKAY, THAT WAS CHEESY. IF ANYONE EVER SAW THIS JOURNAL, I'D BASICALLY DIE OF EMBARRASSMENT.
DITKO
AND PROBABLY DIE I.R.L., TOO.

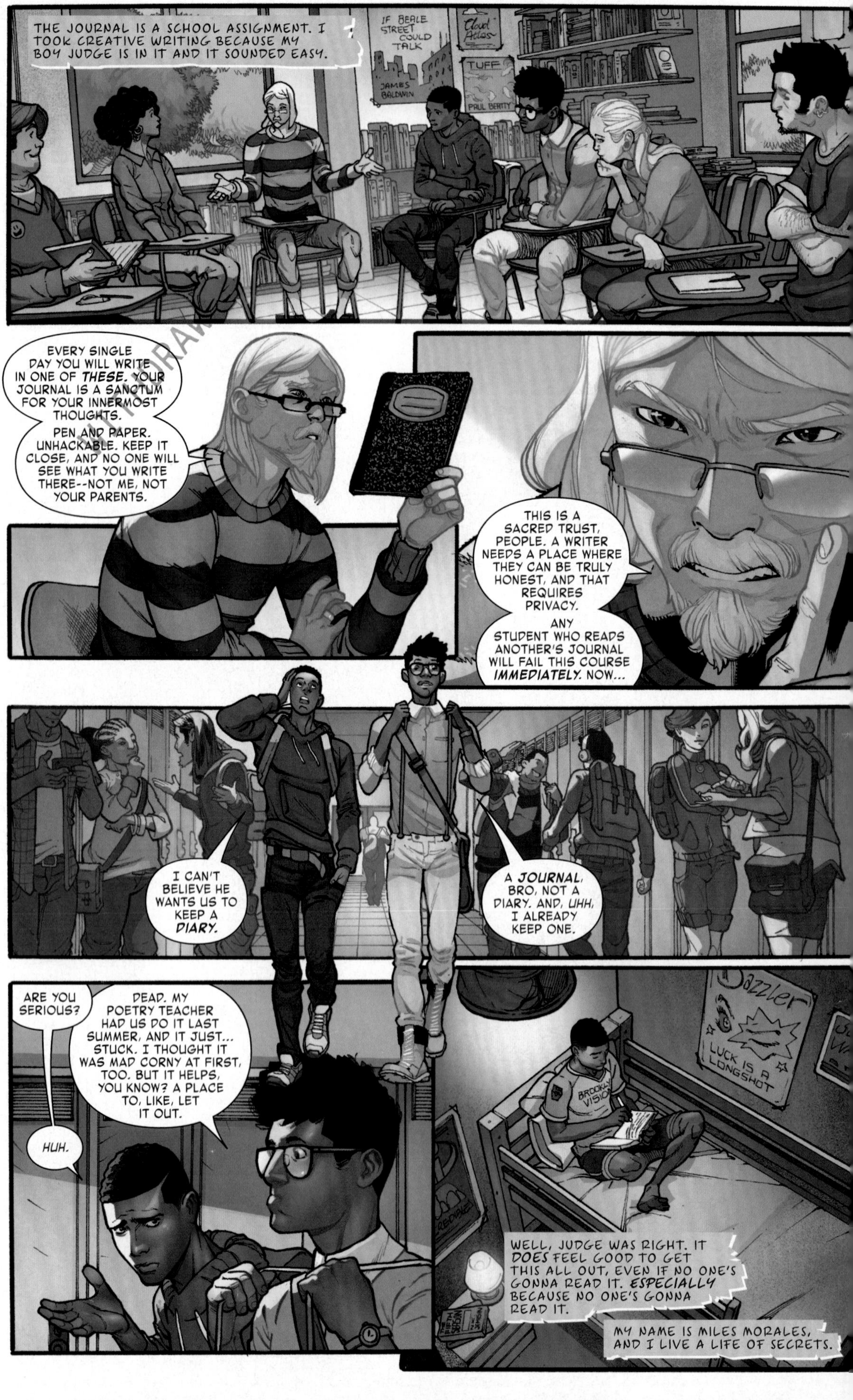

THE JOURNAL IS A SCHOOL ASSIGNMENT. I TOOK CREATIVE WRITING BECAUSE MY BOY JUDGE IS IN IT AND IT SOUNDED EASY.
IF BEALE STREET COULD TALK
JAMES BALDWIN
Cloud Atlas
TUFF
PAUL BEATTY
EVERY SINGLE DAY YOU WILL WRITE IN ONE OF THESE. YOUR JOURNAL IS A SANCTUM FOR YOUR INNERMOST THOUGHTS.
PEN AND PAPER. UNHACKABLE. KEEP IT CLOSE, AND NO ONE WILL SEE WHAT YOU WRITE THERE--NOT ME, NOT YOUR PARENTS.
THIS IS A SACRED TRUST, PEOPLE. A WRITER NEEDS A PLACE WHERE THEY CAN BE TRULY HONEST, AND THAT REQUIRES PRIVACY.
ANY STUDENT WHO READS ANOTHER'S JOURNAL WILL FAIL THIS COURSE IMMEDIATELY. NOW...
I CAN'T BELIEVE HE WANTS US TO KEEP A DIARY.
A JOURNAL, BRO, NOT A DIARY. AND, UHH, I ALREADY KEEP ONE.
ARE YOU SERIOUS?
DEAD. MY POETRY TEACHER HAD US DO IT LAST SUMMER, AND IT JUST... STUCK. I THOUGHT IT WAS MAD CORNY AT FIRST, TOO. BUT IT HELPS, YOU KNOW? A PLACE TO, LIKE, LET IT OUT.
HUH.
Dazzler
LUCK IS A LONGSHOT
BROOKLYN VISIONS
WELL, JUDGE WAS RIGHT. IT DOES FEEL GOOD TO GET THIS ALL OUT, EVEN IF NO ONE'S GONNA READ IT. ESPECIALLY BECAUSE NO ONE'S GONNA READ IT.
MY NAME IS MILES MORALES, AND I LIVE A LIFE OF SECRETS.

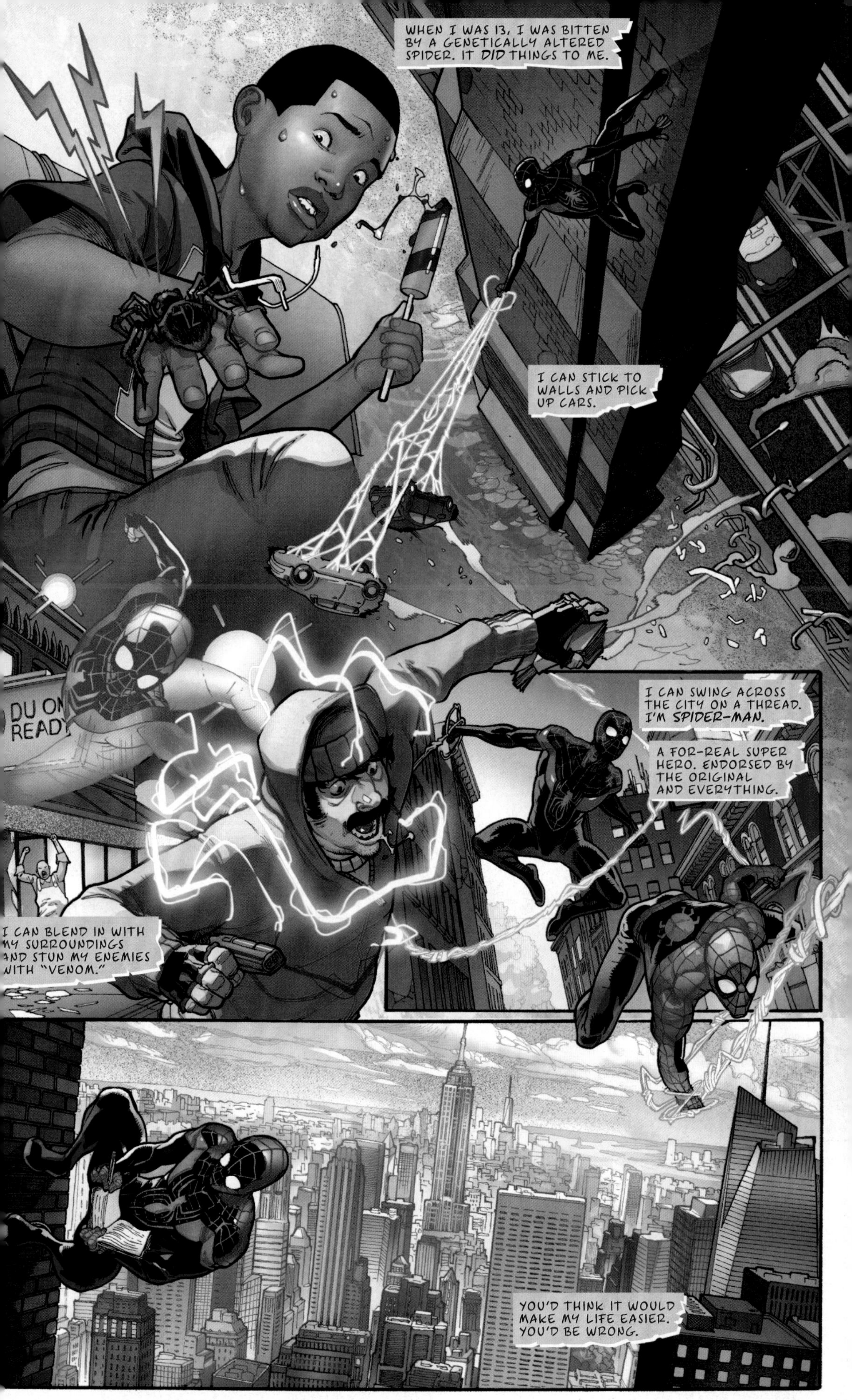

WHEN I WAS 13, I WAS BITTEN BY A GENETICALLY ALTERED SPIDER. IT DID THINGS TO ME.
I CAN STICK TO WALLS AND PICK UP CARS.
I CAN BLEND IN WITH MY SURROUNDINGS AND STUN MY ENEMIES WITH "VENOM."
DU ON READY
I CAN SWING ACROSS THE CITY ON A THREAD. I'M SPIDER-MAN.
A FOR-REAL SUPER HERO. ENDORSED BY THE ORIGINAL AND EVERYTHING.
YOU'D THINK IT WOULD MAKE MY LIFE EASIER. YOU'D BE WRONG.

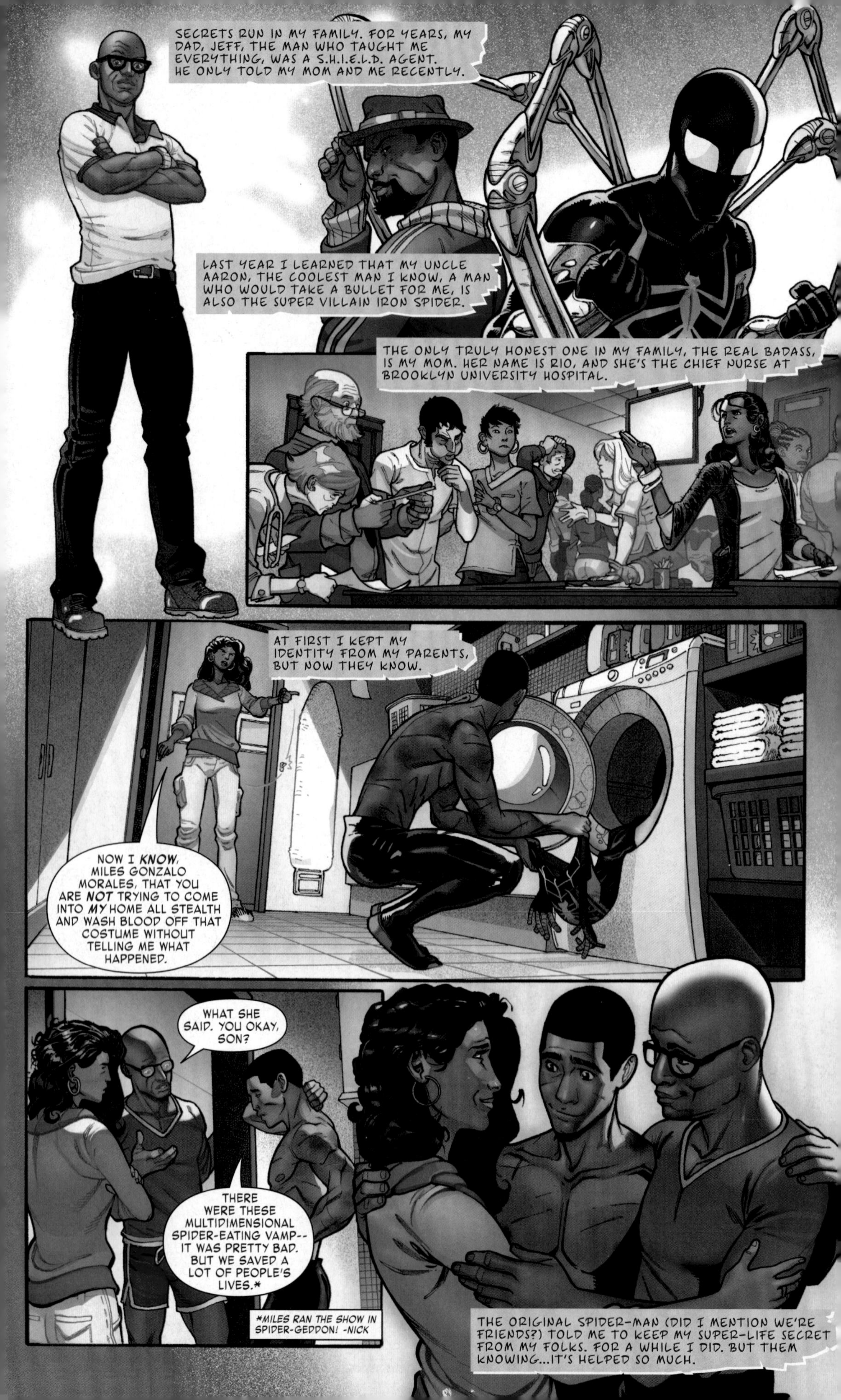
SECRETS RUN IN MY FAMILY. FOR YEARS, MY DAD, JEFF, THE MAN WHO TAUGHT ME EVERYTHING, WAS A S.H.I.E.L.D. AGENT. HE ONLY TOLD MY MOM AND ME RECENTLY.
LAST YEAR I LEARNED THAT MY UNCLE AARON, THE COOLEST MAN I KNOW, A MAN WHO WOULD TAKE A BULLET FOR ME, IS ALSO THE SUPER VILLAIN IRON SPIDER.
THE ONLY TRULY HONEST ONE IN MY FAMILY, THE REAL BADASS, IS MY MOM. HER NAME IS RIO, AND SHE'S THE CHIEF NURSE AT BROOKLYN UNIVERSITY HOSPITAL.
AT FIRST I KEPT MY IDENTITY FROM MY PARENTS, BUT NOW THEY KNOW.
NOW I KNOW, MILES GONZALO MORALES, THAT YOU ARE NOT TRYING TO COME INTO MY HOME ALL STEALTH AND WASH BLOOD OFF THAT COSTUME WITHOUT TELLING ME WHAT HAPPENED.
WHAT SHE SAID. YOU OKAY, SON?
THERE WERE THESE MULTIDIMENSIONAL SPIDER-EATING VAMP-- IT WAS PRETTY BAD. BUT WE SAVED A LOT OF PEOPLE'S LIVES.*
*MILES RAN THE SHOW IN SPIDER-GEDDON! -NICK
THE ORIGINAL SPIDER-MAN (DID I MENTION WE'RE FRIENDS?) TOLD ME TO KEEP MY SUPER-LIFE SECRET FROM MY FOLKS. FOR A WHILE I DID. BUT THEM KNOWING...IT'S HELPED SO MUCH.

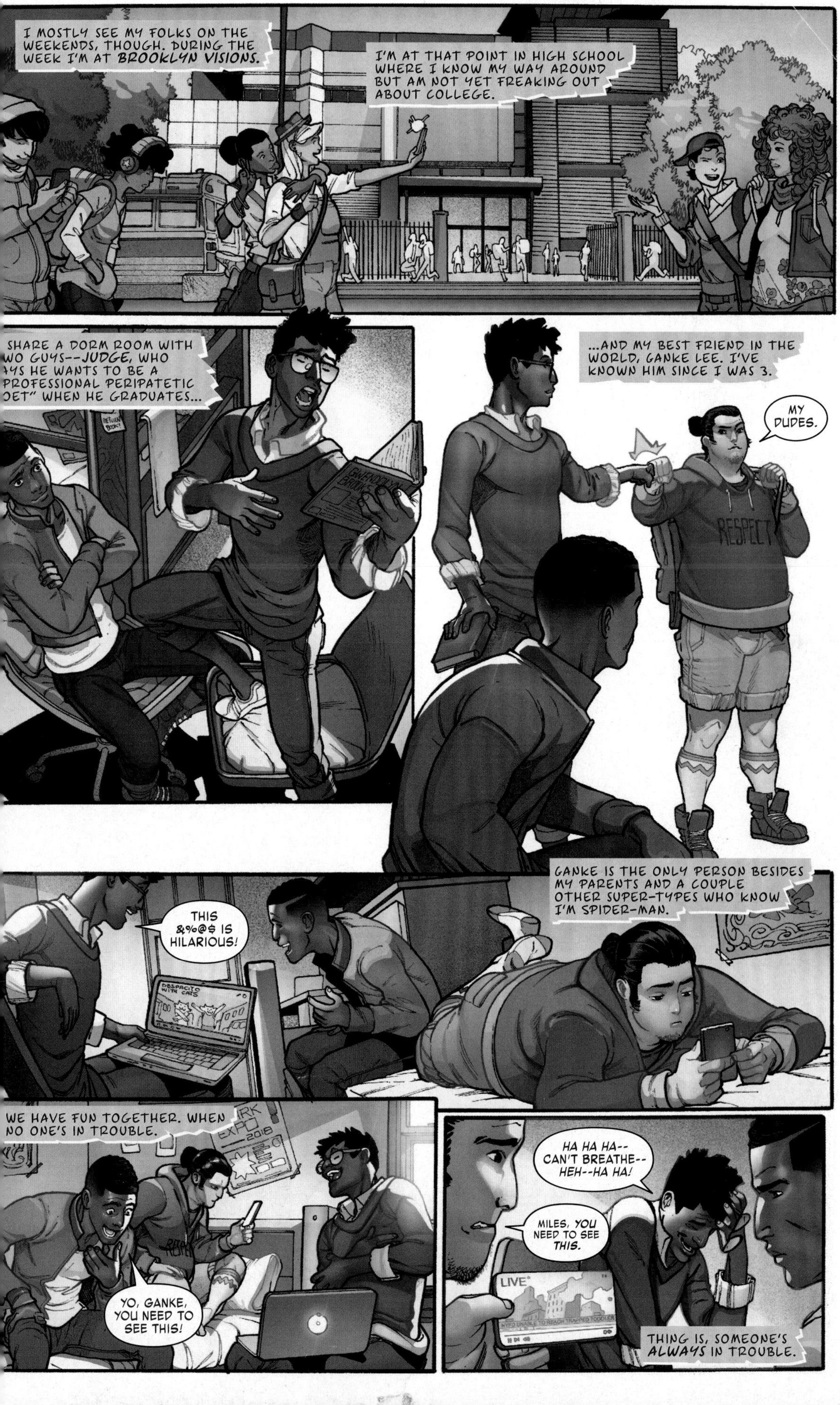
I MOSTLY SEE MY FOLKS ON THE WEEKENDS, THOUGH. DURING THE WEEK I'M AT BROOKLYN VISIONS.
I'M AT THAT POINT IN HIGH SCHOOL WHERE I KNOW MY WAY AROUND BUT AM NOT YET FREAKING OUT ABOUT COLLEGE.
SHARE A DORM ROOM WITH WO GUYS--JUDGE, WHO AYS HE WANTS TO BE A PROFESSIONAL PERIPATETIC OET" WHEN HE GRADUATES...
...AND MY BEST FRIEND IN THE WORLD, GANKE LEE. I'VE KNOWN HIM SINCE I WAS 3.
MY DUDES.
GANKE IS THE ONLY PERSON BESIDES MY PARENTS AND A COUPLE OTHER SUPER-TYPES WHO KNOW I'M SPIDER-MAN.
THIS &%@$ IS HILARIOUS!
DESPACITO WITH CATS
WE HAVE FUN TOGETHER. WHEN NO ONE'S IN TROUBLE.
YO, GANKE, YOU NEED TO SEE THIS!
HA HA HA-- CAN'T BREATHE-- HEH--HA HA!
MILES, YOU NEED TO SEE THIS.
LIVE
THING IS, SOMEONE'S ALWAYS IN TROUBLE.

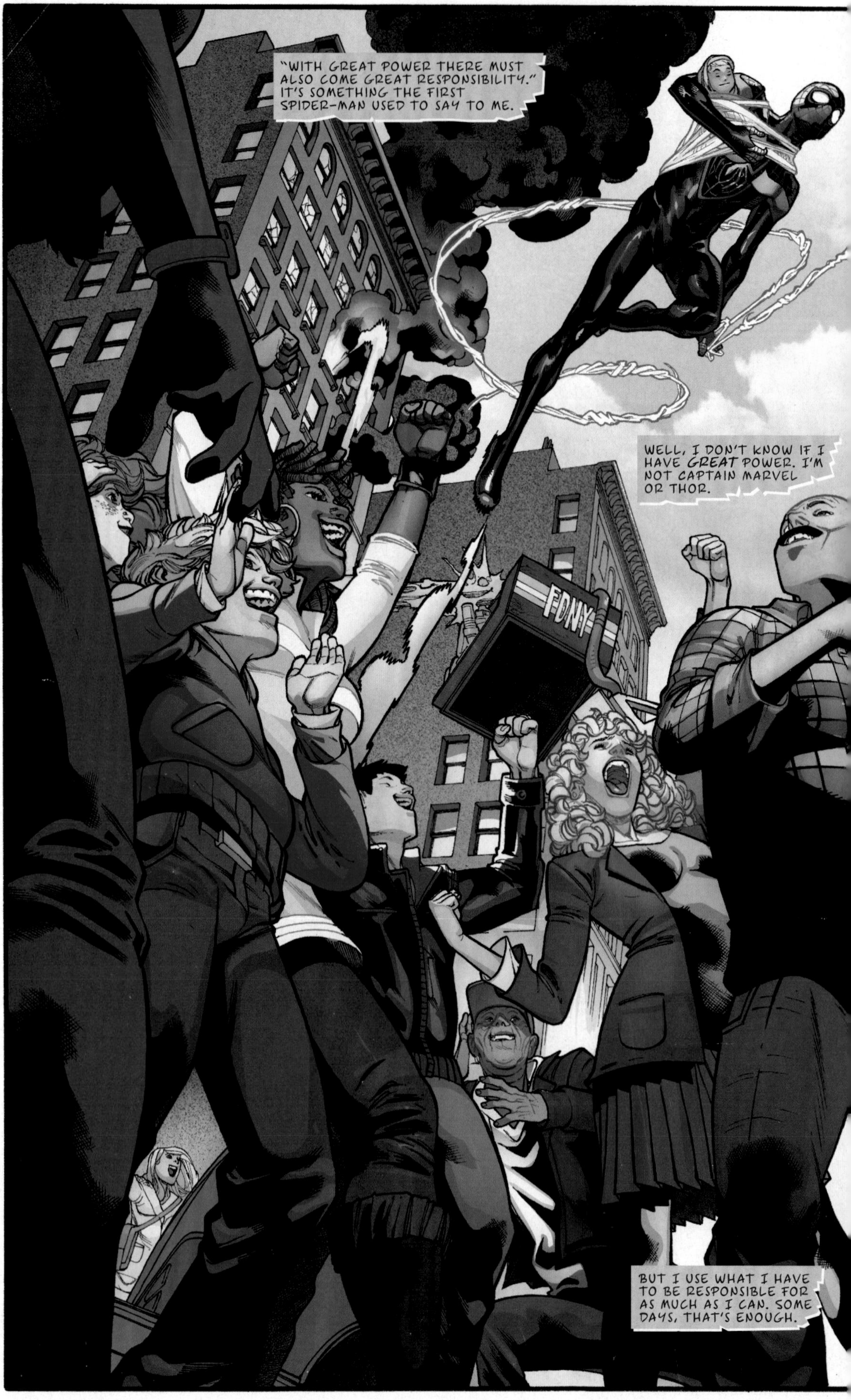
"WITH GREAT POWER THERE MUST ALSO COME GREAT RESPONSIBILITY." IT'S SOMETHING THE FIRST SPIDER-MAN USED TO SAY TO ME.
WELL, I DON'T KNOW IF I HAVE GREAT POWER. I'M NOT CAPTAIN MARVEL OR THOR.
FDNY
BUT I USE WHAT I HAVE TO BE RESPONSIBLE FOR AS MUCH AS I CAN. SOME DAYS, THAT'S ENOUGH.

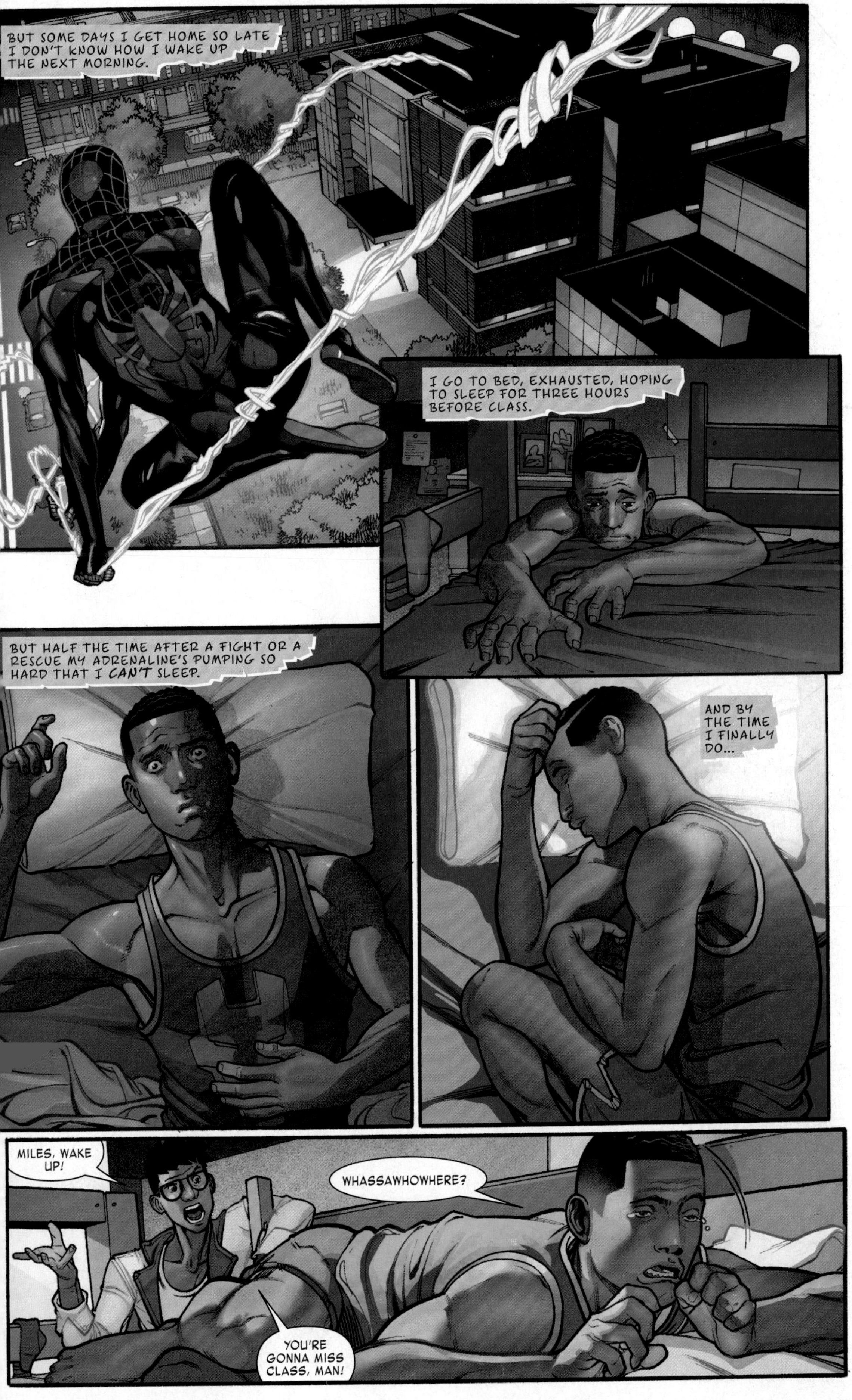
BUT SOME DAYS I GET HOME SO LATE I DON'T KNOW HOW I WAKE UP THE NEXT MORNING.
I GO TO BED, EXHAUSTED, HOPING TO SLEEP FOR THREE HOURS BEFORE CLASS.
BUT HALF THE TIME AFTER A FIGHT OR A RESCUE MY ADRENALINE'S PUMPING SO HARD THAT I CAN'T SLEEP.
AND BY THE TIME I FINALLY DO...
MILES, WAKE UP!
WHASSAWHOWHERE?
YOU'RE GONNA MISS CLASS, MAN!

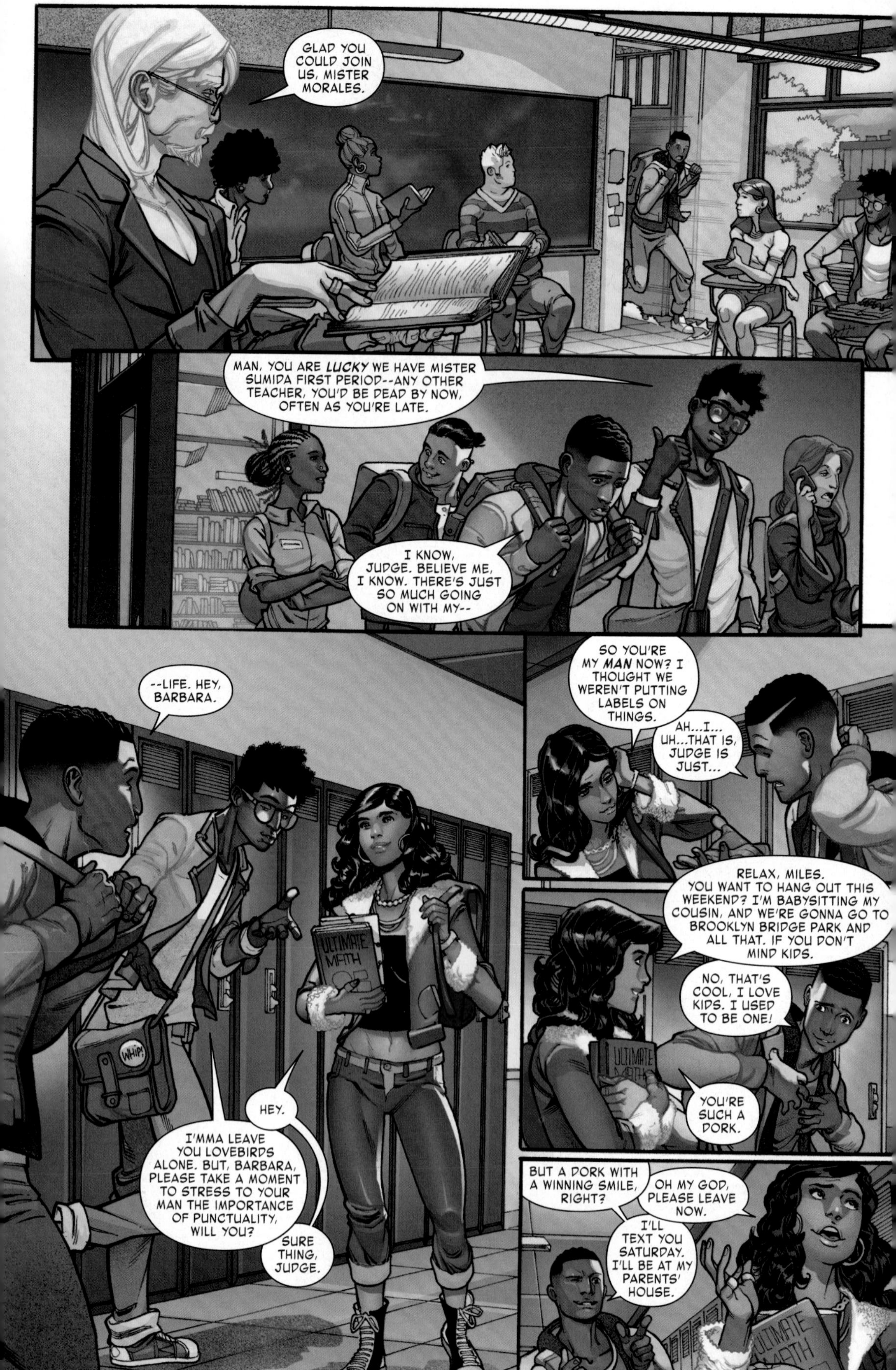
GLAD YOU COULD JOIN US, MISTER MORALES.
MAN, YOU ARE LUCKY WE HAVE MISTER SUMIDA FIRST PERIOD--ANY OTHER TEACHER, YOU'D BE DEAD BY NOW, OFTEN AS YOU'RE LATE.
I KNOW, JUDGE. BELIEVE ME, I KNOW. THERE'S JUST SO MUCH GOING ON WITH MY--
--LIFE. HEY, BARBARA.
HEY.
I'MMA LEAVE YOU LOVEBIRDS ALONE. BUT, BARBARA, PLEASE TAKE A MOMENT TO STRESS TO YOUR MAN THE IMPORTANCE OF PUNCTUALITY, WILL YOU?
SURE THING, JUDGE.
ULTIMATE MATH
WHIP!
SO YOU'RE MY MAN NOW? I THOUGHT WE WEREN'T PUTTING LABELS ON THINGS.
AH...I... UH...THAT IS, JUDGE IS JUST...
RELAX, MILES. YOU WANT TO HANG OUT THIS WEEKEND? I'M BABYSITTING MY COUSIN, AND WE'RE GONNA GO TO BROOKLYN BRIDGE PARK AND ALL THAT. IF YOU DON'T MIND KIDS.
NO, THAT'S COOL, I LOVE KIDS. I USED TO BE ONE!
YOU'RE SUCH A DORK.
BUT A DORK WITH A WINNING SMILE, RIGHT?
OH MY GOD, PLEASE LEAVE NOW.
I'LL TEXT YOU SATURDAY. I'LL BE AT MY PARENTS' HOUSE.

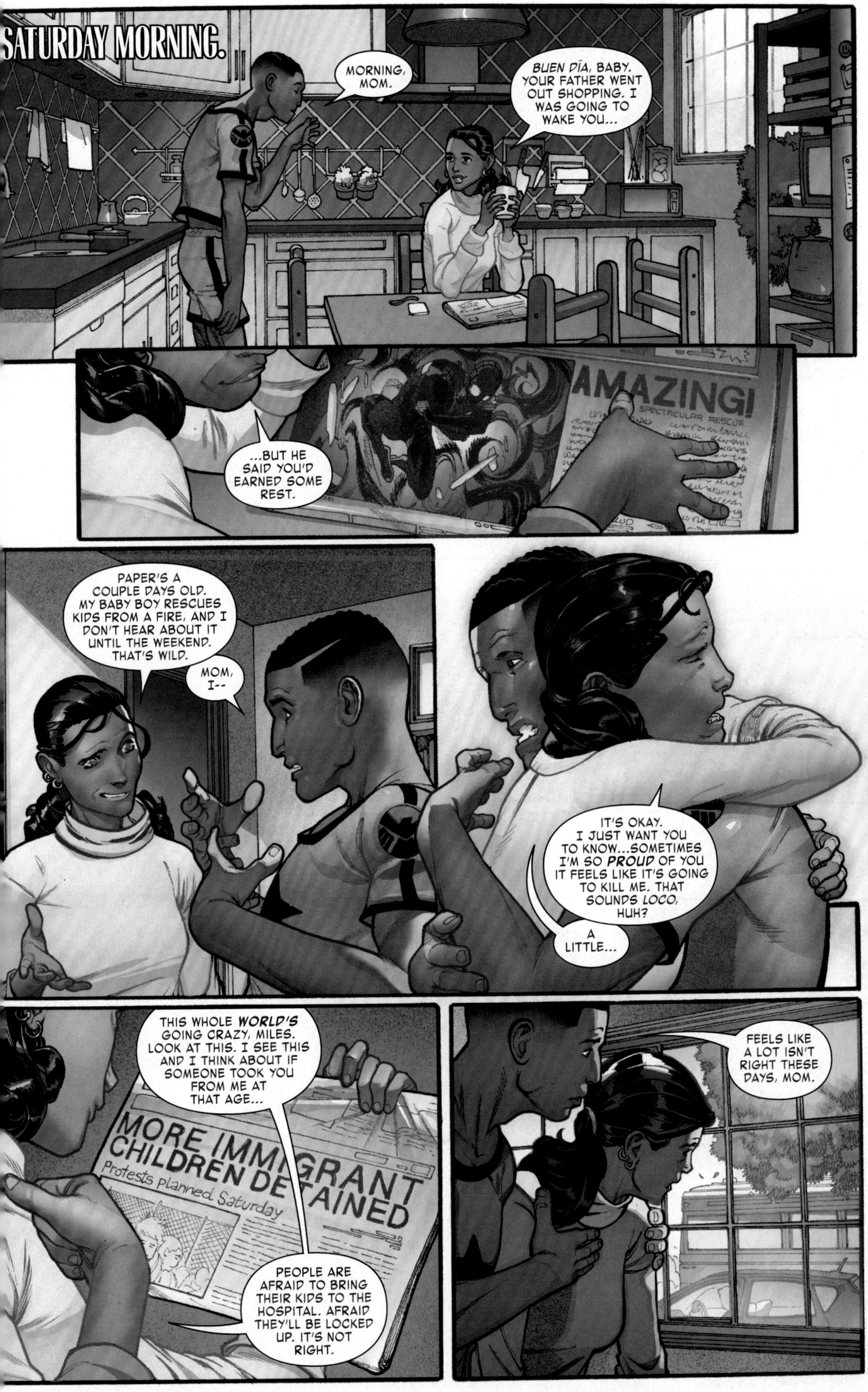
SATURDAY MORNING.
MORNING, MOM.
BUEN DÍA, BABY. YOUR FATHER WENT OUT SHOPPING. I WAS GOING TO WAKE YOU...
AMAZING!
SPECTACULAR RESCUE
...BUT HE SAID YOU'D EARNED SOME REST.
PAPER'S A COUPLE DAYS OLD. MY BABY BOY RESCUES KIDS FROM A FIRE, AND I DON'T HEAR ABOUT IT UNTIL THE WEEKEND. THAT'S WILD.
MOM, I--
IT'S OKAY. I JUST WANT YOU TO KNOW...SOMETIMES I'M SO PROUD OF YOU IT FEELS LIKE IT'S GOING TO KILL ME. THAT SOUNDS LOCO, HUH?
A LITTLE...
THIS WHOLE WORLD'S GOING CRAZY, MILES. LOOK AT THIS. I SEE THIS AND I THINK ABOUT IF SOMEONE TOOK YOU FROM ME AT THAT AGE...
MORE IMMIGRANT CHILDREN DETAINED
Protests Planned Saturday
PEOPLE ARE AFRAID TO BRING THEIR KIDS TO THE HOSPITAL. AFRAID THEY'LL BE LOCKED UP. IT'S NOT RIGHT.
FEELS LIKE A LOT ISN'T RIGHT THESE DAYS, MOM.

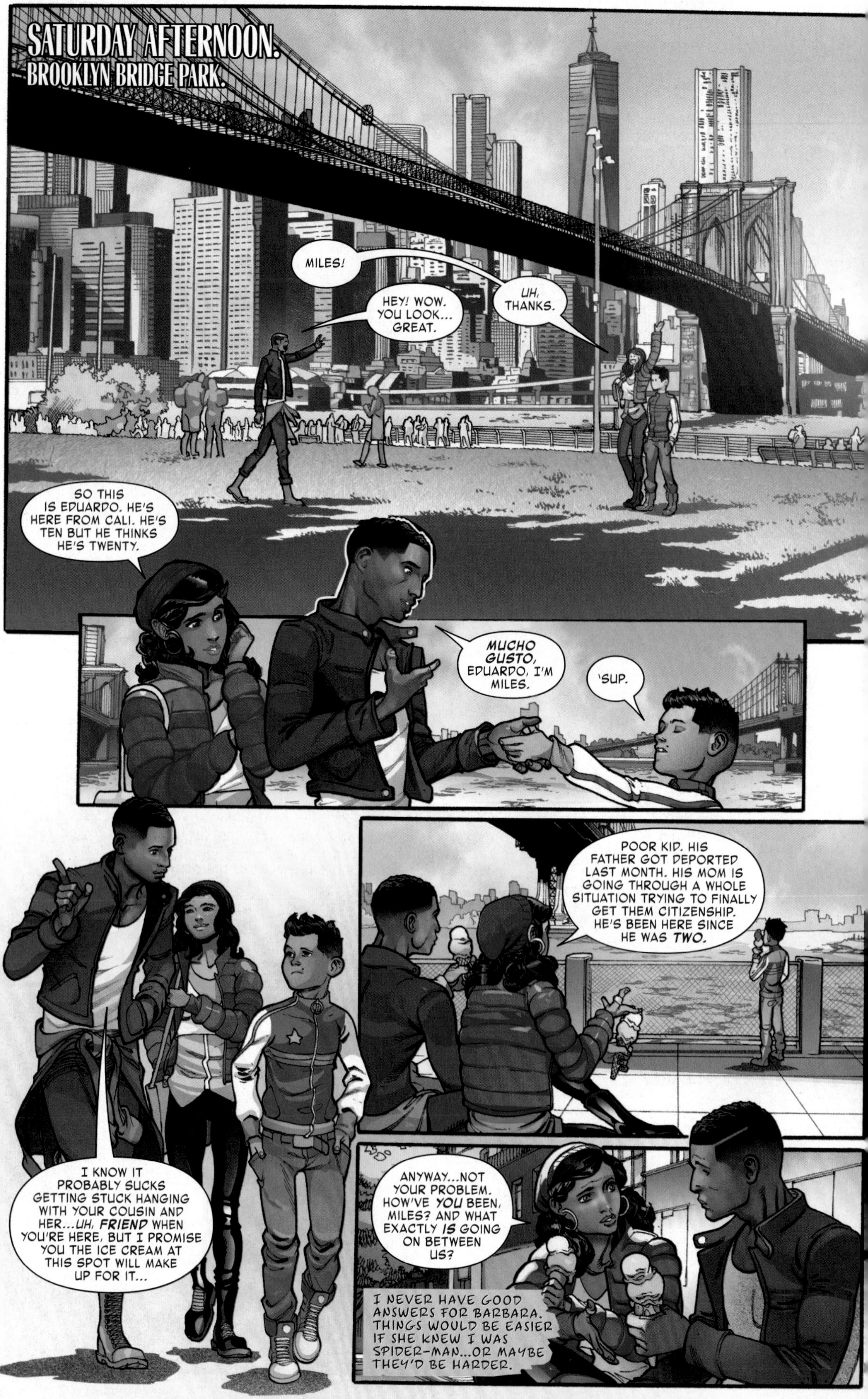
SATURDAY AFTERNOON.
BROOKLYN BRIDGE PARK.
MILES!
HEY! WOW. YOU LOOK... GREAT.
UH, THANKS.
SO THIS IS EDUARDO. HE'S HERE FROM CALI. HE'S TEN BUT HE THINKS HE'S TWENTY.
MUCHO GUSTO, EDUARDO, I'M MILES.
'SUP.
I KNOW IT PROBABLY SUCKS GETTING STUCK HANGING WITH YOUR COUSIN AND HER...UH, FRIEND WHEN YOU'RE HERE, BUT I PROMISE YOU THE ICE CREAM AT THIS SPOT WILL MAKE UP FOR IT...
POOR KID. HIS FATHER GOT DEPORTED LAST MONTH. HIS MOM IS GOING THROUGH A WHOLE SITUATION TRYING TO FINALLY GET THEM CITIZENSHIP. HE'S BEEN HERE SINCE HE WAS TWO.
ANYWAY...NOT YOUR PROBLEM. HOW'VE YOU BEEN, MILES? AND WHAT EXACTLY IS GOING ON BETWEEN US?
I NEVER HAVE GOOD ANSWERS FOR BARBARA. THINGS WOULD BE EASIER IF SHE KNEW I WAS SPIDER-MAN...OR MAYBE THEY'D BE HARDER.

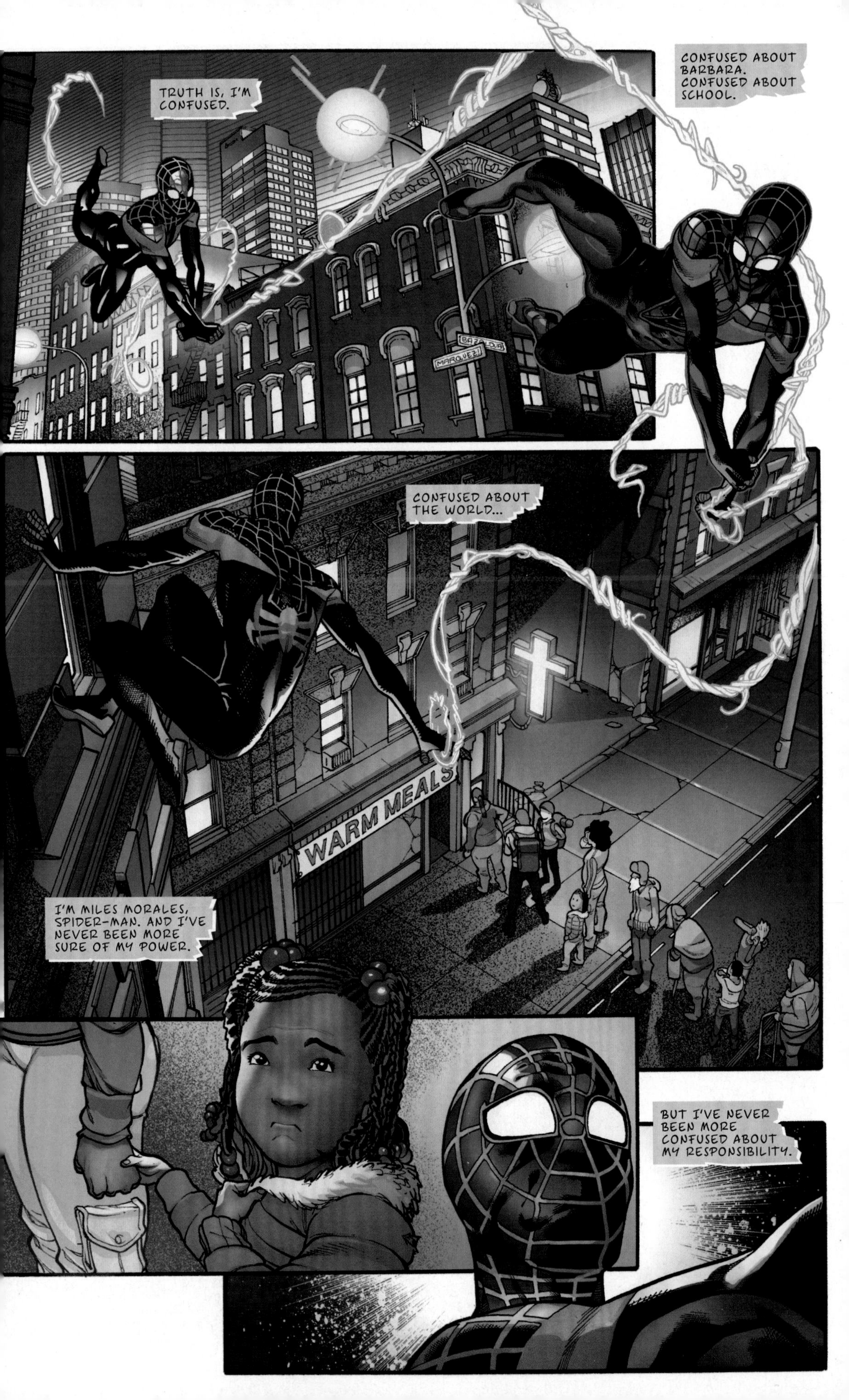
TRUTH IS, I'M CONFUSED.
CONFUSED ABOUT BARBARA. CONFUSED ABOUT SCHOOL.
BAZALDUA
MARQUEZ
CONFUSED ABOUT THE WORLD...
WARM MEALS
I'M MILES MORALES, SPIDER-MAN. AND I'VE NEVER BEEN MORE SURE OF MY POWER.
BUT I'VE NEVER BEEN MORE CONFUSED ABOUT MY RESPONSIBILITY.

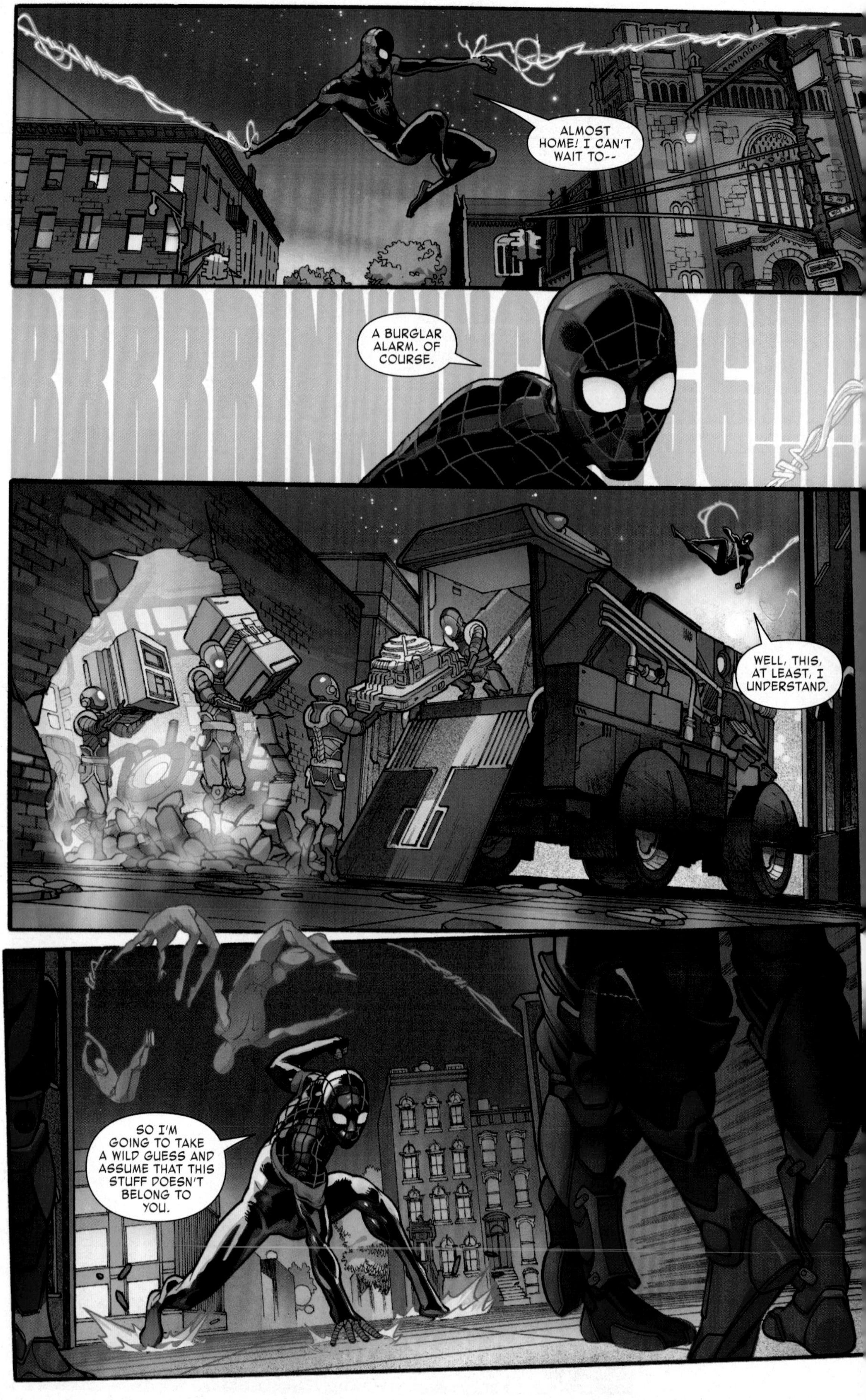
ALMOST HOME! I CAN'T WAIT TO--
A BURGLAR ALARM. OF COURSE.
WELL, THIS, AT LEAST, I UNDERSTAND.
SO I'M GOING TO TAKE A WILD GUESS AND ASSUME THAT THIS STUFF DOESN'T BELONG TO YOU.

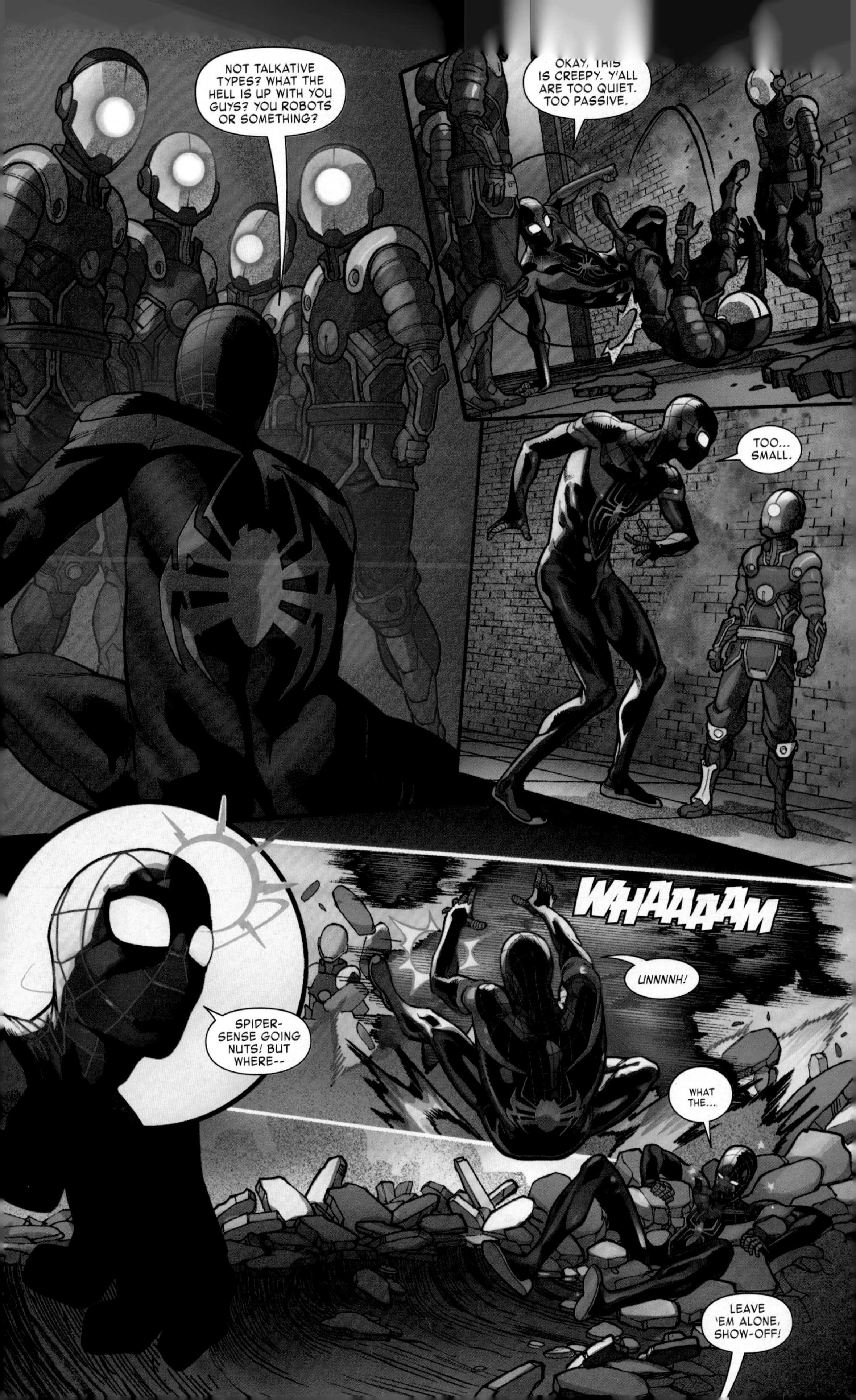
NOT TALKATIVE TYPES? WHAT THE HELL IS UP WITH YOU GUYS? YOU ROBOTS OR SOMETHING?
OKAY, THIS IS CREEPY. Y'ALL ARE TOO QUIET. TOO PASSIVE.
TOO... SMALL.
SPIDER-SENSE GOING NUTS! BUT WHERE--
WHAAAAAM
UNNNNH!
WHAT THE...
LEAVE 'EM ALONE, SHOW-OFF!

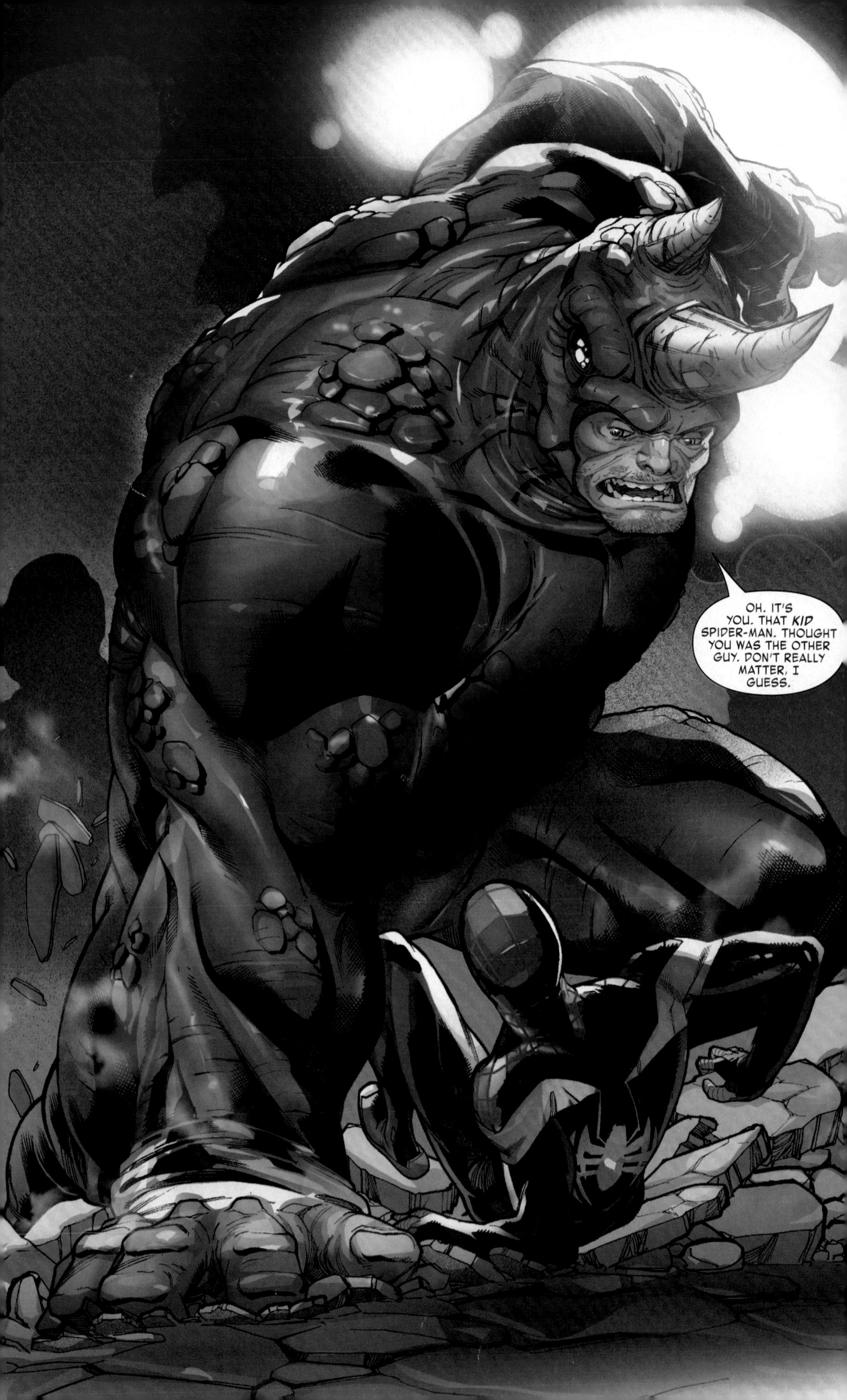
OH. IT'S YOU. THAT KID SPIDER-MAN. THOUGHT YOU WAS THE OTHER GUY. DON'T REALLY MATTER, I GUESS.

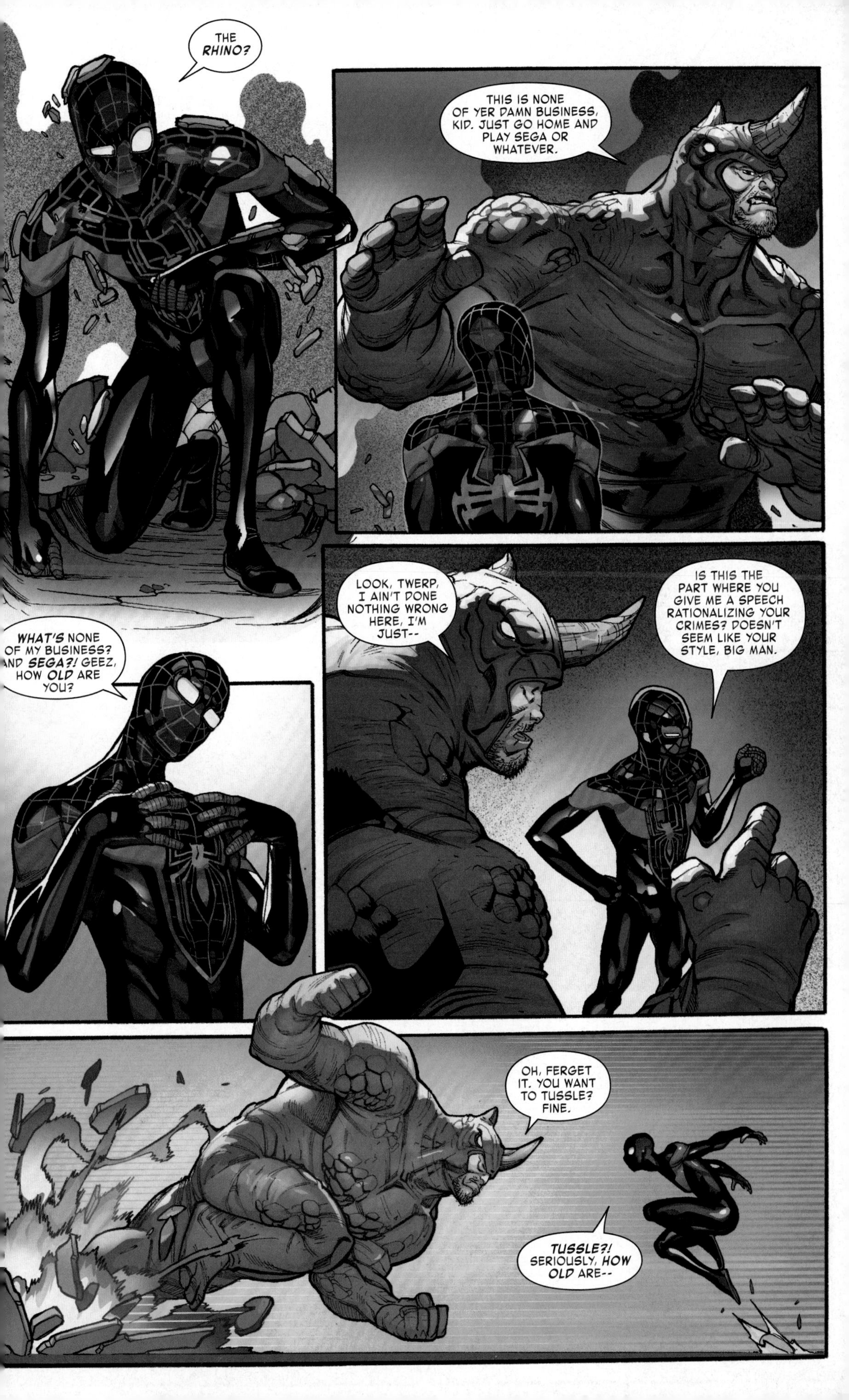
THE *RHINO?*
THIS IS NONE OF YER DAMN BUSINESS, KID. JUST GO HOME AND PLAY SEGA OR WHATEVER.
WHAT'S NONE OF MY BUSINESS? AND *SEGA?!* GEEZ, HOW *OLD* ARE YOU?
LOOK, TWERP, I AIN'T DONE NOTHING WRONG HERE, I'M JUST--
IS THIS THE PART WHERE YOU GIVE ME A SPEECH RATIONALIZING YOUR CRIMES? DOESN'T SEEM LIKE YOUR STYLE, BIG MAN.
OH, FERGET IT. YOU WANT TO TUSSLE? FINE.
TUSSLE?! SERIOUSLY, *HOW OLD* ARE--

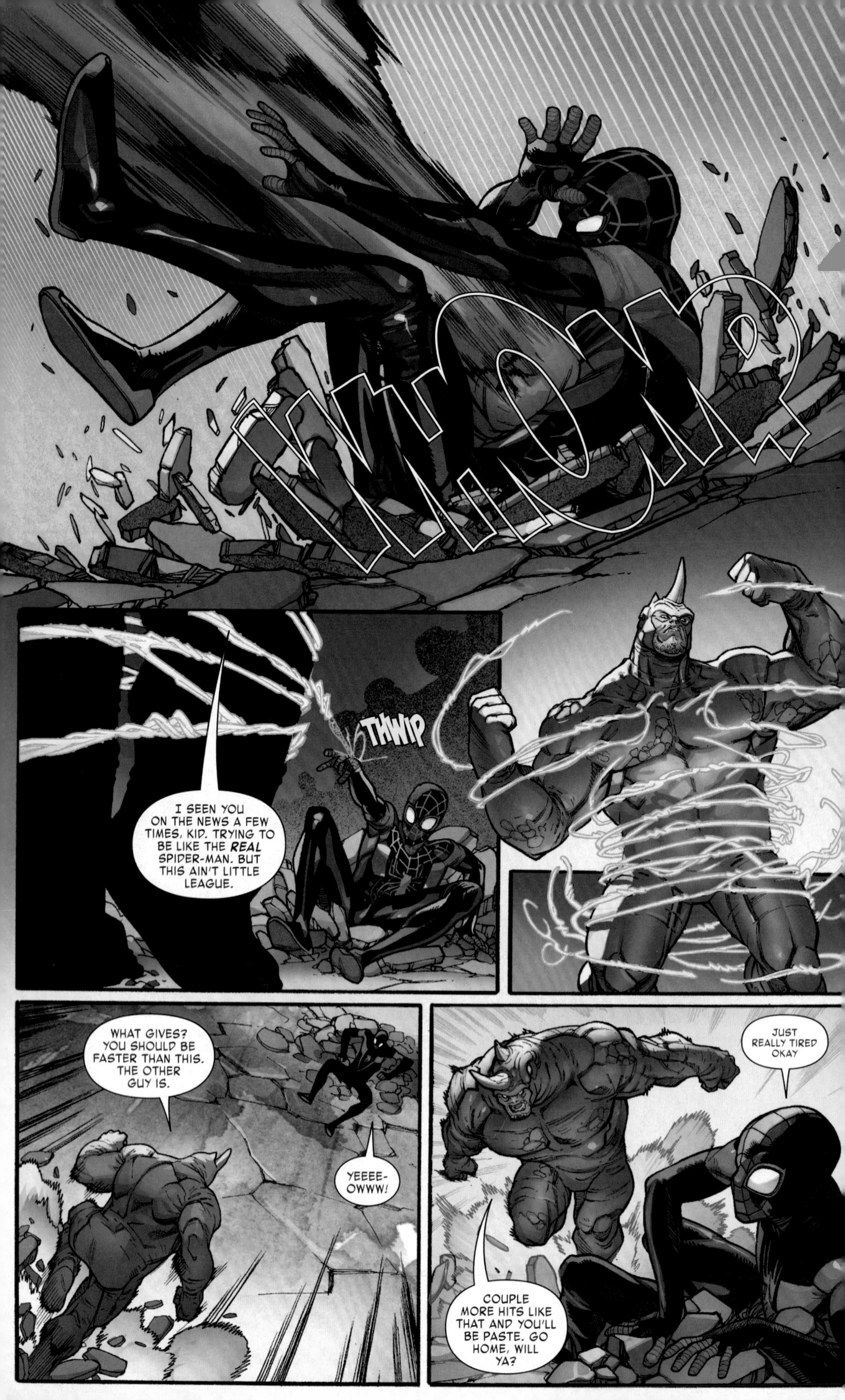
WHOOM
THWIP
I SEEN YOU ON THE NEWS A FEW TIMES, KID. TRYING TO BE LIKE THE REAL SPIDER-MAN. BUT THIS AIN'T LITTLE LEAGUE.
WHAT GIVES? YOU SHOULD BE FASTER THAN THIS. THE OTHER GUY IS.
YEEEE-OWWW!
JUST REALLY TIRED OKAY
COUPLE MORE HITS LIKE THAT AND YOU'LL BE PASTE. GO HOME, WILL YA?

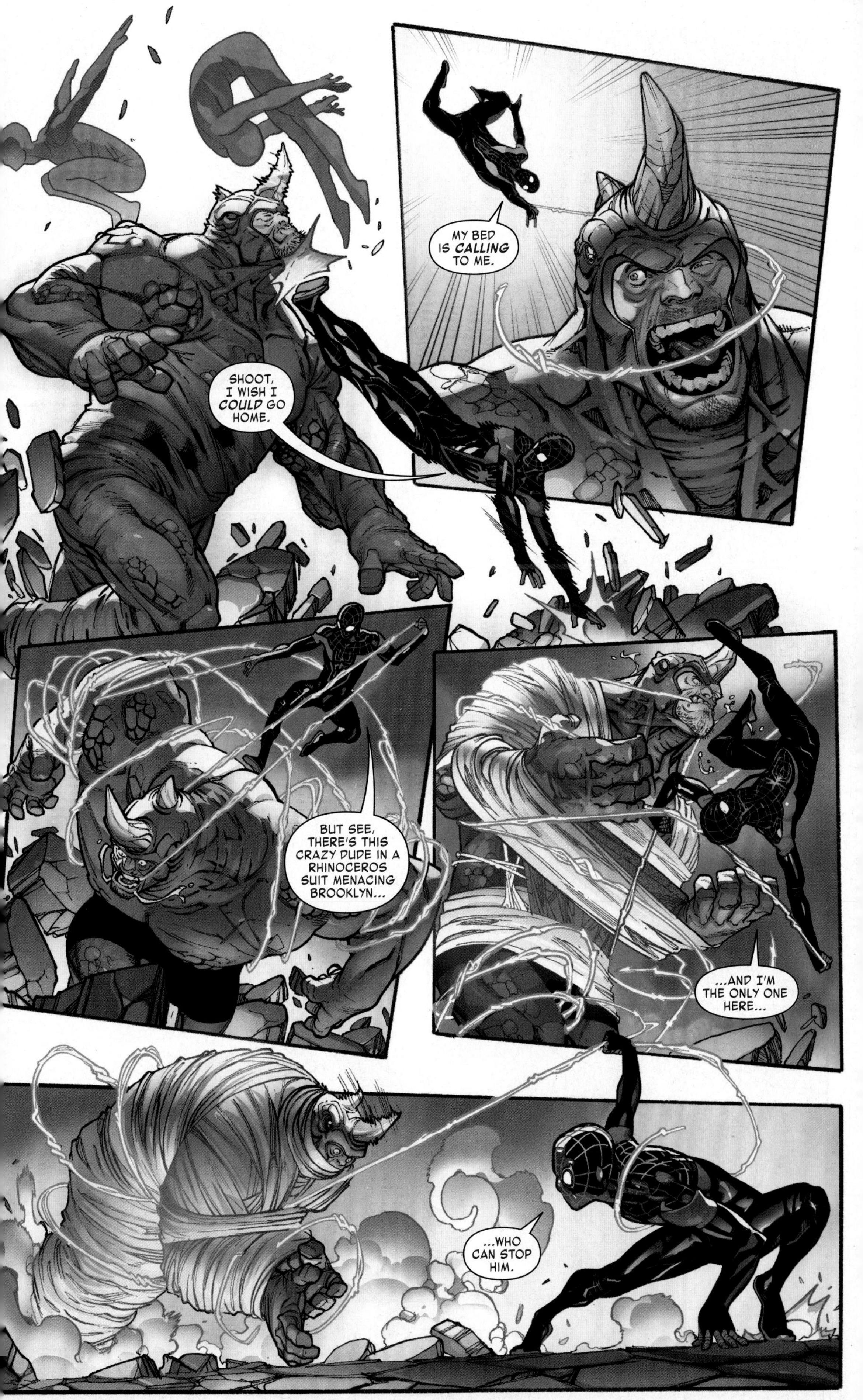
MY BED IS CALLING TO ME.
SHOOT, I WISH I COULD GO HOME.
BUT SEE, THERE'S THIS CRAZY DUDE IN A RHINOCEROS SUIT MENACING BROOKLYN...
...AND I'M THE ONLY ONE HERE...
...WHO CAN STOP HIM.

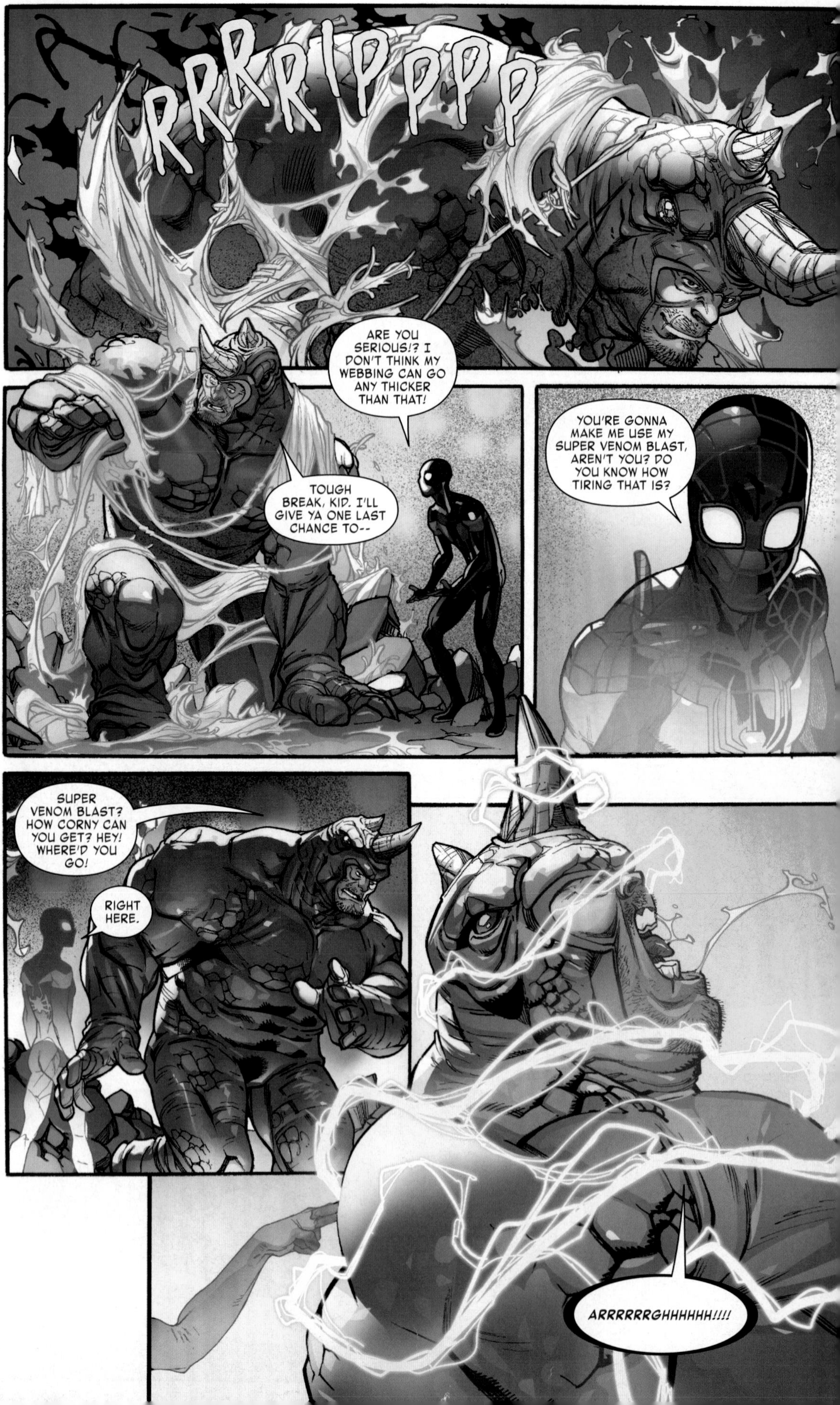
RRRRIPPPP
ARE YOU SERIOUS!? I DON'T THINK MY WEBBING CAN GO ANY THICKER THAN THAT!
TOUGH BREAK, KID. I'LL GIVE YA ONE LAST CHANCE TO--
YOU'RE GONNA MAKE ME USE MY SUPER VENOM BLAST, AREN'T YOU? DO YOU KNOW HOW TIRING THAT IS?
SUPER VENOM BLAST? HOW CORNY CAN YOU GET? HEY! WHERE'D YOU GO!
RIGHT HERE.
ARRRRRRGHHHHHH!!!!

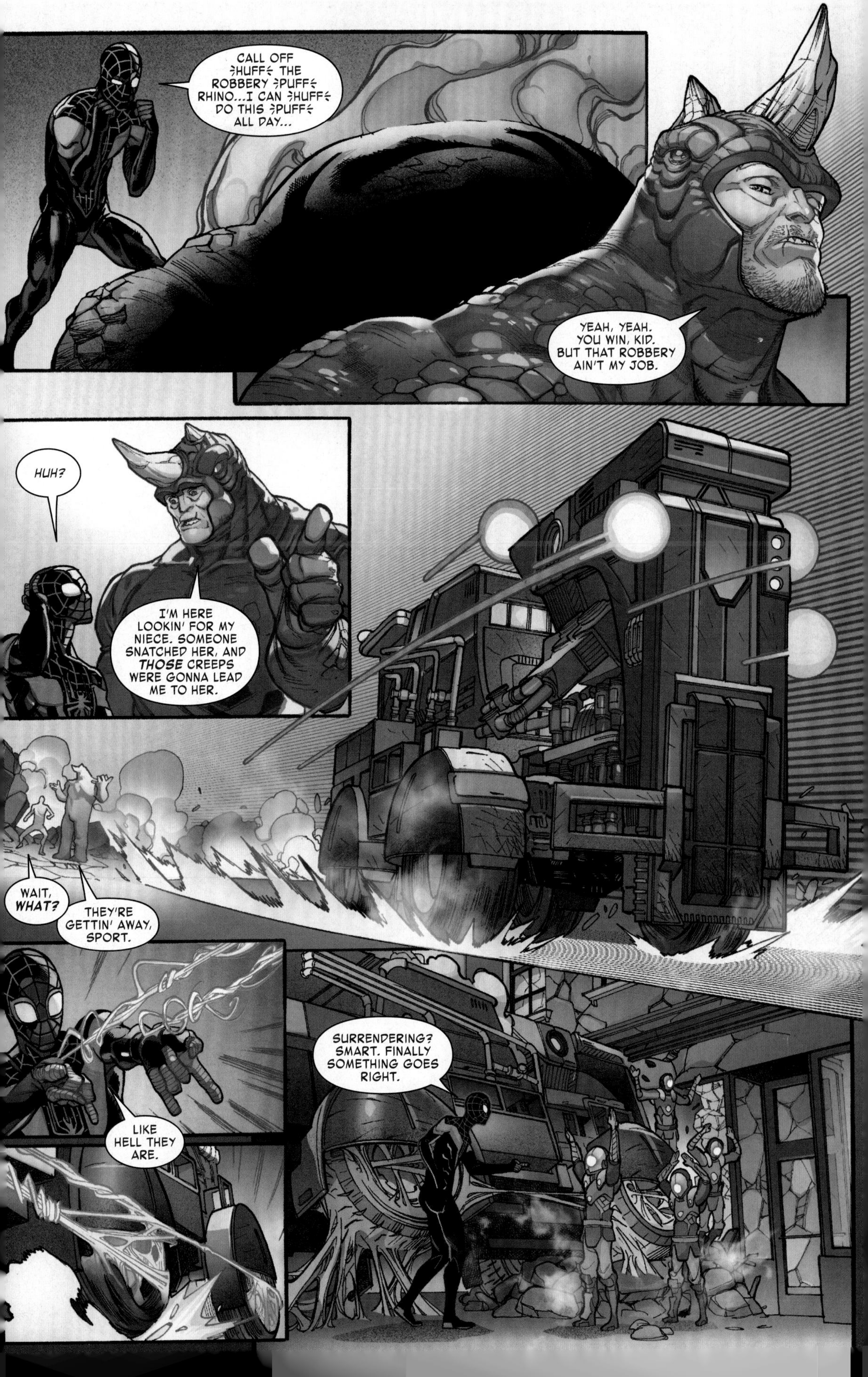
CALL OFF ≶HUFF≶ THE ROBBERY ≶PUFF≶ RHINO...I CAN ≶HUFF≶ DO THIS ≶PUFF≶ ALL DAY...
YEAH, YEAH. YOU WIN, KID. BUT THAT ROBBERY AIN'T MY JOB.
HUH?
I'M HERE LOOKIN' FOR MY NIECE. SOMEONE SNATCHED HER, AND *THOSE* CREEPS WERE GONNA LEAD ME TO HER.
WAIT, **WHAT?**
THEY'RE GETTIN' AWAY, SPORT.
LIKE HELL THEY ARE.
SURRENDERING? SMART. FINALLY SOMETHING GOES RIGHT.

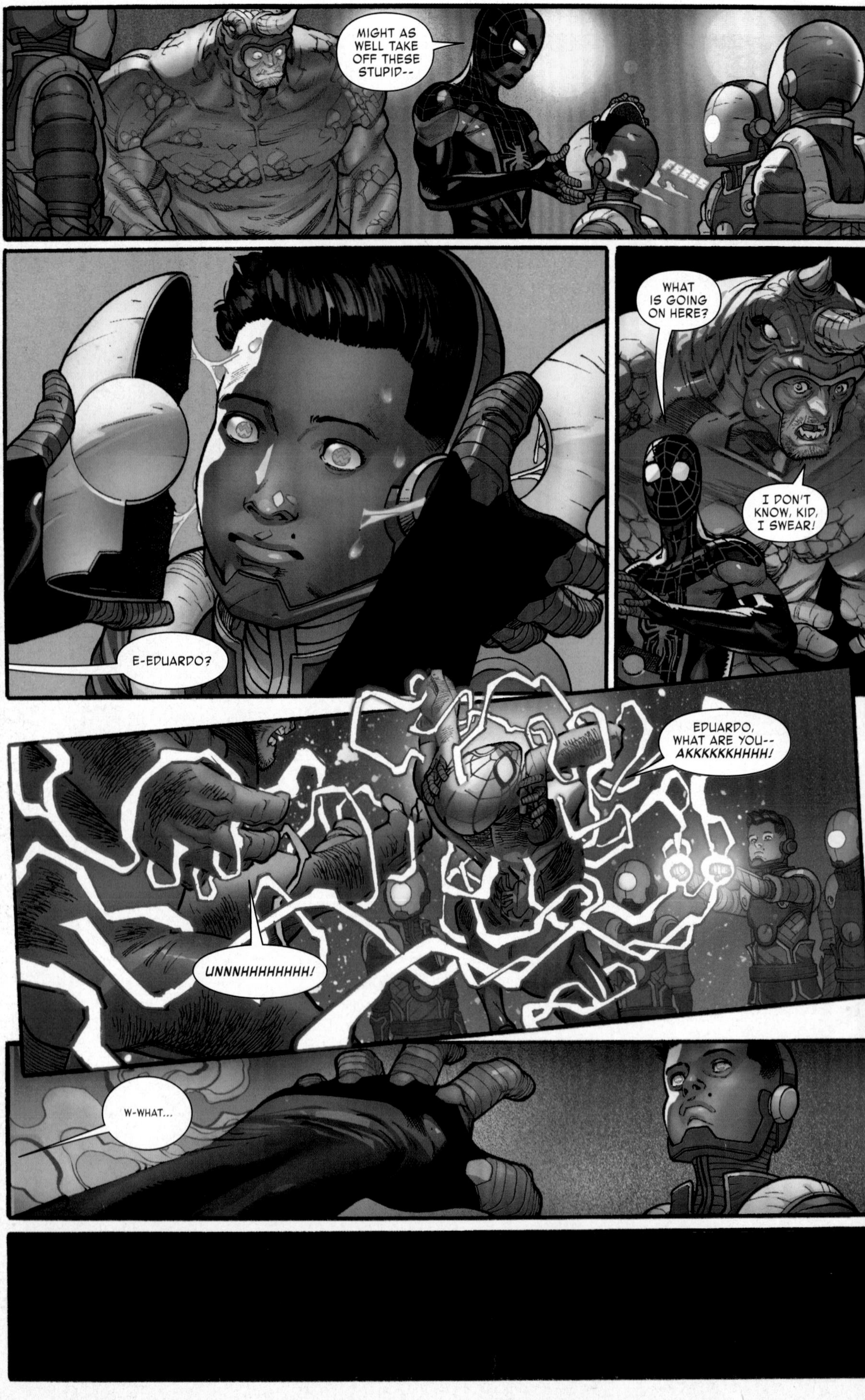
MIGHT AS WELL TAKE OFF THESE STUPID--
FSSSS
E-EDUARDO?
WHAT IS GOING ON HERE?
I DON'T KNOW, KID, I SWEAR!
EDUARDO, WHAT ARE YOU-- AKKKKKKHHHH!
UNNNHHHHHHHH!
W-WHAT...

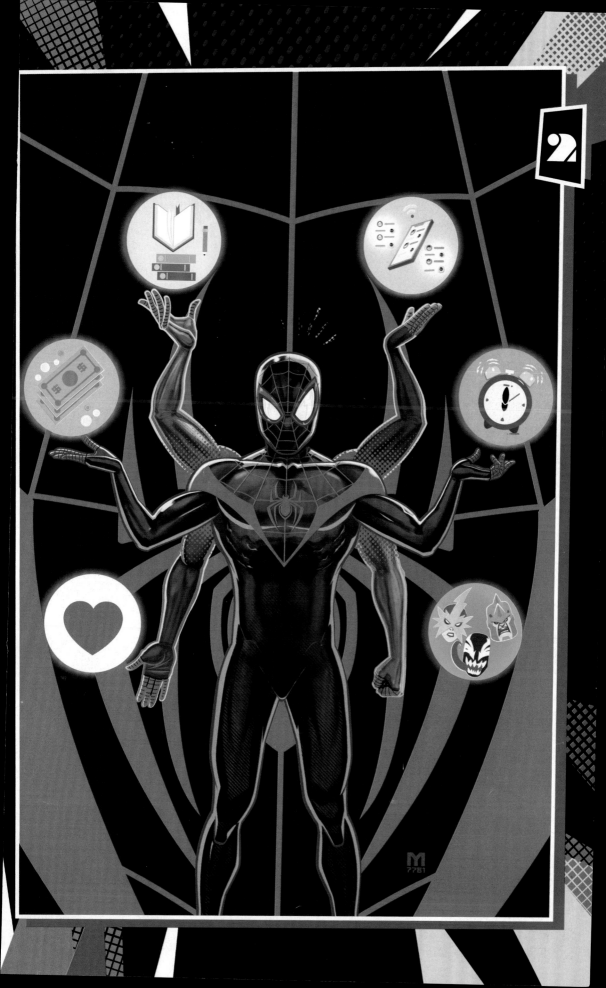

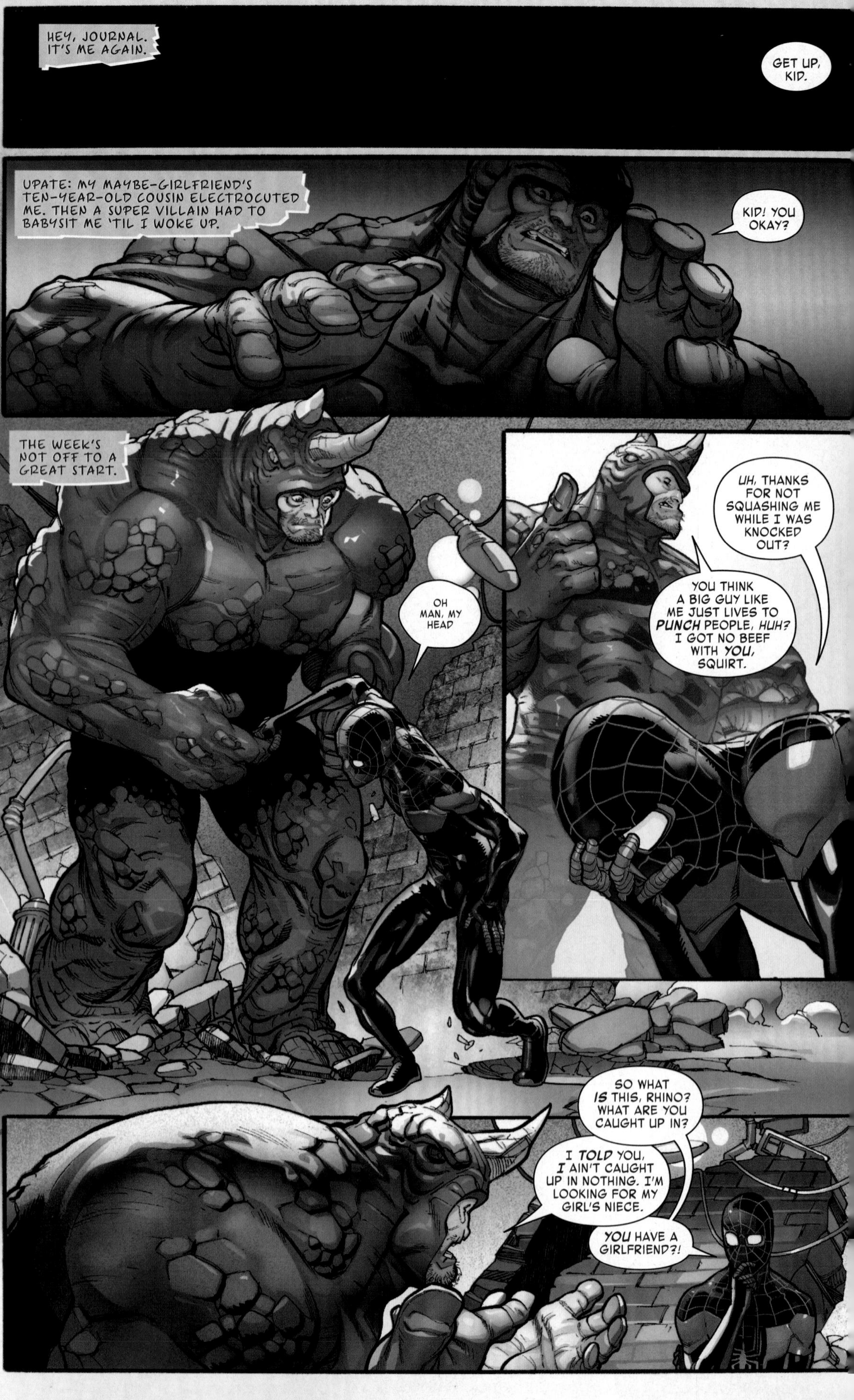
HEY, JOURNAL. IT'S ME AGAIN.
GET UP, KID.
UPATE: MY MAYBE-GIRLFRIEND'S TEN-YEAR-OLD COUSIN ELECTROCUTED ME. THEN A SUPER VILLAIN HAD TO BABYSIT ME 'TIL I WOKE UP.
KID! YOU OKAY?
THE WEEK'S NOT OFF TO A GREAT START.
OH MAN, MY HEAD
UH, THANKS FOR NOT SQUASHING ME WHILE I WAS KNOCKED OUT?
YOU THINK A BIG GUY LIKE ME JUST LIVES TO PUNCH PEOPLE, HUH? I GOT NO BEEF WITH YOU, SQUIRT.
SO WHAT IS THIS, RHINO? WHAT ARE YOU CAUGHT UP IN?
I TOLD YOU, I AIN'T CAUGHT UP IN NOTHING. I'M LOOKING FOR MY GIRL'S NIECE.
YOU HAVE A GIRLFRIEND?!

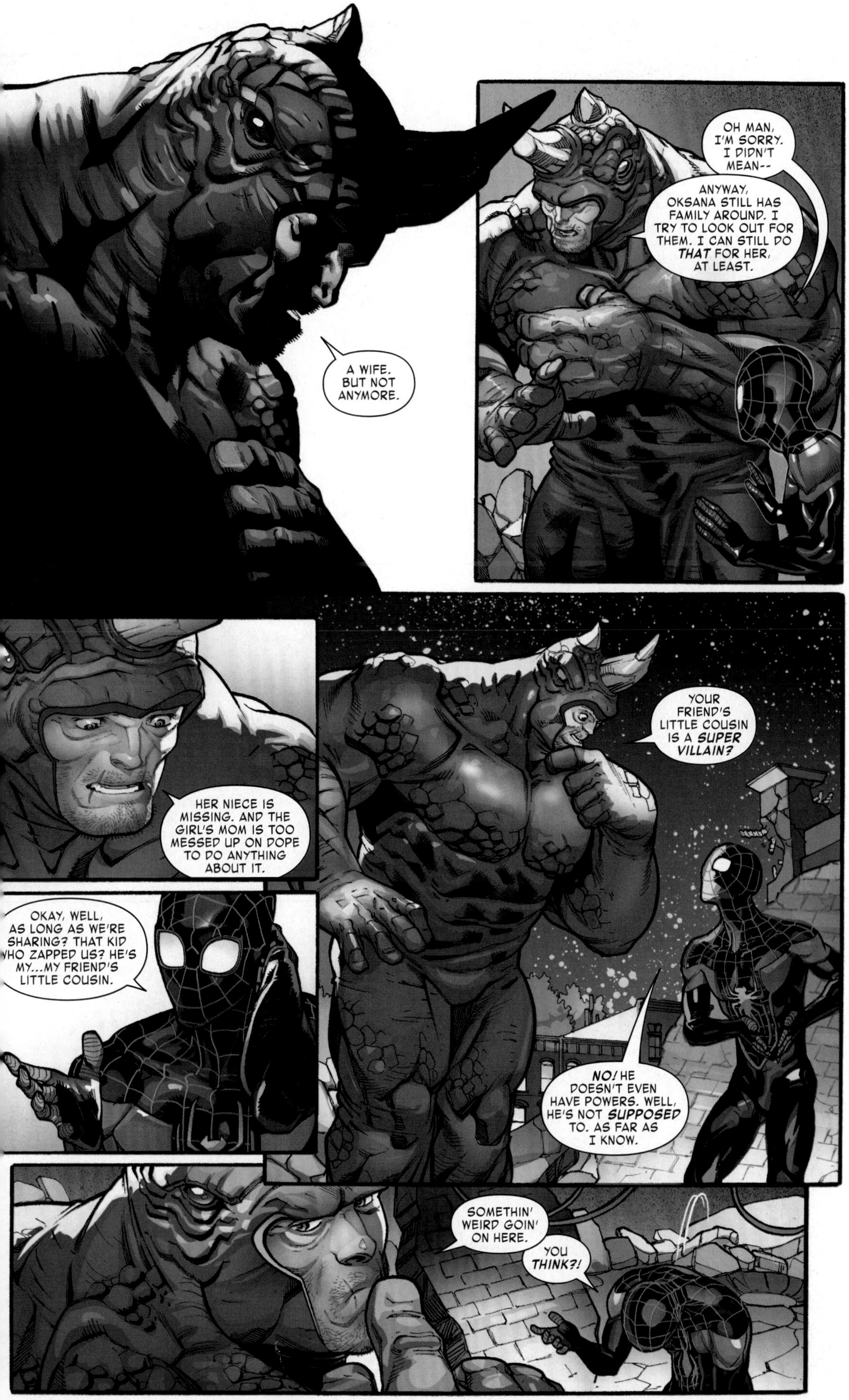
A WIFE. BUT NOT ANYMORE.
OH MAN, I'M SORRY. I DIDN'T MEAN--
ANYWAY, OKSANA STILL HAS FAMILY AROUND. I TRY TO LOOK OUT FOR THEM. I CAN STILL DO THAT FOR HER, AT LEAST.
HER NIECE IS MISSING. AND THE GIRL'S MOM IS TOO MESSED UP ON DOPE TO DO ANYTHING ABOUT IT.
OKAY, WELL, AS LONG AS WE'RE SHARING? THAT KID WHO ZAPPED US? HE'S MY...MY FRIEND'S LITTLE COUSIN.
YOUR FRIEND'S LITTLE COUSIN IS A SUPER VILLAIN?
NO! HE DOESN'T EVEN HAVE POWERS. WELL, HE'S NOT SUPPOSED TO. AS FAR AS I KNOW.
SOMETHIN' WEIRD GOIN' ON HERE.
YOU THINK?!

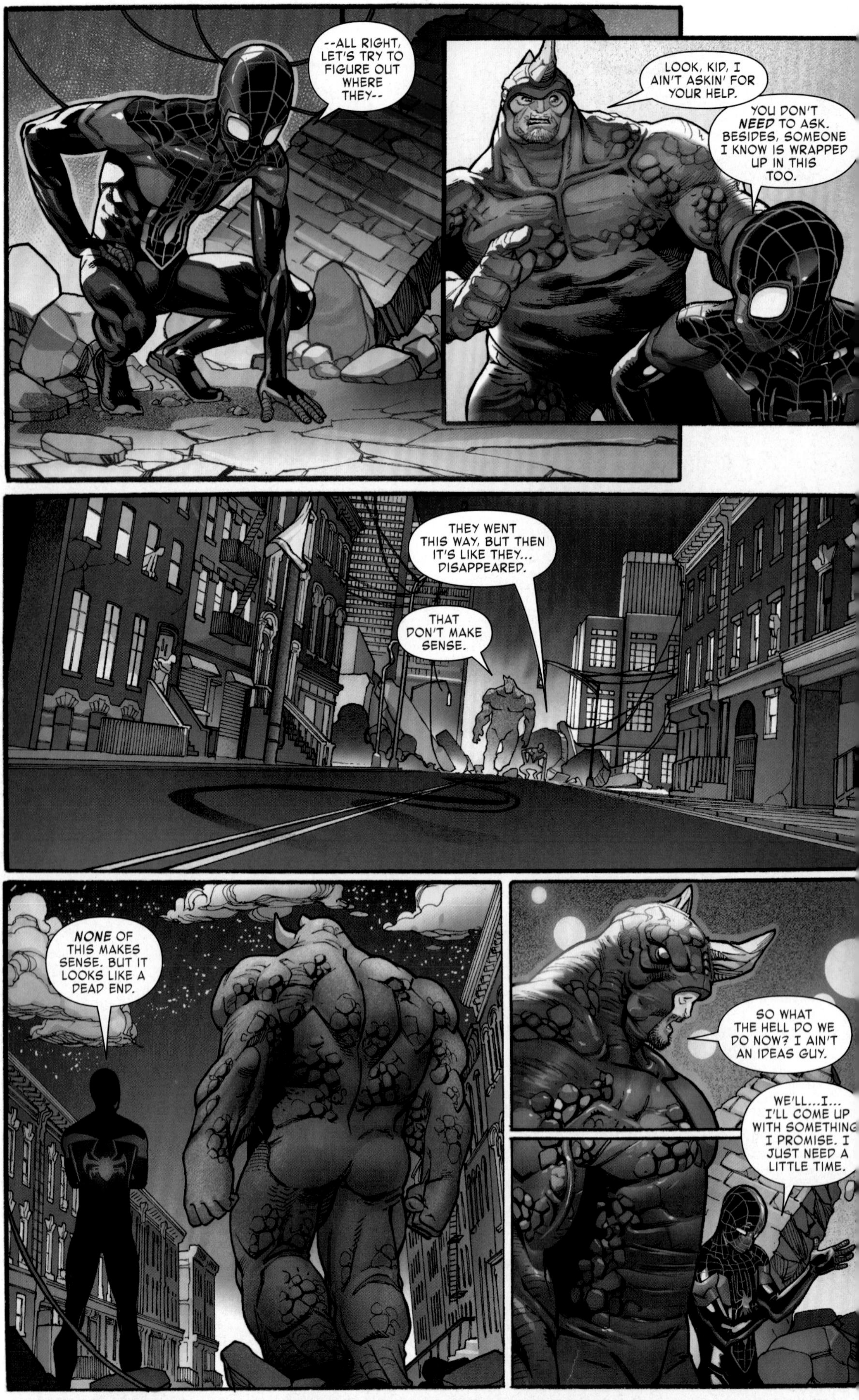
--ALL RIGHT, LET'S TRY TO FIGURE OUT WHERE THEY--
LOOK, KID, I AIN'T ASKIN' FOR YOUR HELP.
YOU DON'T *NEED* TO ASK. BESIDES, SOMEONE I KNOW IS WRAPPED UP IN THIS TOO.
THEY WENT THIS WAY, BUT THEN IT'S LIKE THEY... DISAPPEARED.
THAT DON'T MAKE SENSE.
NONE OF THIS MAKES SENSE. BUT IT LOOKS LIKE A DEAD END.
SO WHAT THE HELL DO WE DO NOW? I AIN'T AN IDEAS GUY.
WE'LL...I... I'LL COME UP WITH SOMETHING I PROMISE. I JUST NEED A LITTLE TIME.

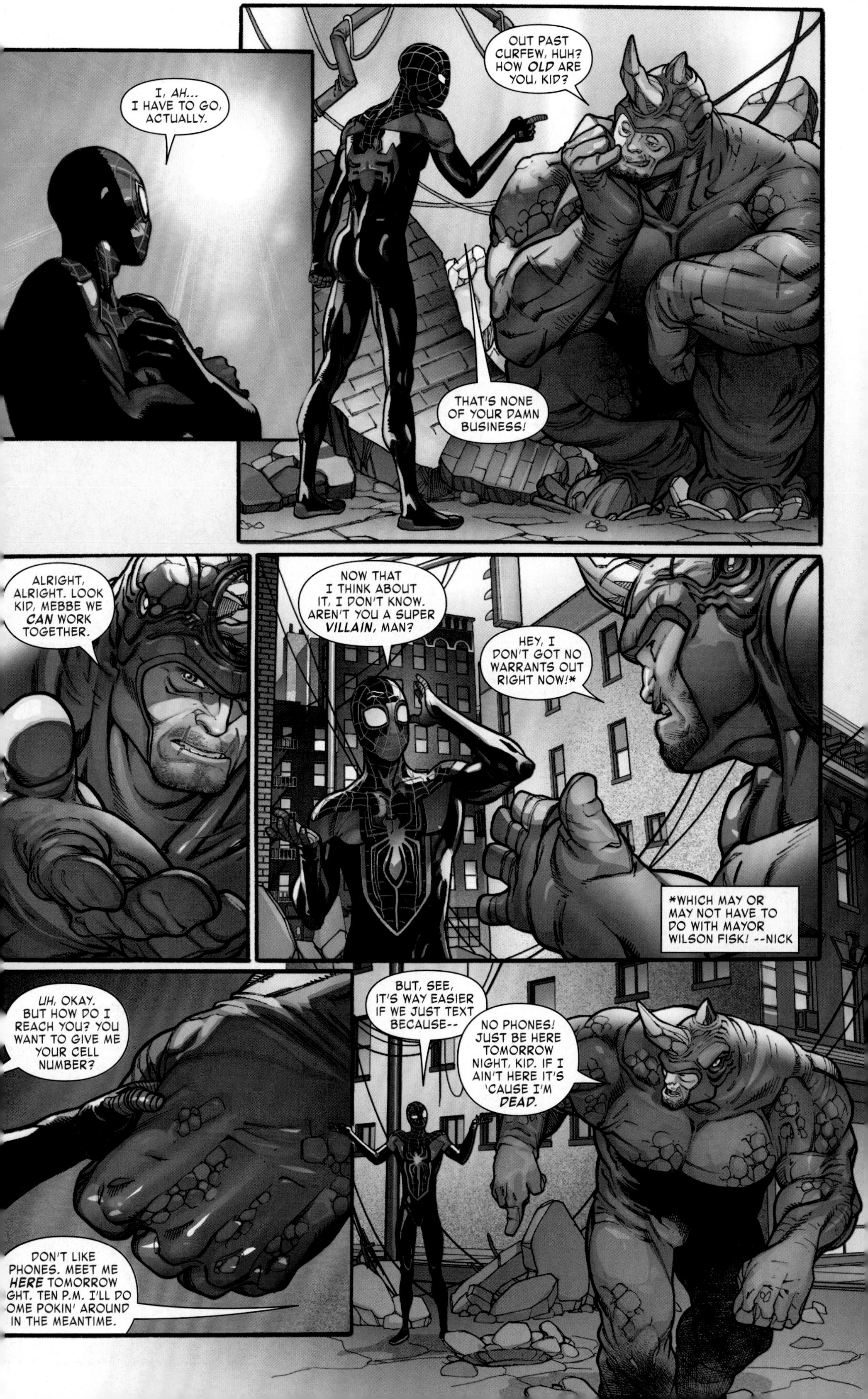

I, *AH...* I HAVE TO GO, ACTUALLY.
OUT PAST CURFEW, HUH? HOW *OLD* ARE YOU, KID?
THAT'S NONE OF YOUR DAMN BUSINESS!
ALRIGHT, ALRIGHT. LOOK KID, MEBBE WE *CAN* WORK TOGETHER.
NOW THAT I THINK ABOUT IT, I DON'T KNOW. AREN'T YOU A SUPER *VILLAIN*, MAN?
HEY, I DON'T GOT NO WARRANTS OUT RIGHT NOW!*
*WHICH MAY OR MAY NOT HAVE TO DO WITH MAYOR WILSON FISK! --NICK
UH, OKAY. BUT HOW DO I REACH YOU? YOU WANT TO GIVE ME YOUR CELL NUMBER?
DON'T LIKE PHONES. MEET ME *HERE* TOMORROW GHT. TEN P.M. I'LL DO OME POKIN' AROUND IN THE MEANTIME.
BUT, SEE, IT'S WAY EASIER IF WE JUST TEXT BECAUSE--
NO PHONES! JUST BE HERE TOMORROW NIGHT, KID. IF I AIN'T HERE IT'S 'CAUSE I'M *DEAD*.

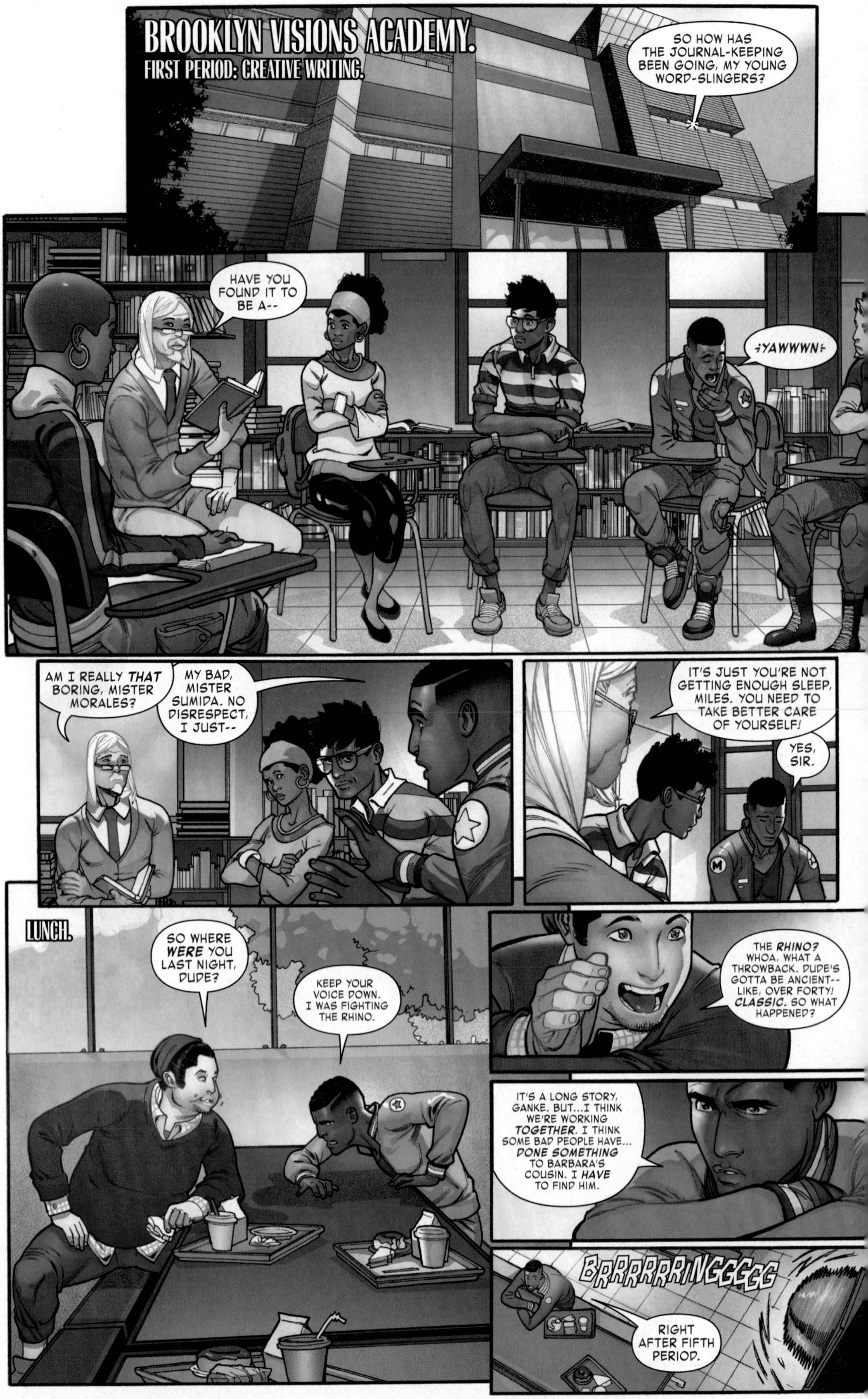

BROOKLYN VISIONS ACADEMY.
FIRST PERIOD: CREATIVE WRITING.
SO HOW HAS THE JOURNAL-KEEPING BEEN GOING, MY YOUNG WORD-SLINGERS?
HAVE YOU FOUND IT TO BE A--
YAWWWN
AM I REALLY THAT BORING, MISTER MORALES?
MY BAD, MISTER SUMIDA. NO DISRESPECT, I JUST--
IT'S JUST YOU'RE NOT GETTING ENOUGH SLEEP, MILES. YOU NEED TO TAKE BETTER CARE OF YOURSELF!
YES, SIR.
LUNCH.
SO WHERE WERE YOU LAST NIGHT, DUDE?
KEEP YOUR VOICE DOWN. I WAS FIGHTING THE RHINO.
THE RHINO? WHOA, WHAT A THROWBACK. DUDE'S GOTTA BE ANCIENT--LIKE, OVER FORTY! CLASSIC. SO WHAT HAPPENED?
IT'S A LONG STORY, GANKE. BUT...I THINK WE'RE WORKING TOGETHER. I THINK SOME BAD PEOPLE HAVE... DONE SOMETHING TO BARBARA'S COUSIN. I HAVE TO FIND HIM.
BRRRRRRINGGGGG
RIGHT AFTER FIFTH PERIOD.

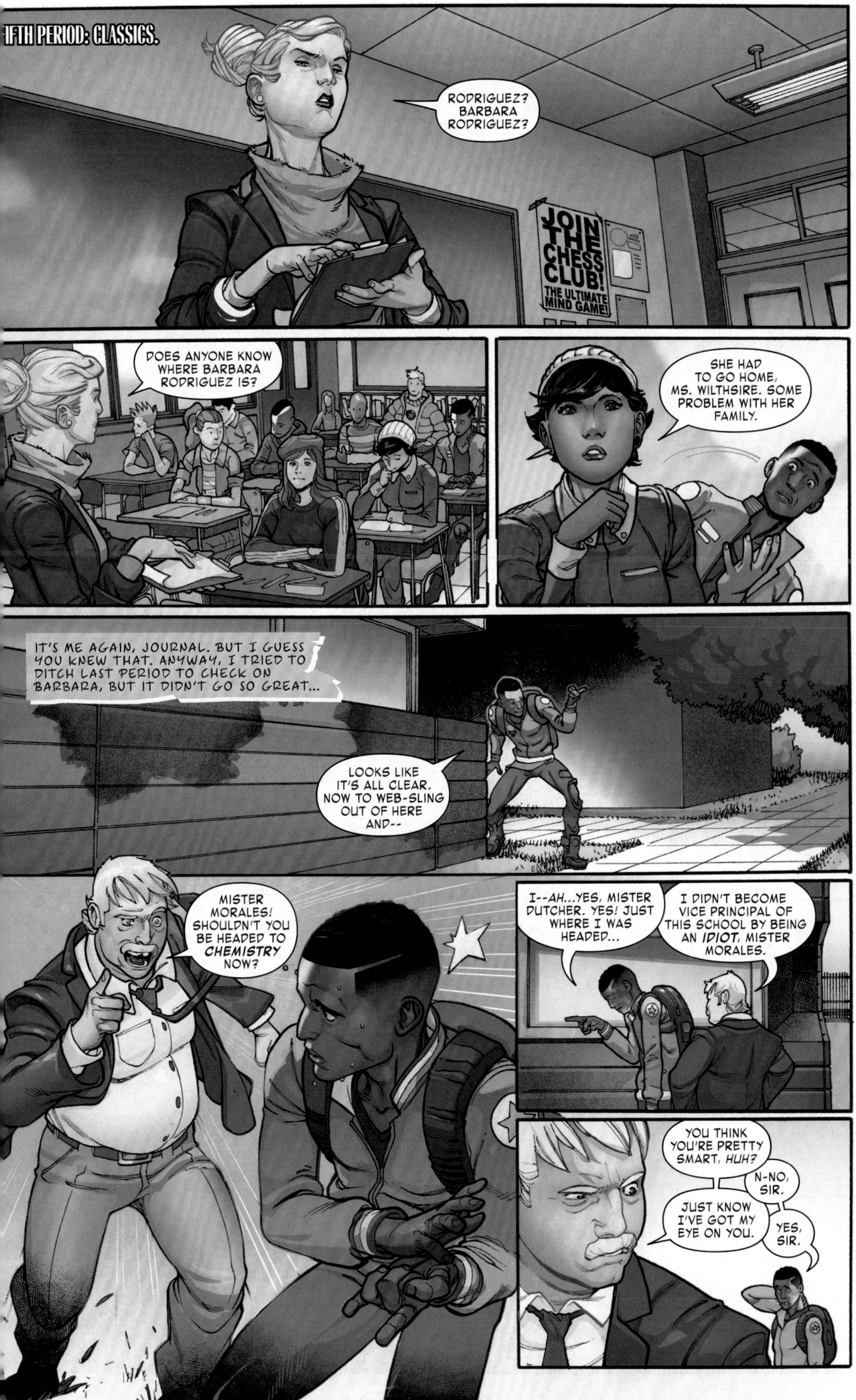
FIFTH PERIOD: CLASSICS.
RODRIGUEZ? BARBARA RODRIGUEZ?
JOIN THE CHESS CLUB! THE ULTIMATE MIND GAME!
DOES ANYONE KNOW WHERE BARBARA RODRIGUEZ IS?
SHE HAD TO GO HOME, MS. WILTHSIRE. SOME PROBLEM WITH HER FAMILY.
IT'S ME AGAIN, JOURNAL. BUT I GUESS YOU KNEW THAT. ANYWAY, I TRIED TO DITCH LAST PERIOD TO CHECK ON BARBARA, BUT IT DIDN'T GO SO GREAT...
LOOKS LIKE IT'S ALL CLEAR. NOW TO WEB-SLING OUT OF HERE AND--
MISTER MORALES! SHOULDN'T YOU BE HEADED TO CHEMISTRY NOW?
I--AH...YES, MISTER DUTCHER. YES! JUST WHERE I WAS HEADED...
I DIDN'T BECOME VICE PRINCIPAL OF THIS SCHOOL BY BEING AN IDIOT, MISTER MORALES.
YOU THINK YOU'RE PRETTY SMART, HUH?
N-NO, SIR.
JUST KNOW I'VE GOT MY EYE ON YOU.
YES, SIR.

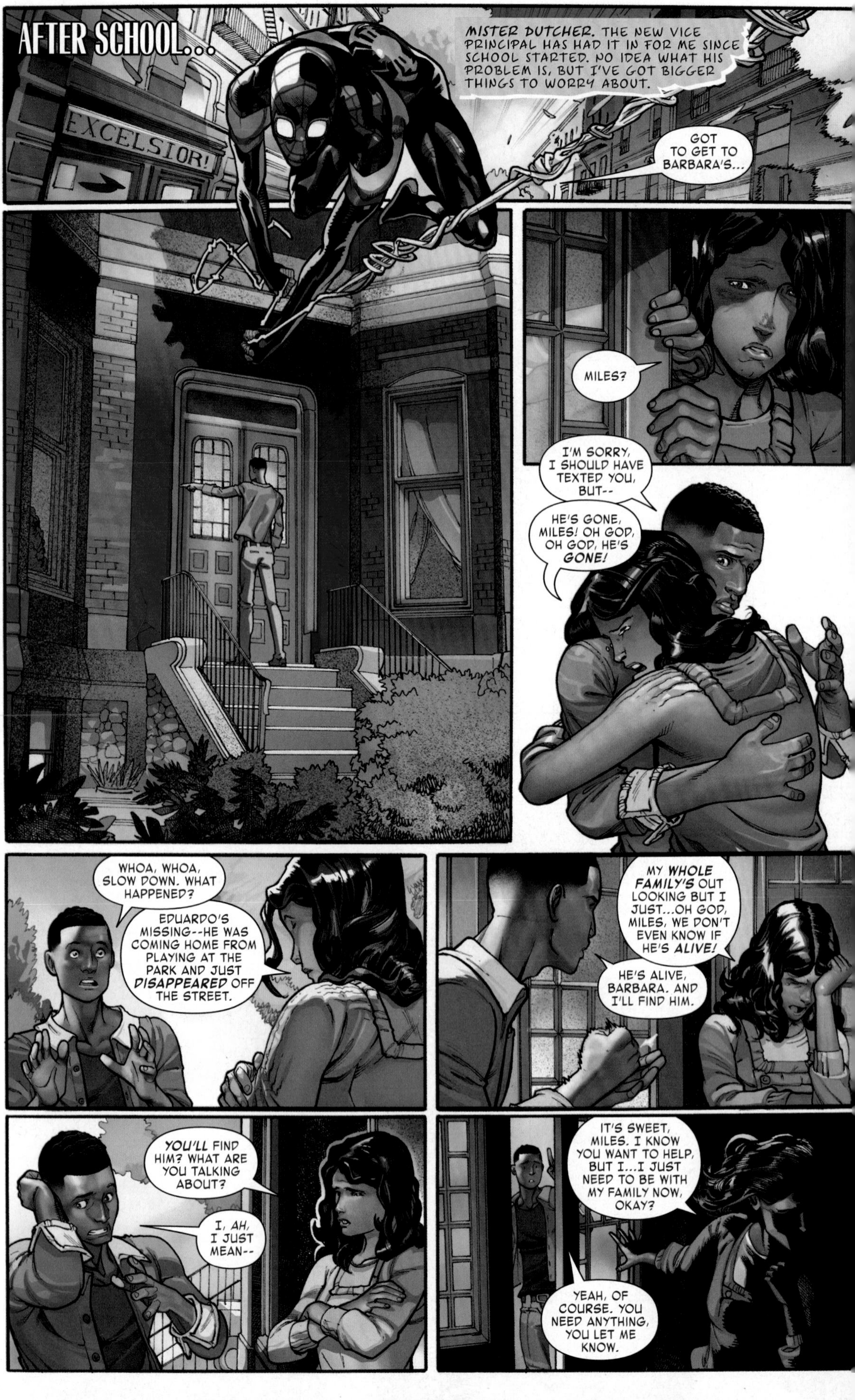
AFTER SCHOOL...
MISTER DUTCHER. THE NEW VICE PRINCIPAL HAS HAD IT IN FOR ME SINCE SCHOOL STARTED. NO IDEA WHAT HIS PROBLEM IS, BUT I'VE GOT BIGGER THINGS TO WORRY ABOUT.
EXCELSIOR!
GOT TO GET TO BARBARA'S...
MILES?
I'M SORRY, I SHOULD HAVE TEXTED YOU, BUT--
HE'S GONE, MILES! OH GOD, OH GOD, HE'S GONE!
WHOA, WHOA, SLOW DOWN. WHAT HAPPENED?
EDUARDO'S MISSING--HE WAS COMING HOME FROM PLAYING AT THE PARK AND JUST DISAPPEARED OFF THE STREET.
MY WHOLE FAMILY'S OUT LOOKING BUT I JUST...OH GOD, MILES, WE DON'T EVEN KNOW IF HE'S ALIVE!
HE'S ALIVE, BARBARA. AND I'LL FIND HIM.
YOU'LL FIND HIM? WHAT ARE YOU TALKING ABOUT?
I, AH, I JUST MEAN--
IT'S SWEET, MILES. I KNOW YOU WANT TO HELP, BUT I...I JUST NEED TO BE WITH MY FAMILY NOW, OKAY?
YEAH, OF COURSE. YOU NEED ANYTHING, YOU LET ME KNOW.

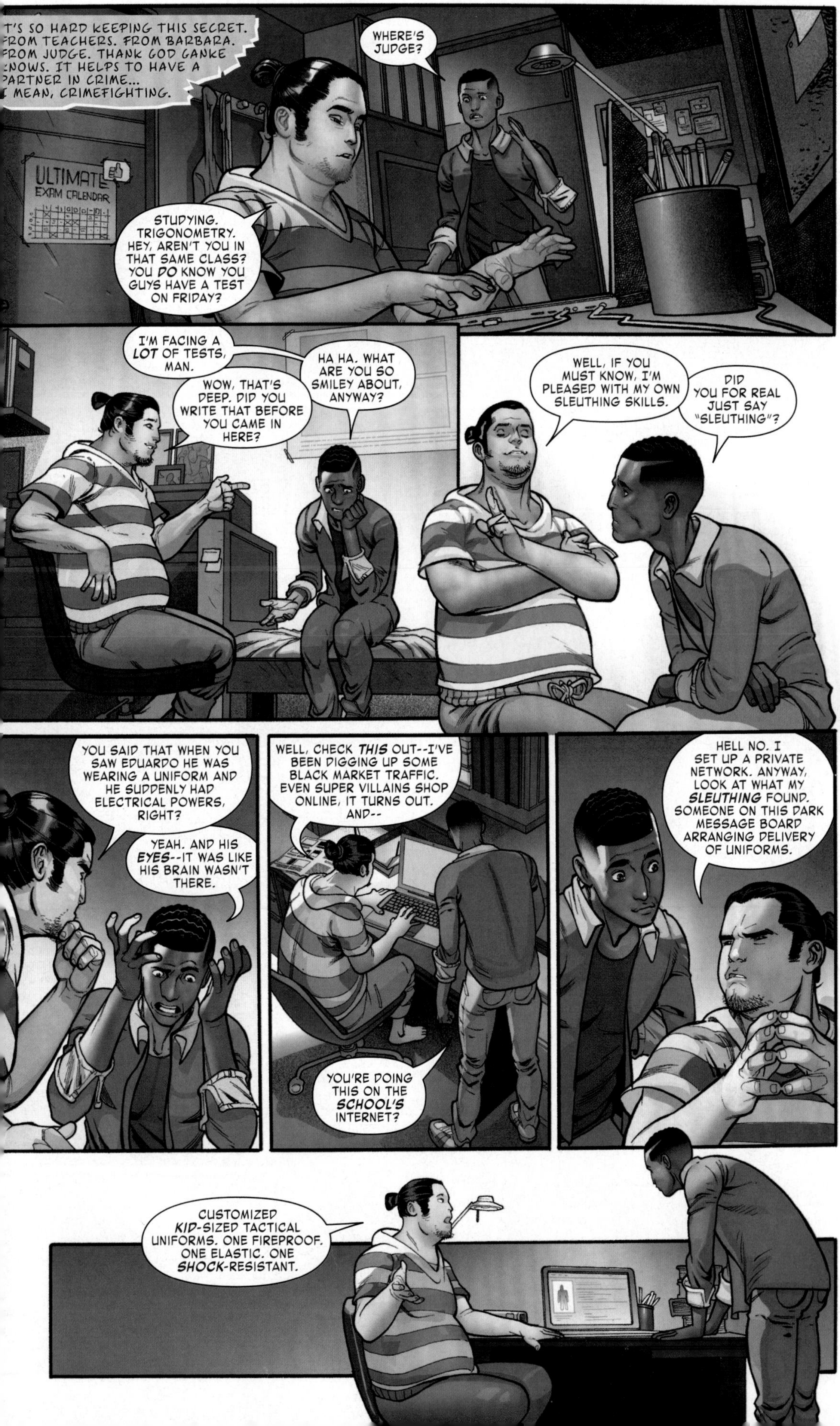

T'S SO HARD KEEPING THIS SECRET. FROM TEACHERS. FROM BARBARA. FROM JUDGE. THANK GOD GANKE KNOWS. IT HELPS TO HAVE A PARTNER IN CRIME... I MEAN, CRIMEFIGHTING.
WHERE'S JUDGE?
ULTIMATE EXAM CALENDAR
STUDYING. TRIGONOMETRY. HEY, AREN'T YOU IN THAT SAME CLASS? YOU DO KNOW YOU GUYS HAVE A TEST ON FRIDAY?
I'M FACING A LOT OF TESTS, MAN.
WOW, THAT'S DEEP. DID YOU WRITE THAT BEFORE YOU CAME IN HERE?
HA HA. WHAT ARE YOU SO SMILEY ABOUT, ANYWAY?
WELL, IF YOU MUST KNOW, I'M PLEASED WITH MY OWN SLEUTHING SKILLS.
DID YOU FOR REAL JUST SAY "SLEUTHING"?
YOU SAID THAT WHEN YOU SAW EDUARDO HE WAS WEARING A UNIFORM AND HE SUDDENLY HAD ELECTRICAL POWERS, RIGHT?
YEAH. AND HIS EYES--IT WAS LIKE HIS BRAIN WASN'T THERE.
WELL, CHECK THIS OUT--I'VE BEEN DIGGING UP SOME BLACK MARKET TRAFFIC. EVEN SUPER VILLAINS SHOP ONLINE, IT TURNS OUT. AND--
YOU'RE DOING THIS ON THE SCHOOL'S INTERNET?
HELL NO. I SET UP A PRIVATE NETWORK. ANYWAY, LOOK AT WHAT MY SLEUTHING FOUND. SOMEONE ON THIS DARK MESSAGE BOARD ARRANGING DELIVERY OF UNIFORMS.
CUSTOMIZED KID-SIZED TACTICAL UNIFORMS. ONE FIREPROOF. ONE ELASTIC. ONE SHOCK-RESISTANT.

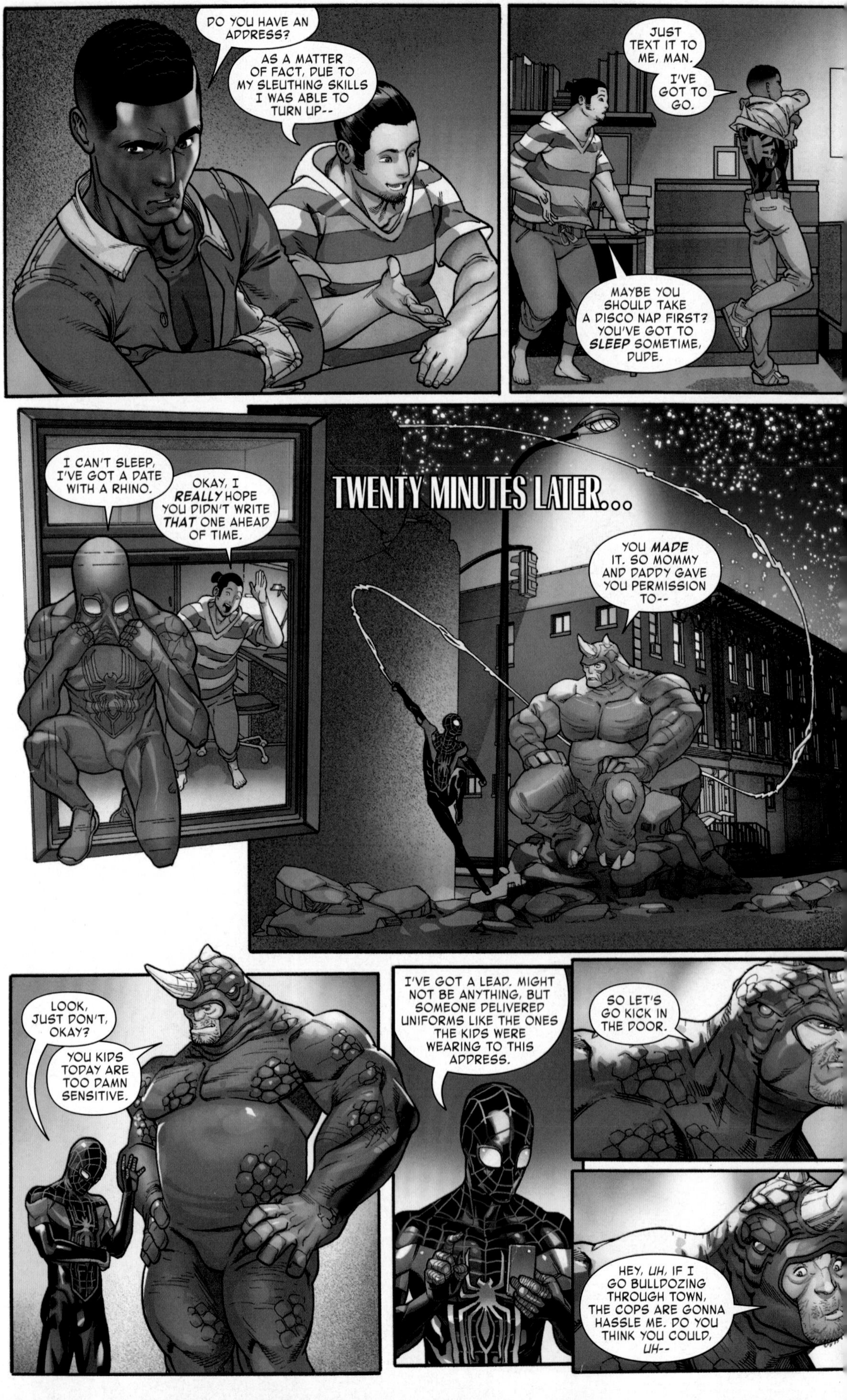
DO YOU HAVE AN ADDRESS?
AS A MATTER OF FACT, DUE TO MY SLEUTHING SKILLS I WAS ABLE TO TURN UP--
JUST TEXT IT TO ME, MAN.
I'VE GOT TO GO.
MAYBE YOU SHOULD TAKE A DISCO NAP FIRST? YOU'VE GOT TO SLEEP SOMETIME, DUDE.
I CAN'T SLEEP, I'VE GOT A DATE WITH A RHINO.
OKAY, I REALLY HOPE YOU DIDN'T WRITE THAT ONE AHEAD OF TIME.
TWENTY MINUTES LATER...
YOU MADE IT. SO MOMMY AND DADDY GAVE YOU PERMISSION TO--
LOOK, JUST DON'T, OKAY?
YOU KIDS TODAY ARE TOO DAMN SENSITIVE.
I'VE GOT A LEAD. MIGHT NOT BE ANYTHING, BUT SOMEONE DELIVERED UNIFORMS LIKE THE ONES THE KIDS WERE WEARING TO THIS ADDRESS.
SO LET'S GO KICK IN THE DOOR.
HEY, UH, IF I GO BULLDOZING THROUGH TOWN, THE COPS ARE GONNA HASSLE ME. DO YOU THINK YOU COULD, UH--

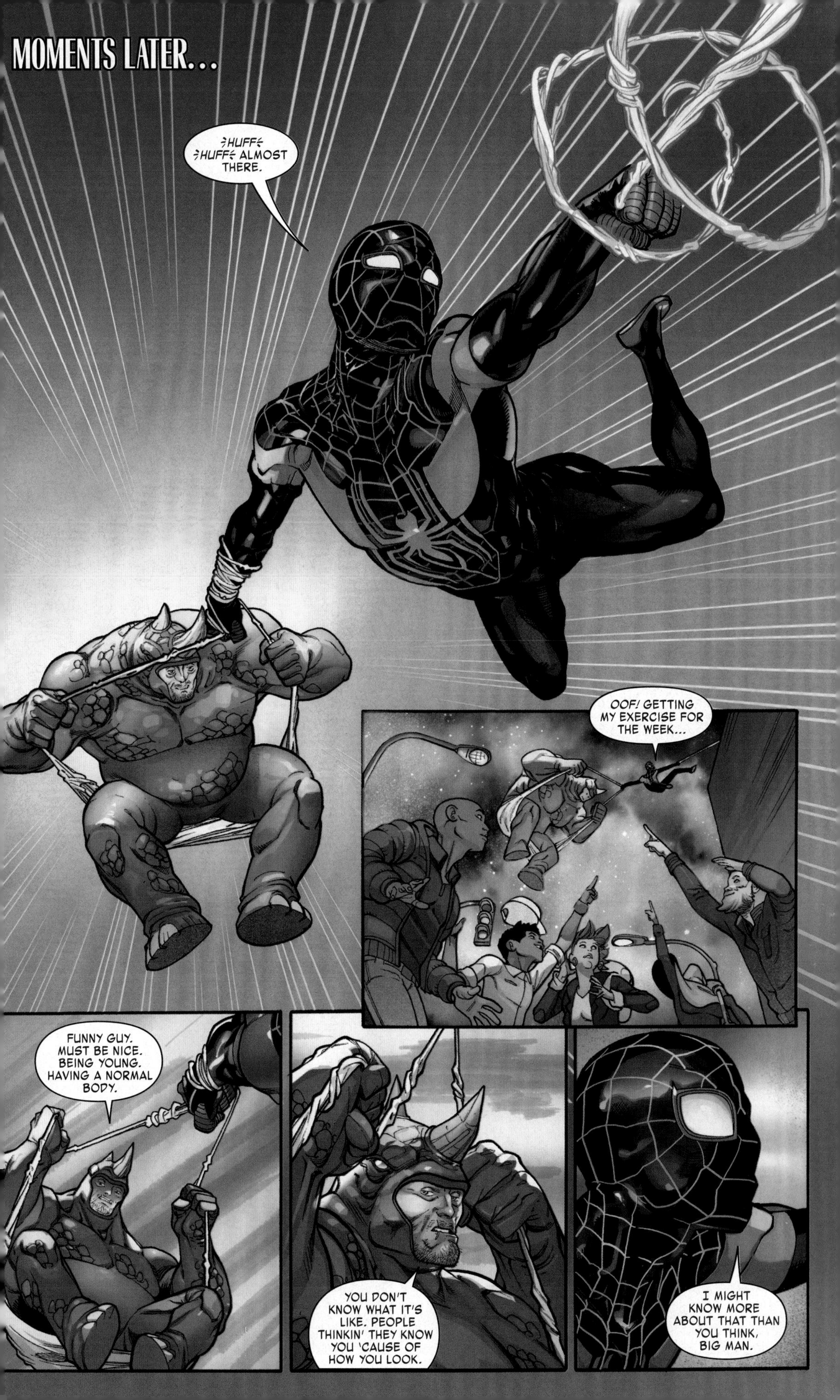

MOMENTS LATER...
HUFF HUFF ALMOST THERE.
OOF! GETTING MY EXERCISE FOR THE WEEK...
FUNNY GUY. MUST BE NICE. BEING YOUNG. HAVING A NORMAL BODY.
YOU DON'T KNOW WHAT IT'S LIKE. PEOPLE THINKIN' THEY KNOW YOU 'CAUSE OF HOW YOU LOOK.
I MIGHT KNOW MORE ABOUT THAT THAN YOU THINK, BIG MAN.

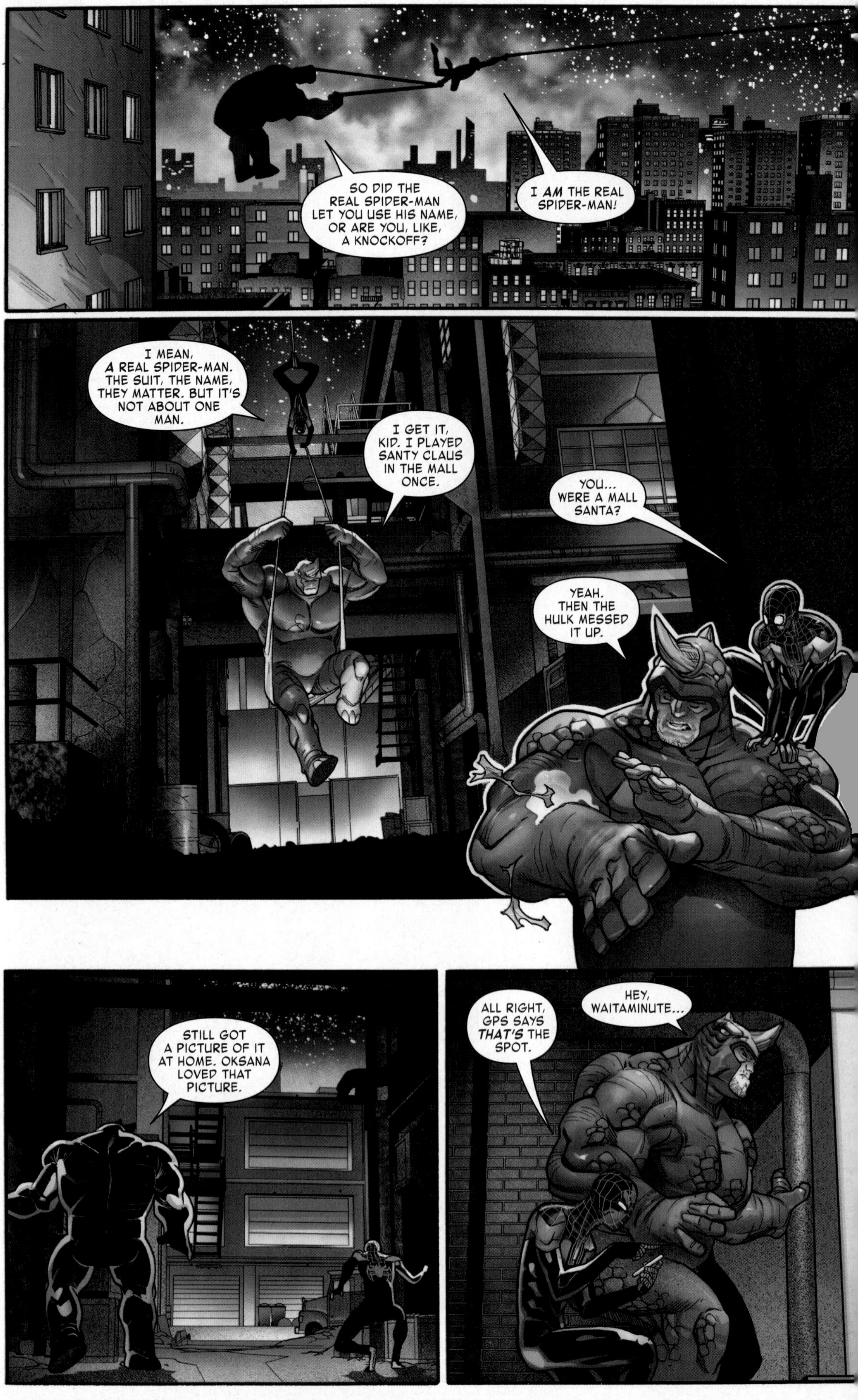
SO DID THE REAL SPIDER-MAN LET YOU USE HIS NAME, OR ARE YOU, LIKE, A KNOCKOFF?
I AM THE REAL SPIDER-MAN!
I MEAN, A REAL SPIDER-MAN. THE SUIT, THE NAME, THEY MATTER. BUT IT'S NOT ABOUT ONE MAN.
I GET IT, KID. I PLAYED SANTY CLAUS IN THE MALL ONCE.
YOU... WERE A MALL SANTA?
YEAH. THEN THE HULK MESSED IT UP.
STILL GOT A PICTURE OF IT AT HOME. OKSANA LOVED THAT PICTURE.
ALL RIGHT, GPS SAYS THAT'S THE SPOT.
HEY, WAITAMINUTE...

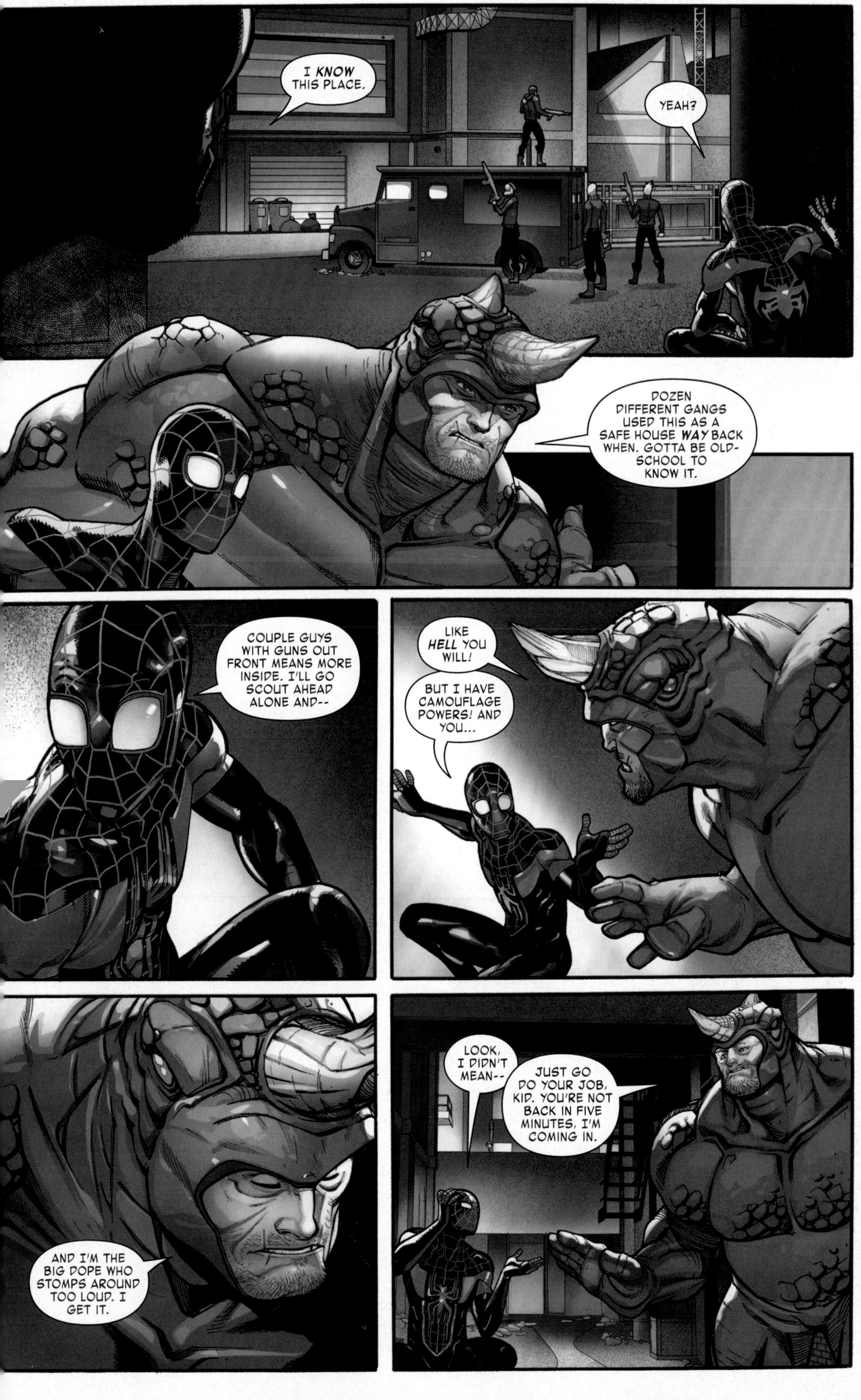
I KNOW THIS PLACE.
YEAH?
DOZEN DIFFERENT GANGS USED THIS AS A SAFE HOUSE WAY BACK WHEN. GOTTA BE OLD-SCHOOL TO KNOW IT.
COUPLE GUYS WITH GUNS OUT FRONT MEANS MORE INSIDE. I'LL GO SCOUT AHEAD ALONE AND--
LIKE HELL YOU WILL!
BUT I HAVE CAMOUFLAGE POWERS! AND YOU...
AND I'M THE BIG DOPE WHO STOMPS AROUND TOO LOUD. I GET IT.
LOOK, I DIDN'T MEAN--
JUST GO DO YOUR JOB, KID. YOU'RE NOT BACK IN FIVE MINUTES, I'M COMING IN.

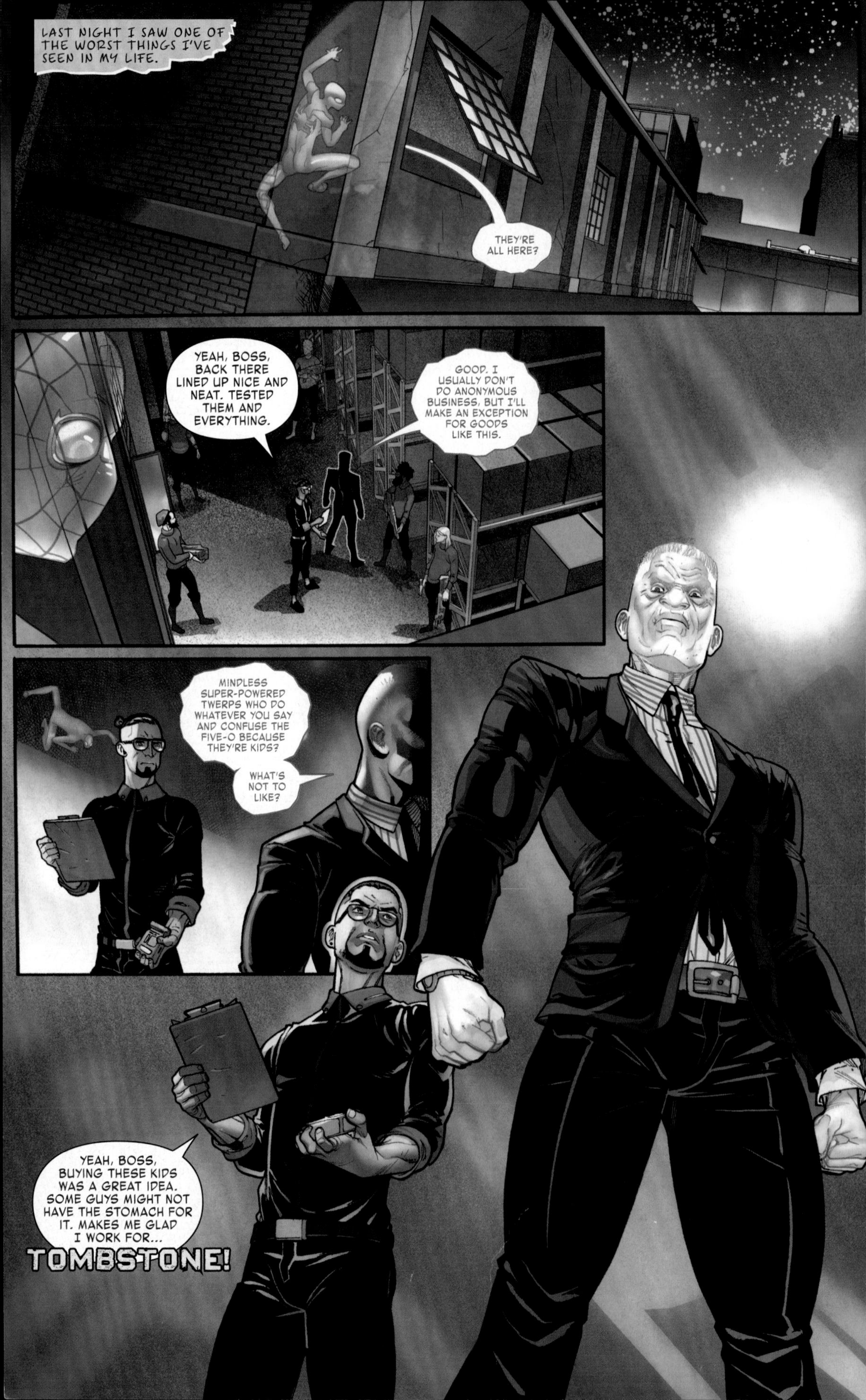
LAST NIGHT I SAW ONE OF THE WORST THINGS I'VE SEEN IN MY LIFE.
THEY'RE ALL HERE?
YEAH, BOSS, BACK THERE LINED UP NICE AND NEAT. TESTED THEM AND EVERYTHING.
GOOD. I USUALLY DON'T DO ANONYMOUS BUSINESS, BUT I'LL MAKE AN EXCEPTION FOR GOODS LIKE THIS.
MINDLESS SUPER-POWERED TWERPS WHO DO WHATEVER YOU SAY AND CONFUSE THE FIVE-O BECAUSE THEY'RE KIDS?
WHAT'S NOT TO LIKE?
YEAH, BOSS, BUYING THESE KIDS WAS A GREAT IDEA. SOME GUYS MIGHT NOT HAVE THE STOMACH FOR IT. MAKES ME GLAD I WORK FOR...
TOMBSTONE!

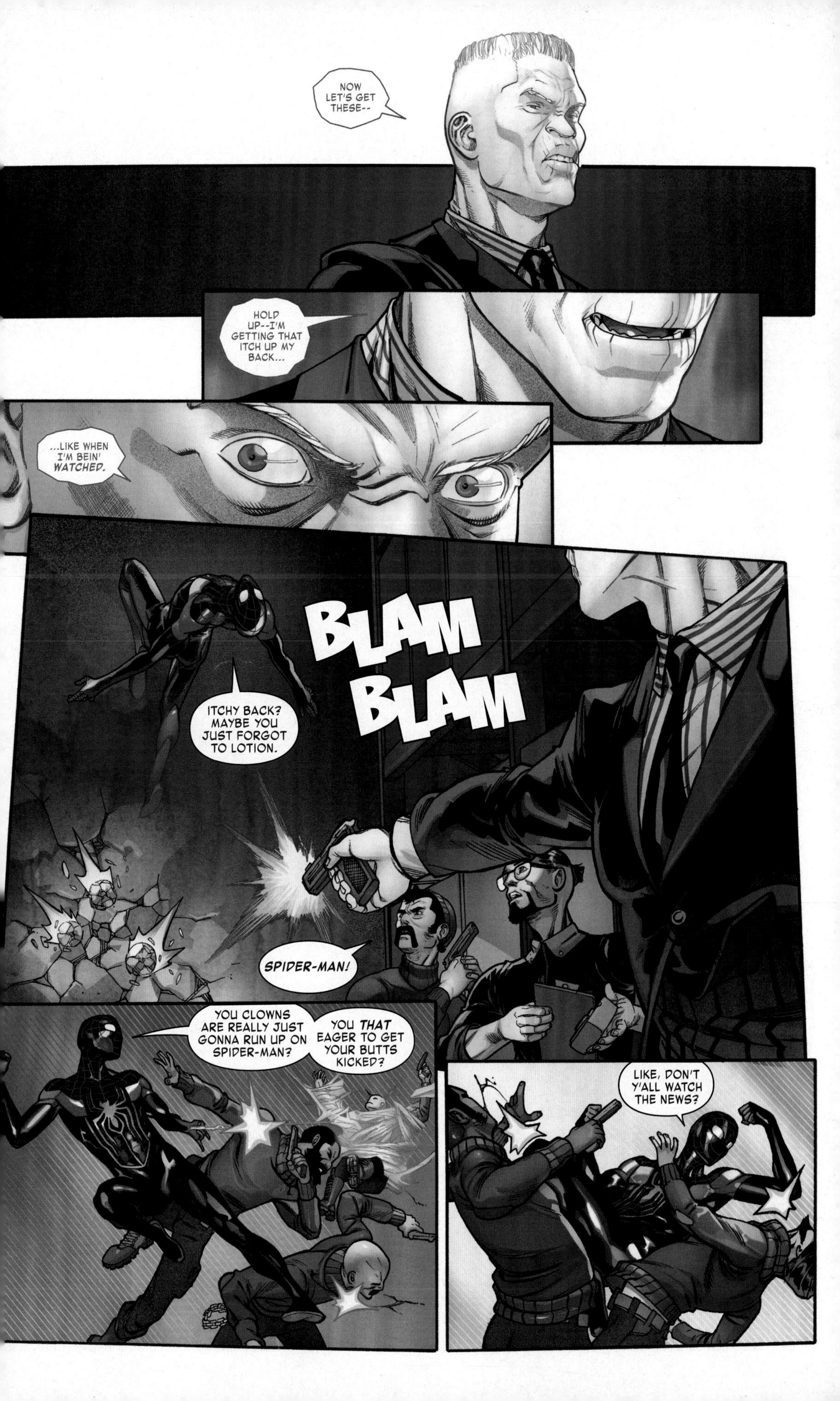

NOW LET'S GET THESE--
HOLD UP--I'M GETTING THAT ITCH UP MY BACK...
...LIKE WHEN I'M BEIN' *WATCHED.*
BLAM BLAM
ITCHY BACK? MAYBE YOU JUST FORGOT TO LOTION.
SPIDER-MAN!
YOU CLOWNS ARE REALLY JUST GONNA RUN UP ON SPIDER-MAN?
YOU *THAT* EAGER TO GET YOUR BUTTS KICKED?
LIKE, DON'T Y'ALL WATCH THE NEWS?

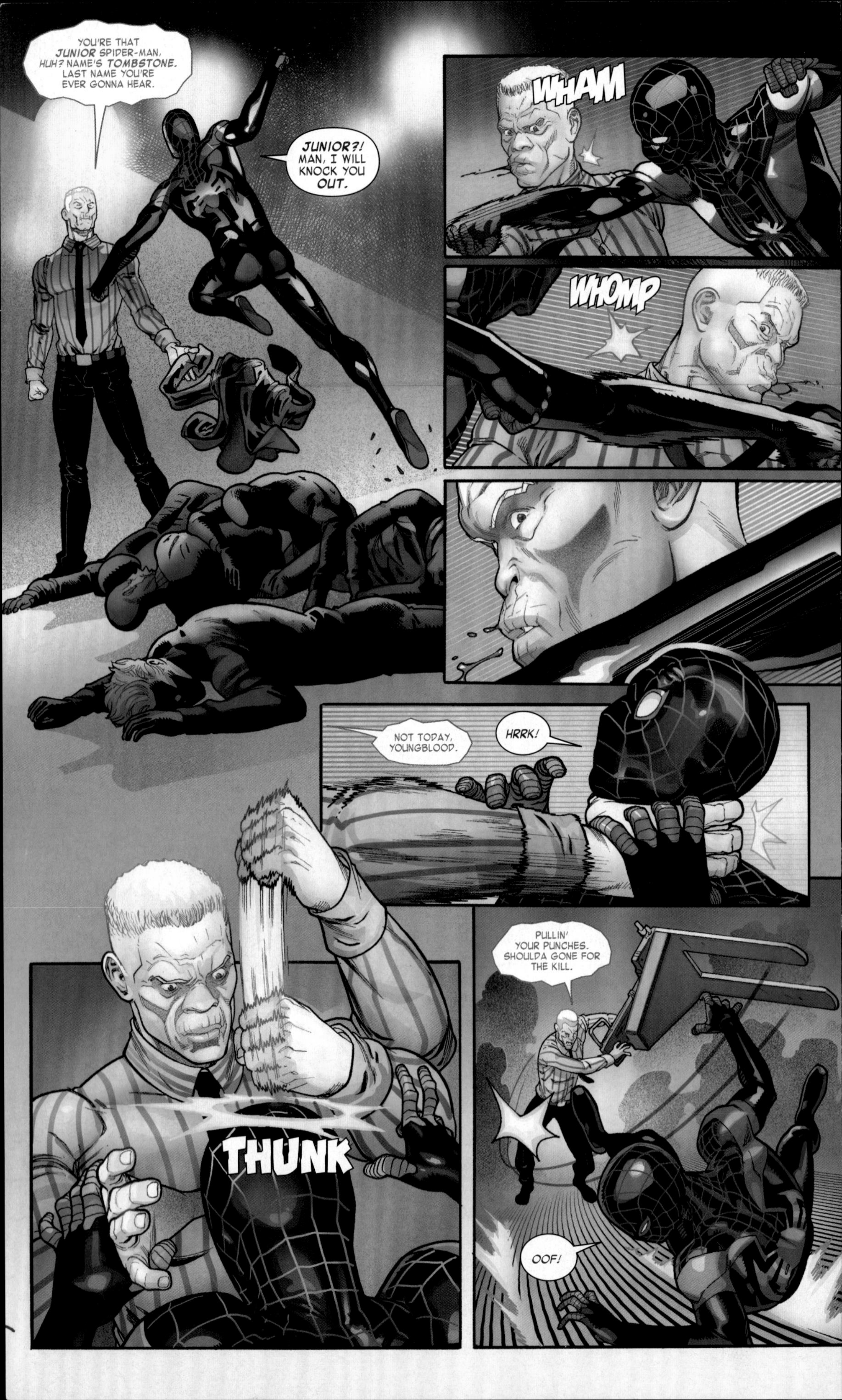
YOU'RE THAT JUNIOR SPIDER-MAN, HUH? NAME'S TOMBSTONE. LAST NAME YOU'RE EVER GONNA HEAR.
JUNIOR?! MAN, I WILL KNOCK YOU OUT.
WHAM
WHOMP
NOT TODAY, YOUNGBLOOD.
HRRK!
THUNK
PULLIN' YOUR PUNCHES. SHOULDA GONE FOR THE KILL.
OOF!

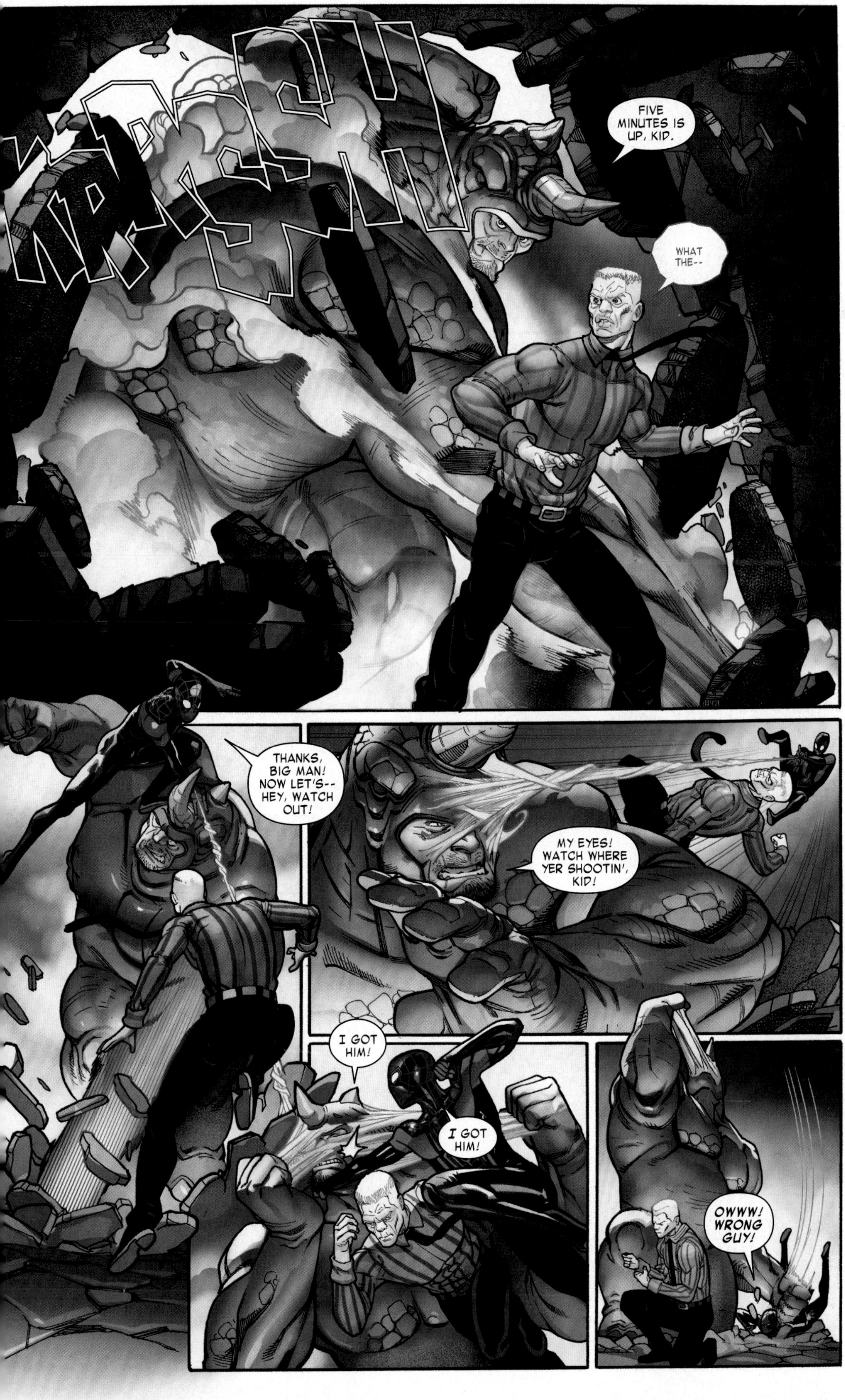
KRAKOOM
FIVE MINUTES IS UP, KID.
WHAT THE--
THANKS, BIG MAN! NOW LET'S-- HEY, WATCH OUT!
MY EYES! WATCH WHERE YER SHOOTIN', KID!
I GOT HIM!
I GOT HIM!
OWWW! WRONG GUY!

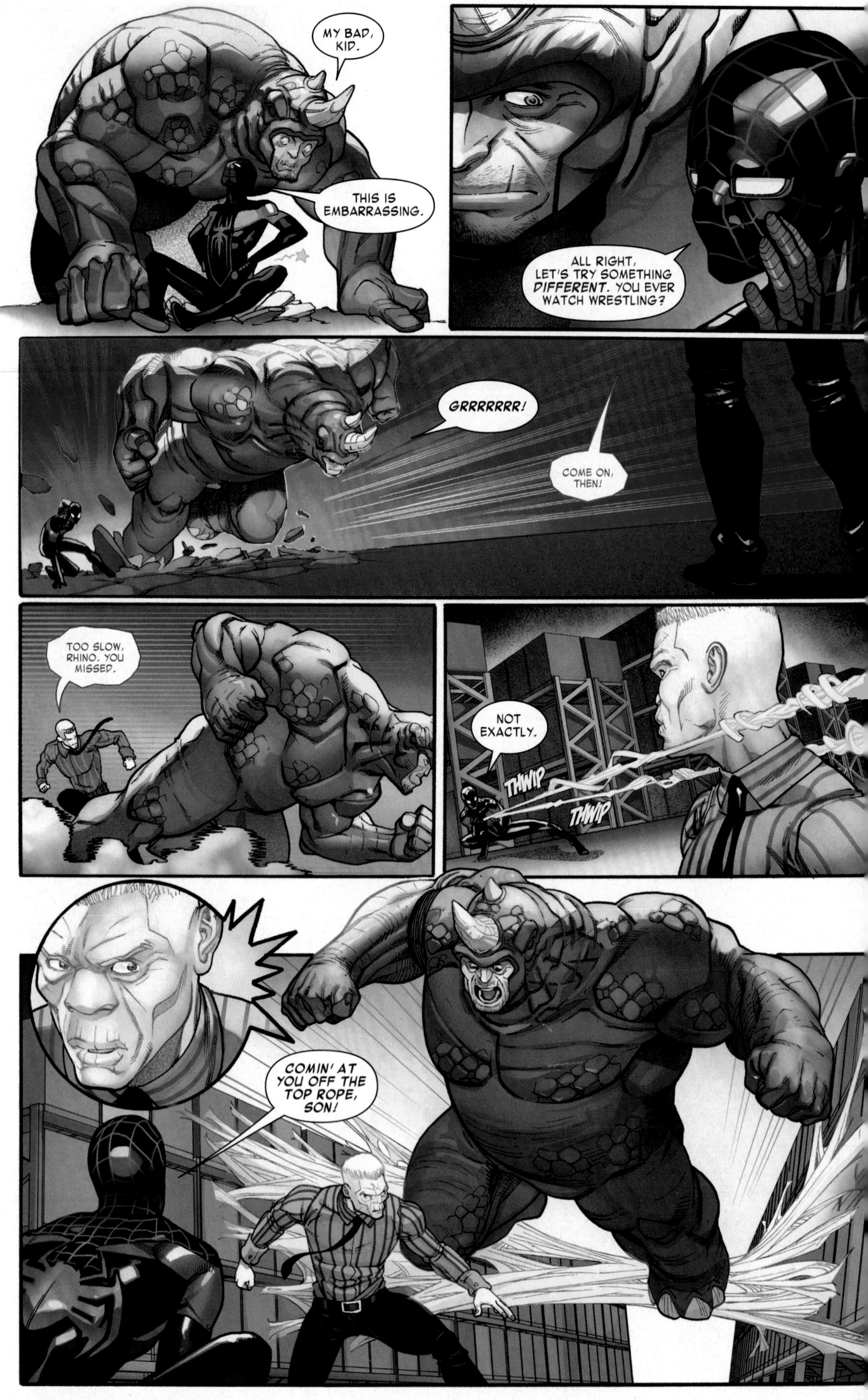
MY BAD, KID.
THIS IS EMBARRASSING.
ALL RIGHT, LET'S TRY SOMETHING DIFFERENT. YOU EVER WATCH WRESTLING?
GRRRRRRR!
COME ON, THEN!
TOO SLOW, RHINO. YOU MISSED.
NOT EXACTLY.
THWIP
THWIP
COMIN' AT YOU OFF THE TOP ROPE, SON!

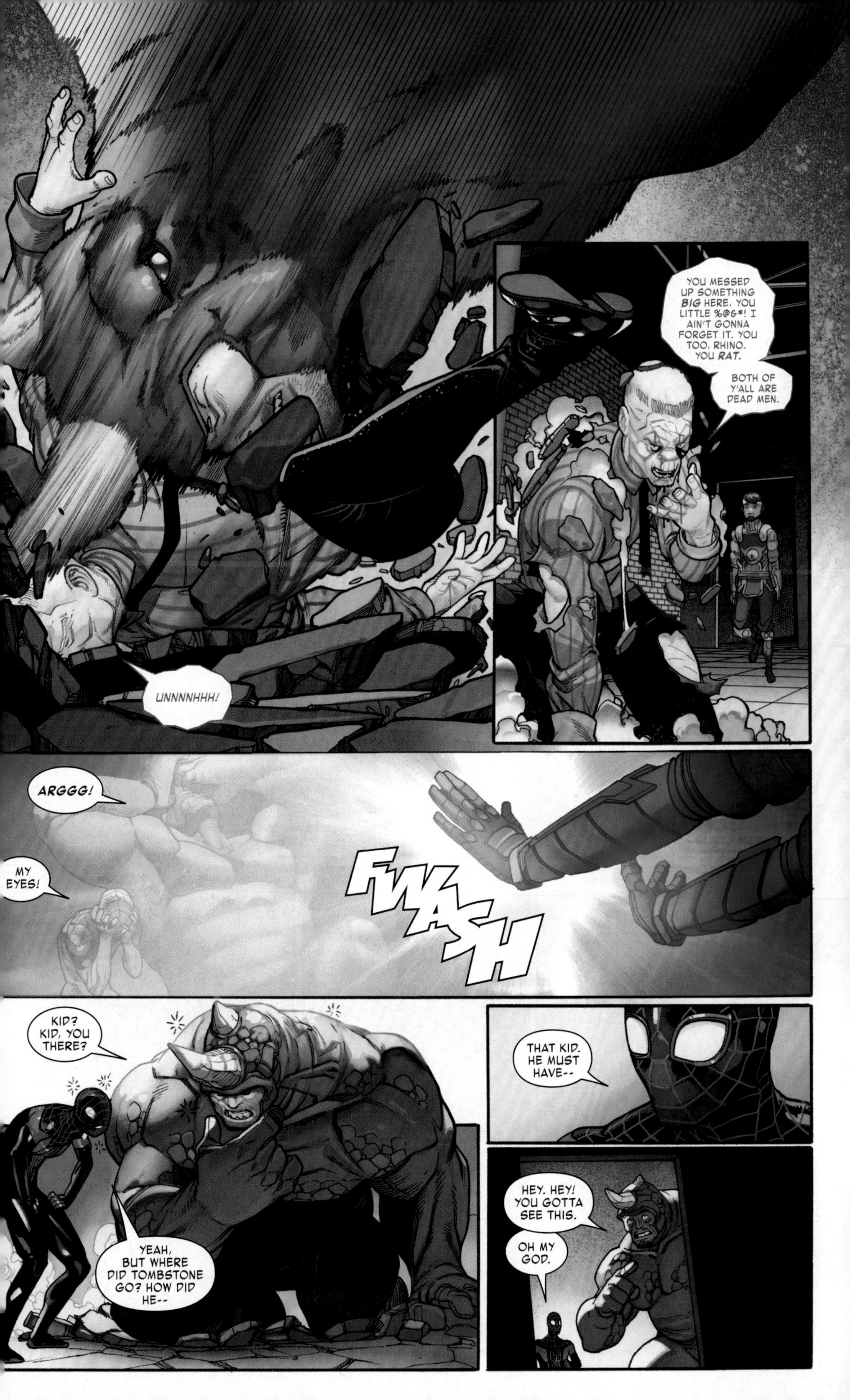
UNNNNHHH!
YOU MESSED UP SOMETHING BIG HERE, YOU LITTLE %@&*! I AIN'T GONNA FORGET IT. YOU TOO, RHINO. YOU RAT.
BOTH OF Y'ALL ARE DEAD MEN.
ARGGG!
MY EYES!
FWASH
KID? KID, YOU THERE?
YEAH, BUT WHERE DID TOMBSTONE GO? HOW DID HE--
THAT KID. HE MUST HAVE--
HEY. HEY! YOU GOTTA SEE THIS.
OH MY GOD.

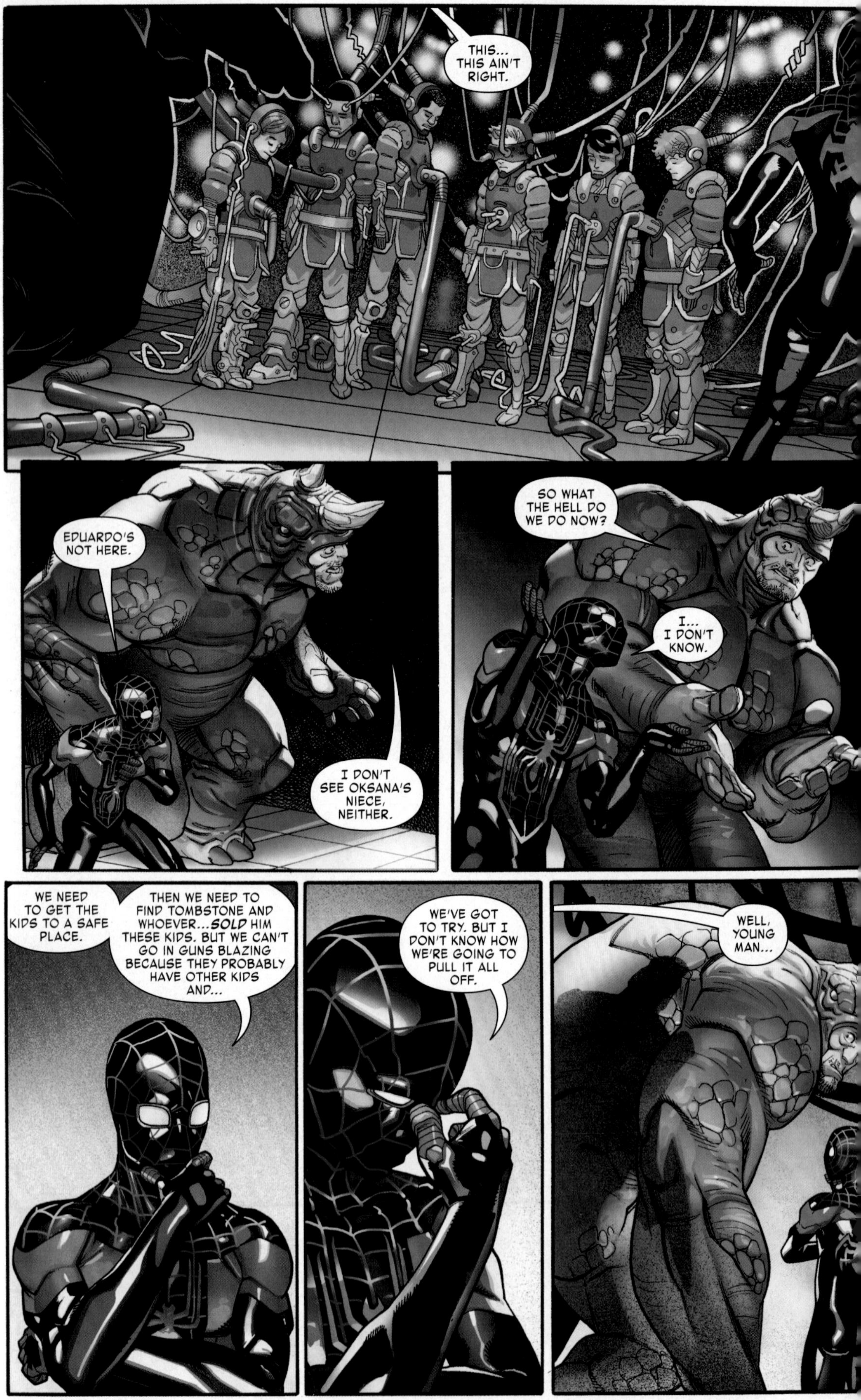
THIS... THIS AIN'T RIGHT.
EDUARDO'S NOT HERE.
I DON'T SEE OKSANA'S NIECE, NEITHER.
SO WHAT THE HELL DO WE DO NOW?
I... I DON'T KNOW.
WE NEED TO GET THE KIDS TO A SAFE PLACE.
THEN WE NEED TO FIND TOMBSTONE AND WHOEVER...SOLD HIM THESE KIDS. BUT WE CAN'T GO IN GUNS BLAZING BECAUSE THEY PROBABLY HAVE OTHER KIDS AND...
WE'VE GOT TO TRY. BUT I DON'T KNOW HOW WE'RE GOING TO PULL IT ALL OFF.
WELL, YOUNG MAN...

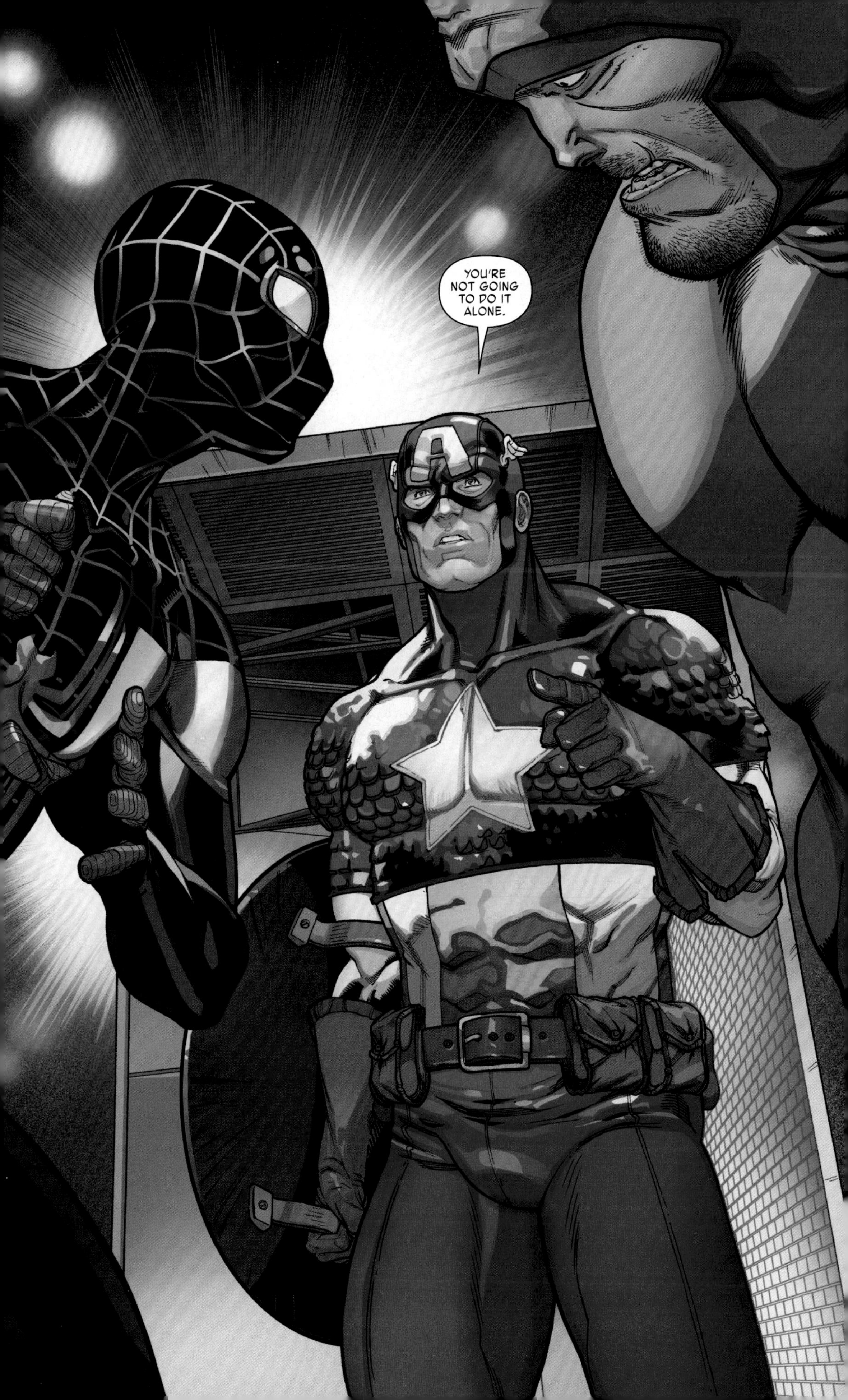
YOU'RE NOT GOING TO DO IT ALONE.

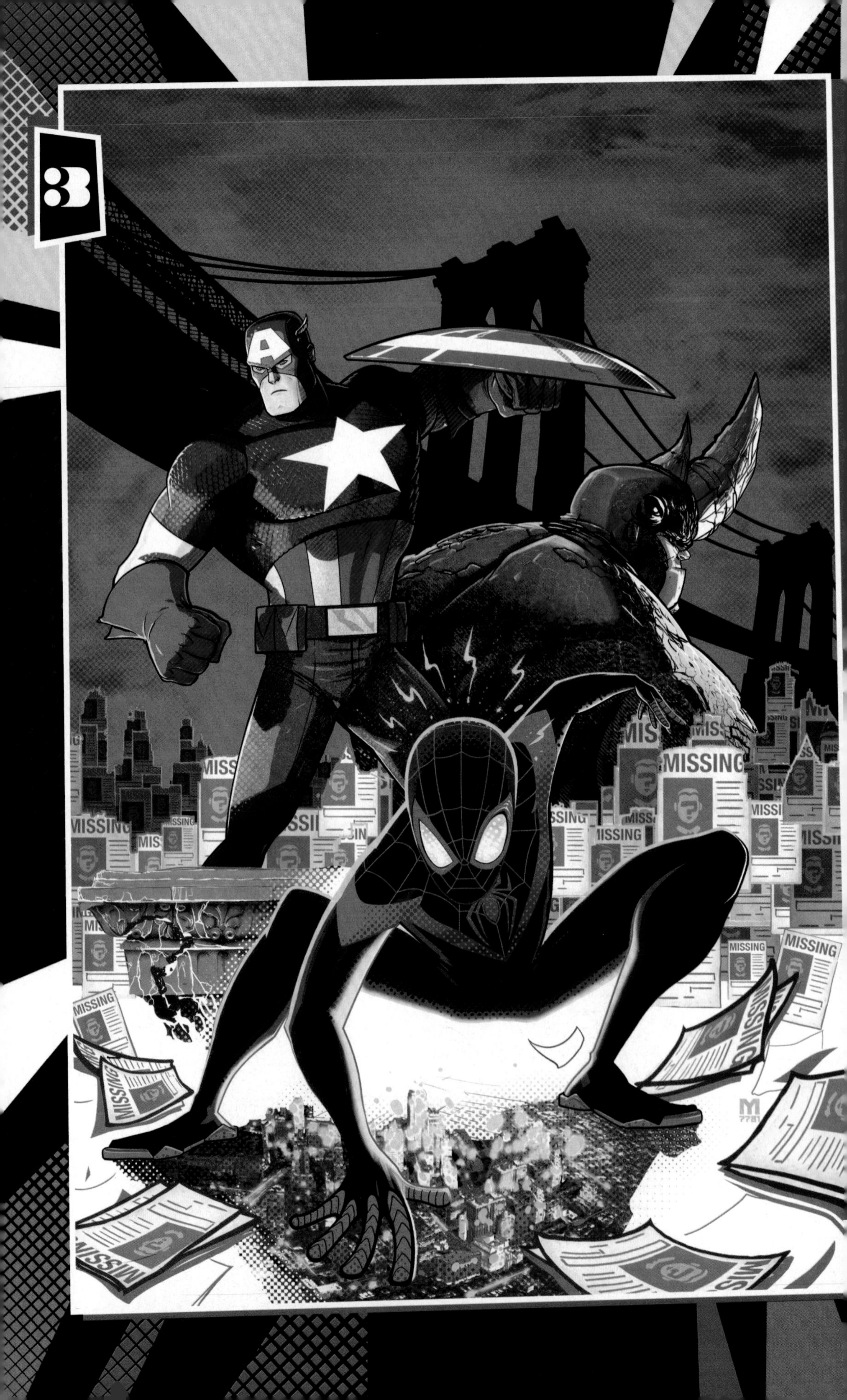

3
MISSING
MISSING
MISSING
MISSING
MISSING
MISSING
MISSING

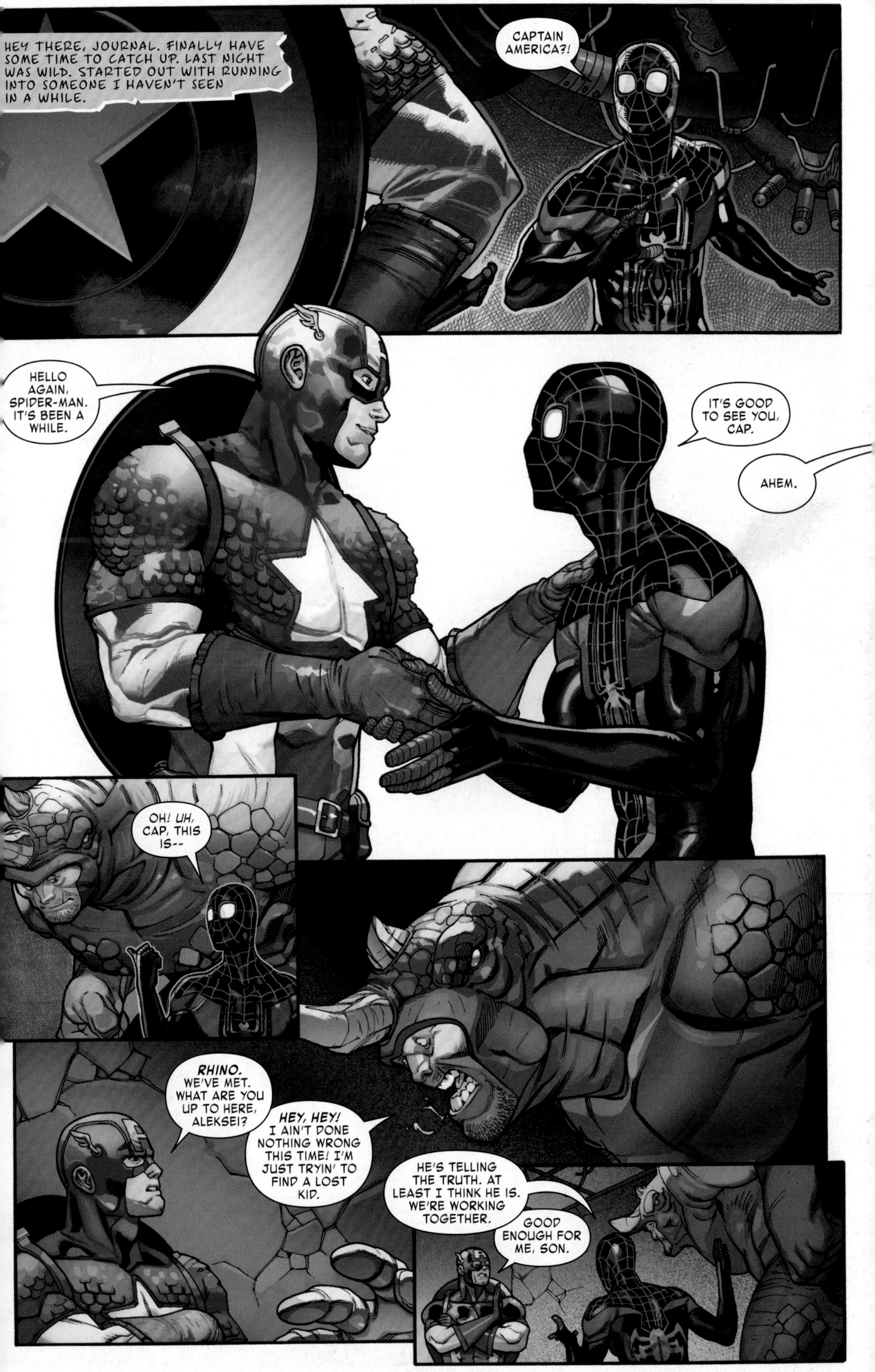
HEY THERE, JOURNAL. FINALLY HAVE SOME TIME TO CATCH UP. LAST NIGHT WAS WILD. STARTED OUT WITH RUNNING INTO SOMEONE I HAVEN'T SEEN IN A WHILE.
CAPTAIN AMERICA?!
HELLO AGAIN, SPIDER-MAN. IT'S BEEN A WHILE.
IT'S GOOD TO SEE YOU, CAP.
AHEM.
OH! UH, CAP, THIS IS--
RHINO. WE'VE MET. WHAT ARE YOU UP TO HERE, ALEKSEI?
HEY, HEY! I AIN'T DONE NOTHING WRONG THIS TIME! I'M JUST TRYIN' TO FIND A LOST KID.
HE'S TELLING THE TRUTH. AT LEAST I THINK HE IS. WE'RE WORKING TOGETHER.
GOOD ENOUGH FOR ME, SON.

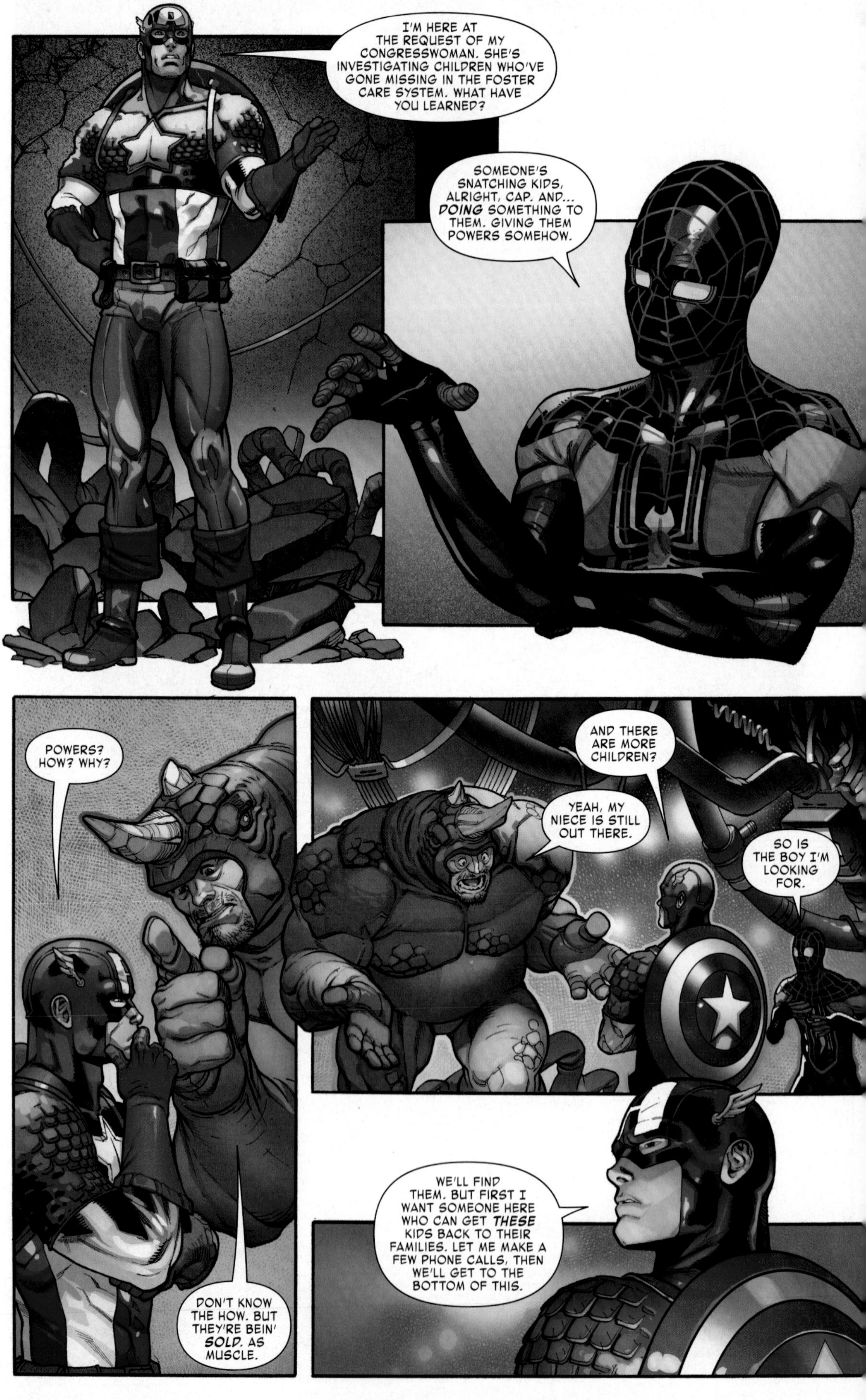
I'M HERE AT THE REQUEST OF MY CONGRESSWOMAN. SHE'S INVESTIGATING CHILDREN WHO'VE GONE MISSING IN THE FOSTER CARE SYSTEM. WHAT HAVE YOU LEARNED?
SOMEONE'S SNATCHING KIDS, ALRIGHT, CAP. AND... *DOING* SOMETHING TO THEM. GIVING THEM POWERS SOMEHOW.
POWERS? HOW? WHY?
DON'T KNOW THE HOW. BUT THEY'RE BEIN' *SOLD*. AS MUSCLE.
AND THERE ARE MORE CHILDREN?
YEAH, MY NIECE IS STILL OUT THERE.
SO IS THE BOY I'M LOOKING FOR.
WE'LL FIND THEM. BUT FIRST I WANT SOMEONE HERE WHO CAN GET *THESE* KIDS BACK TO THEIR FAMILIES. LET ME MAKE A FEW PHONE CALLS, THEN WE'LL GET TO THE BOTTOM OF THIS.

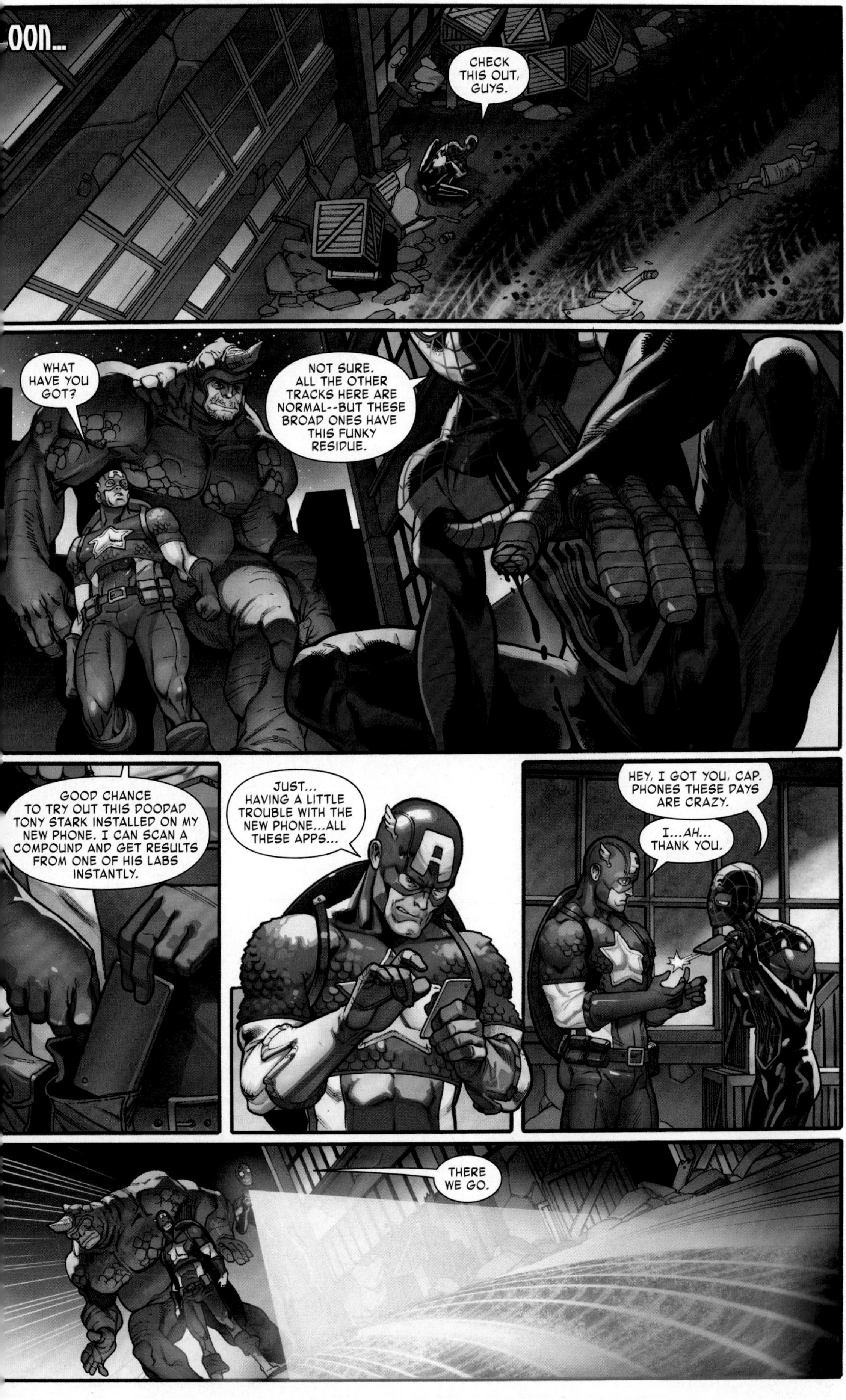
...OON...
CHECK THIS OUT, GUYS.
WHAT HAVE YOU GOT?
NOT SURE. ALL THE OTHER TRACKS HERE ARE NORMAL--BUT THESE BROAD ONES HAVE THIS FUNKY RESIDUE.
GOOD CHANCE TO TRY OUT THIS DOODAD TONY STARK INSTALLED ON MY NEW PHONE. I CAN SCAN A COMPOUND AND GET RESULTS FROM ONE OF HIS LABS INSTANTLY.
JUST... HAVING A LITTLE TROUBLE WITH THE NEW PHONE...ALL THESE APPS...
HEY, I GOT YOU, CAP. PHONES THESE DAYS ARE CRAZY.
I...AH... THANK YOU.
THERE WE GO.

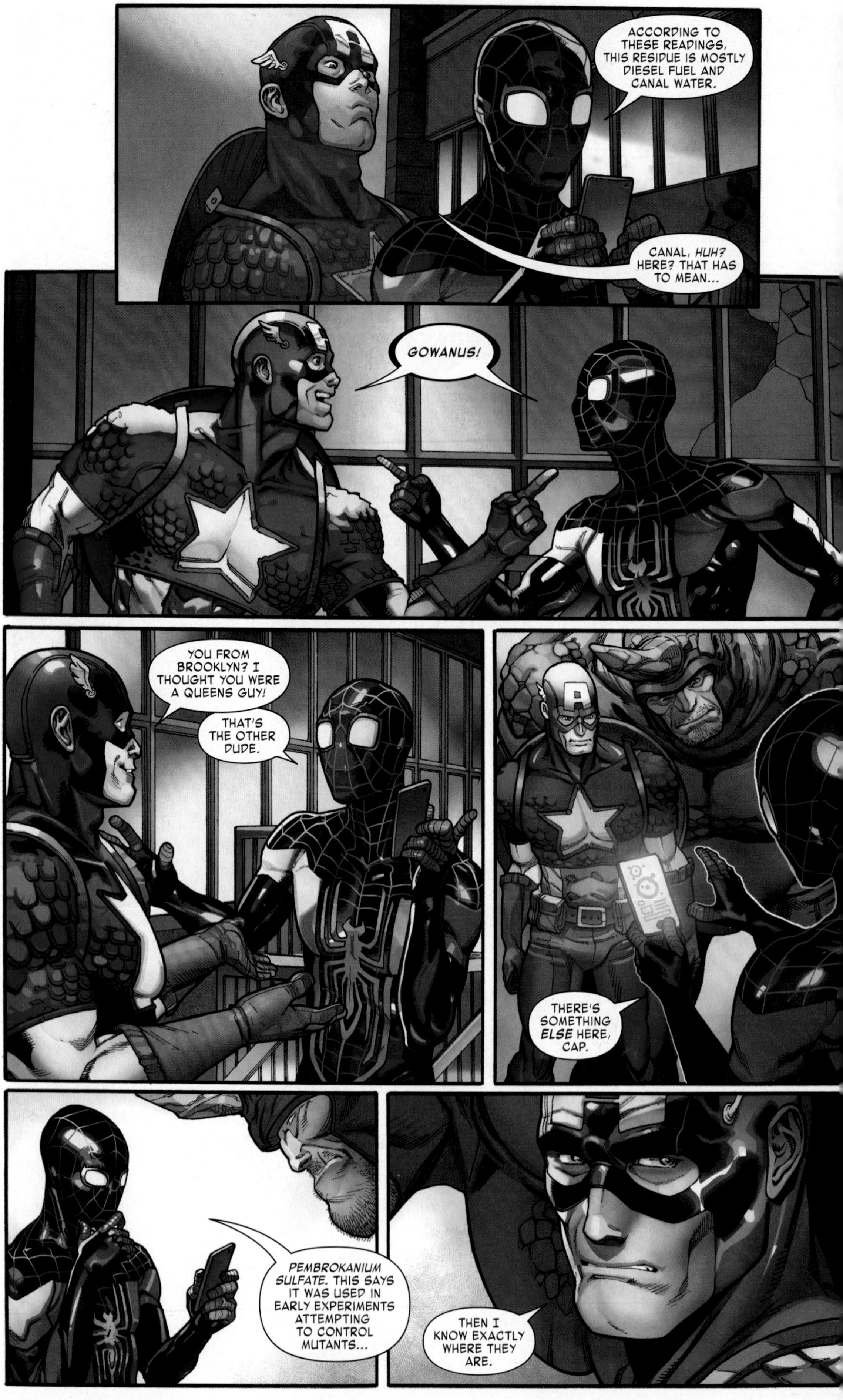
ACCORDING TO THESE READINGS, THIS RESIDUE IS MOSTLY DIESEL FUEL AND CANAL WATER.
CANAL, *HUH?* HERE? THAT HAS TO MEAN...
GOWANUS!
YOU FROM BROOKLYN? I THOUGHT YOU WERE A QUEENS GUY!
THAT'S THE OTHER DUDE.
THERE'S SOMETHING ***ELSE*** HERE, CAP.
PEMBROKANIUM SULFATE. THIS SAYS IT WAS USED IN EARLY EXPERIMENTS ATTEMPTING TO CONTROL MUTANTS...
THEN I KNOW EXACTLY WHERE THEY ARE.

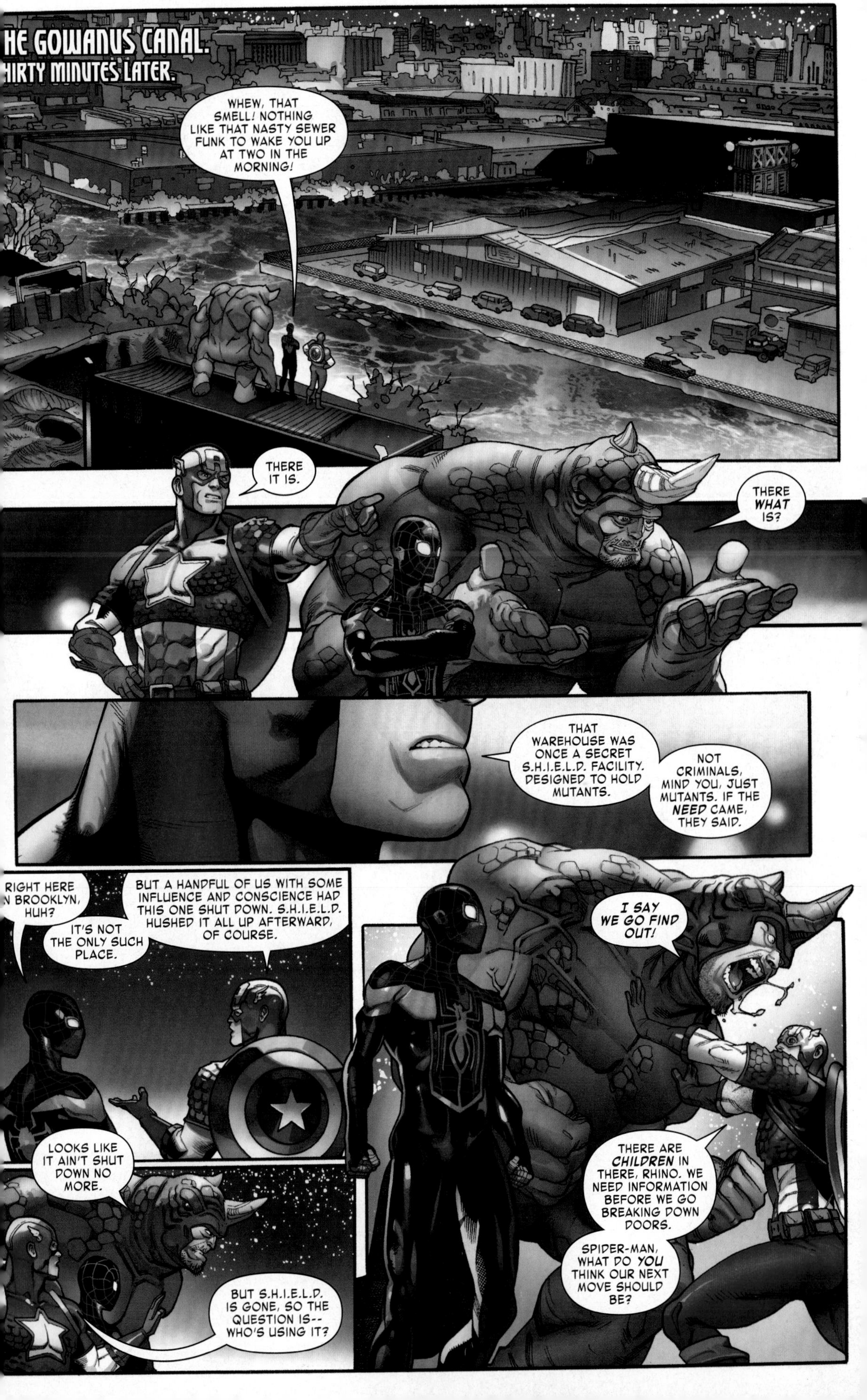

HE GOWANUS CANAL.
HIRTY MINUTES LATER.
WHEW, THAT SMELL! NOTHING LIKE THAT NASTY SEWER FUNK TO WAKE YOU UP AT TWO IN THE MORNING!
THERE IT IS.
THERE WHAT IS?
THAT WAREHOUSE WAS ONCE A SECRET S.H.I.E.L.D. FACILITY. DESIGNED TO HOLD MUTANTS.
NOT CRIMINALS, MIND YOU, JUST MUTANTS. IF THE NEED CAME, THEY SAID.
RIGHT HERE N BROOKLYN, HUH?
IT'S NOT THE ONLY SUCH PLACE.
BUT A HANDFUL OF US WITH SOME INFLUENCE AND CONSCIENCE HAD THIS ONE SHUT DOWN. S.H.I.E.L.D. HUSHED IT ALL UP AFTERWARD, OF COURSE.
LOOKS LIKE IT AIN'T SHUT DOWN NO MORE.
BUT S.H.I.E.L.D. IS GONE, SO THE QUESTION IS-- WHO'S USING IT?
I SAY WE GO FIND OUT!
THERE ARE CHILDREN IN THERE, RHINO. WE NEED INFORMATION BEFORE WE GO BREAKING DOWN DOORS.
SPIDER-MAN, WHAT DO YOU THINK OUR NEXT MOVE SHOULD BE?

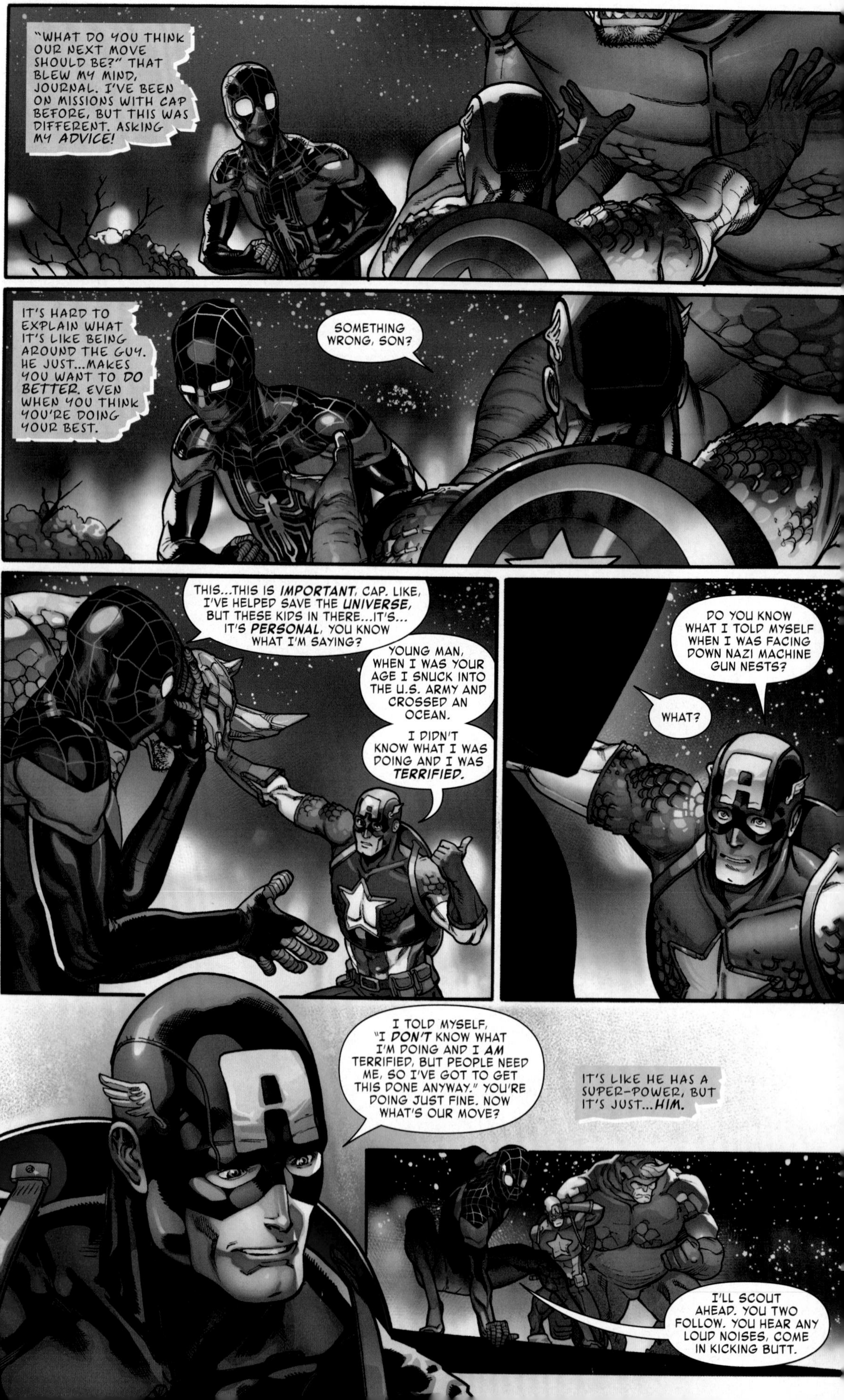
"WHAT DO YOU THINK OUR NEXT MOVE SHOULD BE?" THAT BLEW MY MIND, JOURNAL. I'VE BEEN ON MISSIONS WITH CAP BEFORE, BUT THIS WAS DIFFERENT. ASKING MY ADVICE!
IT'S HARD TO EXPLAIN WHAT IT'S LIKE BEING AROUND THE GUY. HE JUST...MAKES YOU WANT TO DO BETTER. EVEN WHEN YOU THINK YOU'RE DOING YOUR BEST.
SOMETHING WRONG, SON?
THIS...THIS IS IMPORTANT, CAP. LIKE, I'VE HELPED SAVE THE UNIVERSE, BUT THESE KIDS IN THERE...IT'S... IT'S PERSONAL, YOU KNOW WHAT I'M SAYING?
YOUNG MAN, WHEN I WAS YOUR AGE I SNUCK INTO THE U.S. ARMY AND CROSSED AN OCEAN.
I DIDN'T KNOW WHAT I WAS DOING AND I WAS TERRIFIED.
DO YOU KNOW WHAT I TOLD MYSELF WHEN I WAS FACING DOWN NAZI MACHINE GUN NESTS?
WHAT?
I TOLD MYSELF, "I DON'T KNOW WHAT I'M DOING AND I AM TERRIFIED, BUT PEOPLE NEED ME, SO I'VE GOT TO GET THIS DONE ANYWAY." YOU'RE DOING JUST FINE. NOW WHAT'S OUR MOVE?
IT'S LIKE HE HAS A SUPER-POWER, BUT IT'S JUST...HIM.
I'LL SCOUT AHEAD. YOU TWO FOLLOW. YOU HEAR ANY LOUD NOISES, COME IN KICKING BUTT.

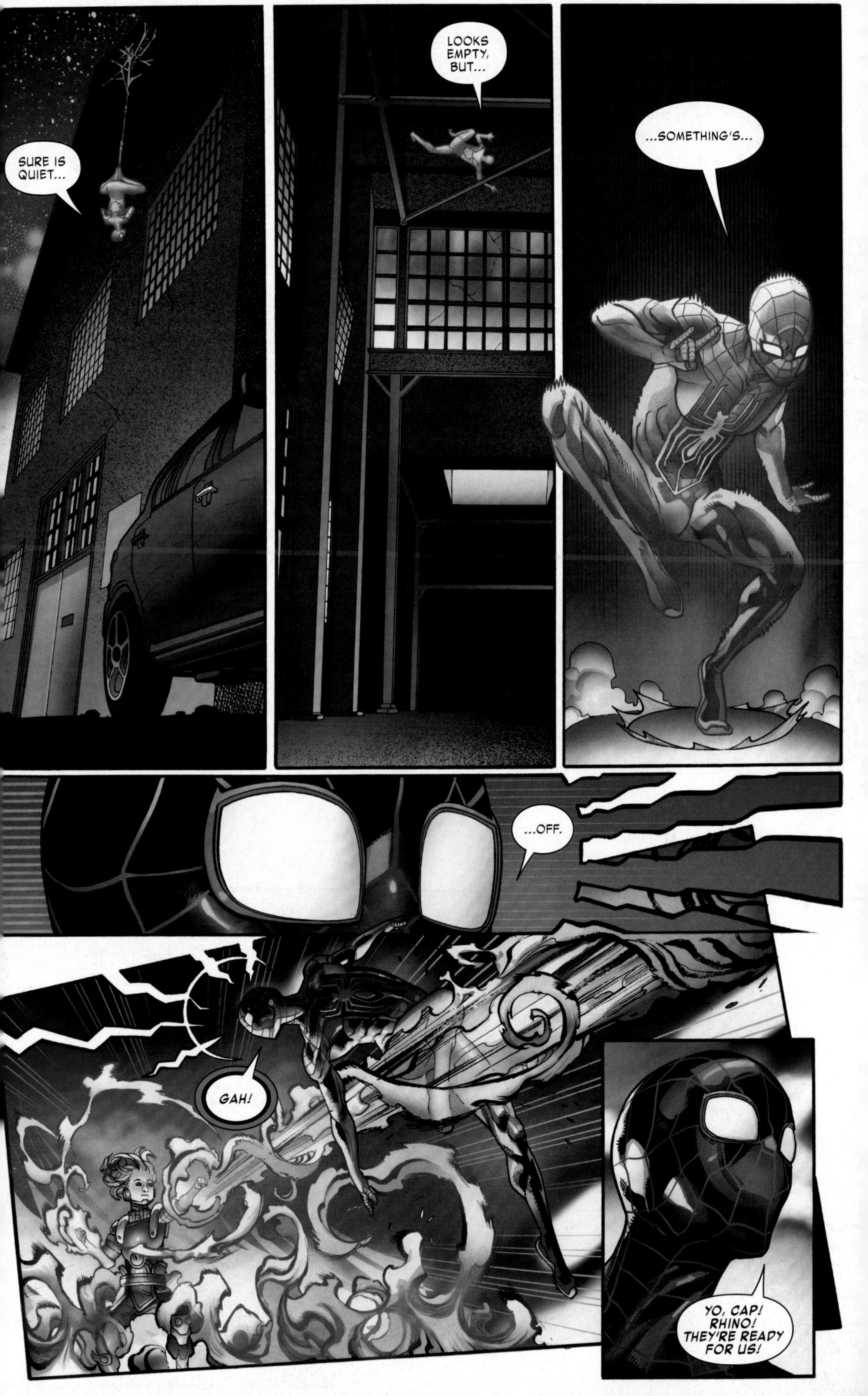
SURE IS QUIET...
LOOKS EMPTY, BUT...
...SOMETHING'S...
...OFF.
GAH!
YO, CAP! RHINO! THEY'RE READY FOR US!

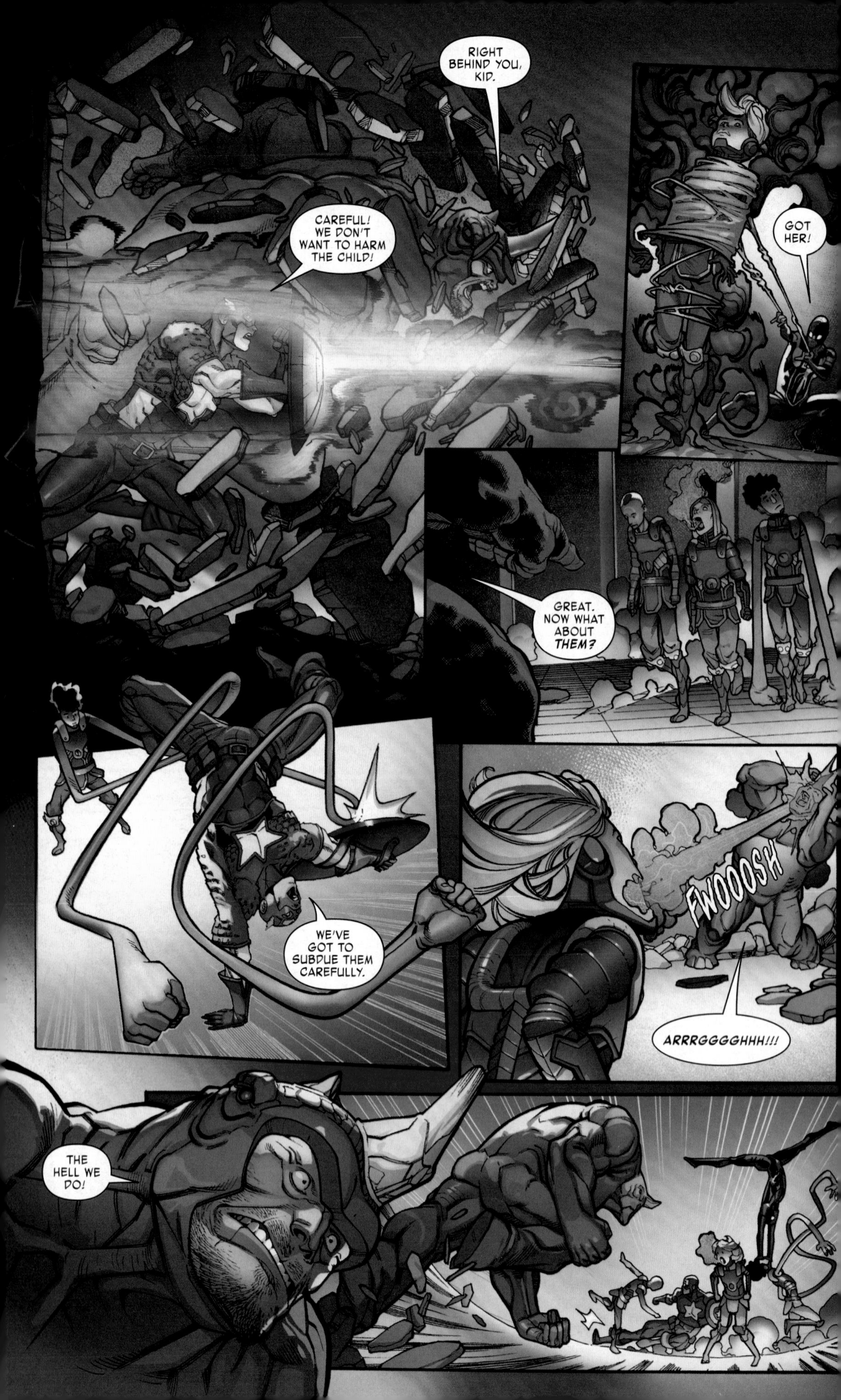
RIGHT BEHIND YOU, KID.
CAREFUL! WE DON'T WANT TO HARM THE CHILD!
GOT HER!
GREAT. NOW WHAT ABOUT THEM?
WE'VE GOT TO SUBDUE THEM CAREFULLY.
FWOOOSH
ARRRGGGGHHH!!!
THE HELL WE DO!

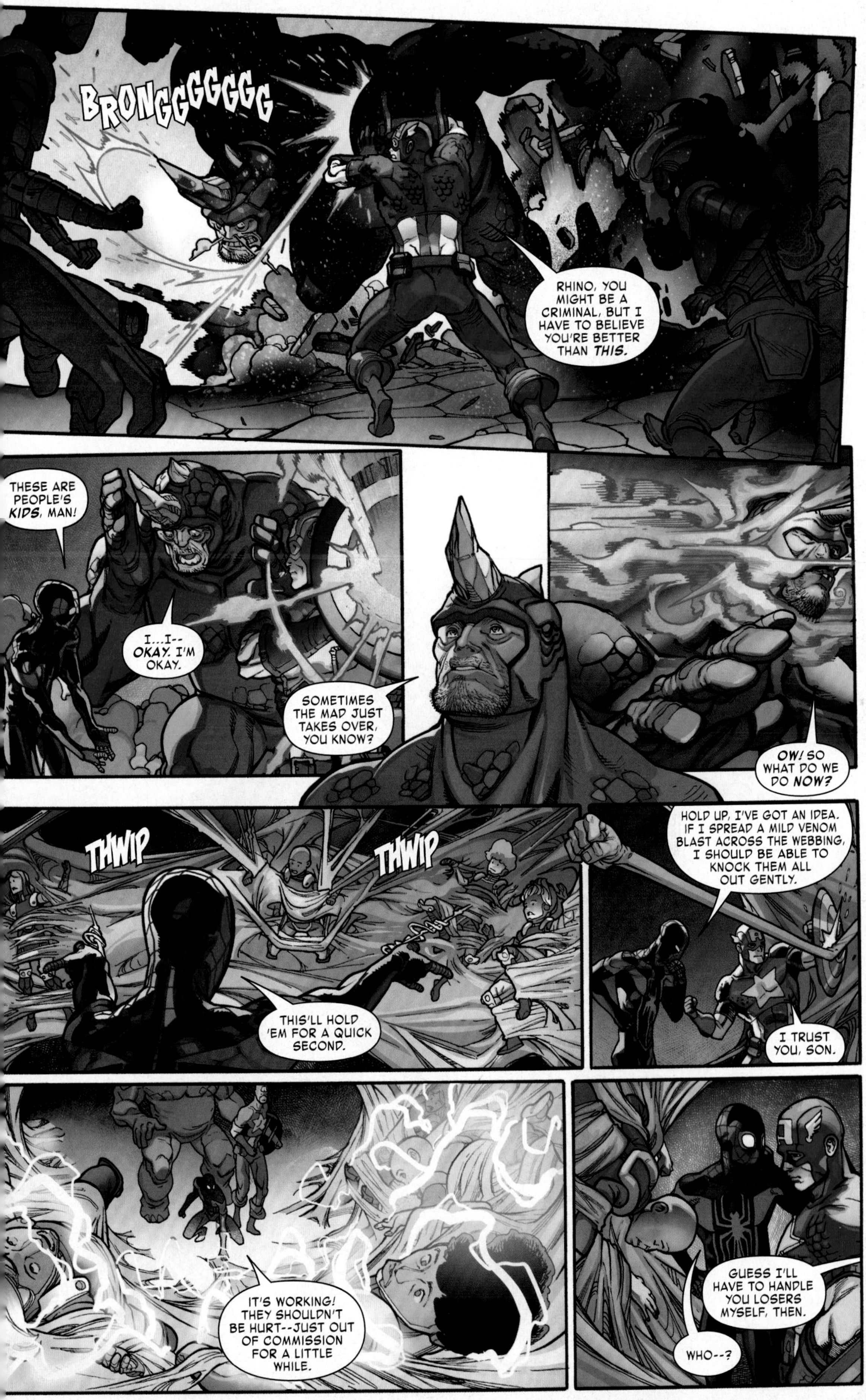
BRONGGGGGGG
RHINO, YOU MIGHT BE A CRIMINAL, BUT I HAVE TO BELIEVE YOU'RE BETTER THAN THIS.
THESE ARE PEOPLE'S KIDS, MAN!
I...I-- OKAY. I'M OKAY.
SOMETIMES THE MAD JUST TAKES OVER, YOU KNOW?
OW! SO WHAT DO WE DO NOW?
THWIP
THWIP
THIS'LL HOLD 'EM FOR A QUICK SECOND.
HOLD UP, I'VE GOT AN IDEA. IF I SPREAD A MILD VENOM BLAST ACROSS THE WEBBING, I SHOULD BE ABLE TO KNOCK THEM ALL OUT GENTLY.
I TRUST YOU, SON.
IT'S WORKING! THEY SHOULDN'T BE HURT--JUST OUT OF COMMISSION FOR A LITTLE WHILE.
GUESS I'LL HAVE TO HANDLE YOU LOSERS MYSELF, THEN.
WHO--?

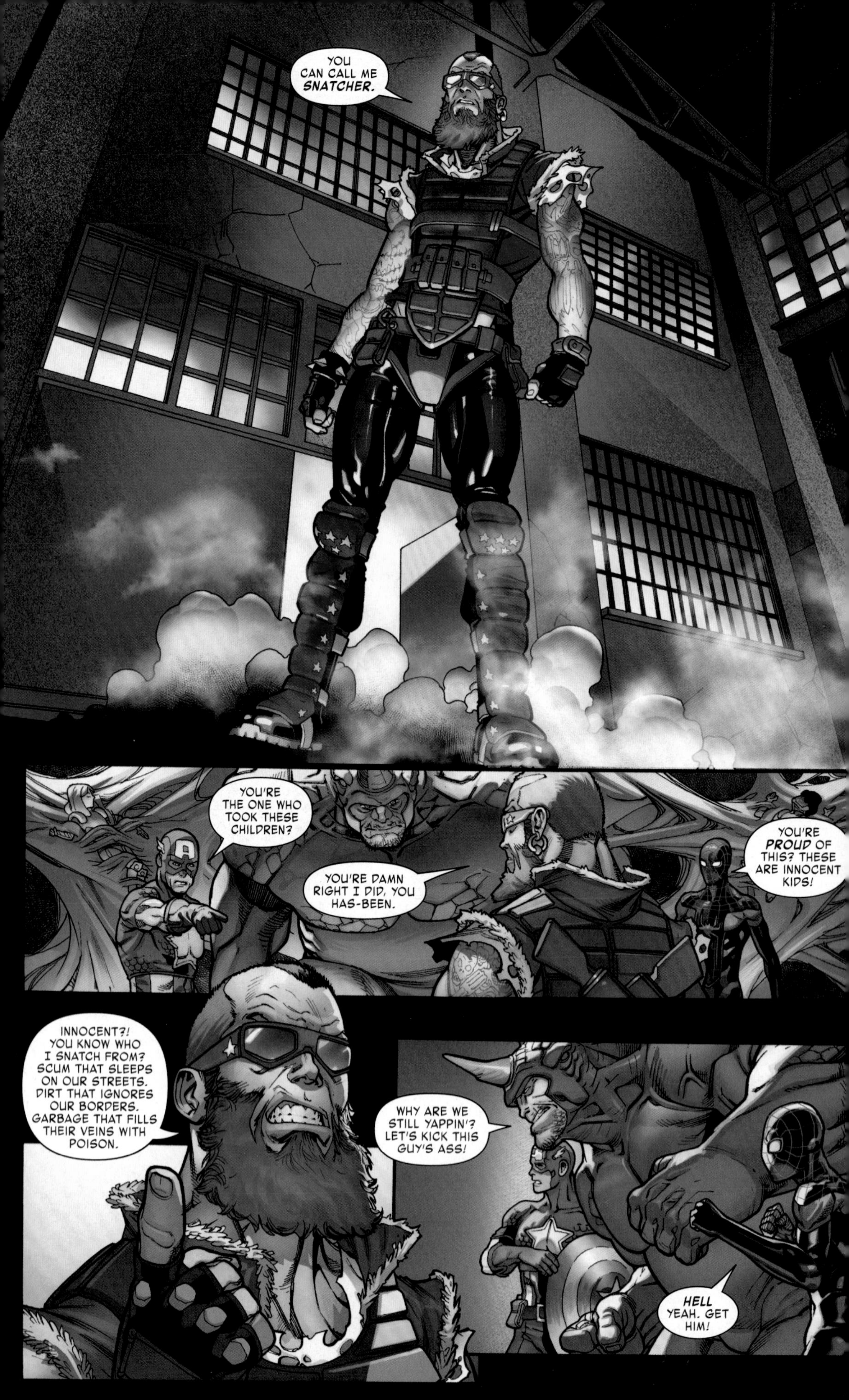
YOU CAN CALL ME *SNATCHER.*
YOU'RE THE ONE WHO TOOK THESE CHILDREN?
YOU'RE DAMN RIGHT I DID, YOU HAS-BEEN.
YOU'RE *PROUD* OF THIS? THESE ARE INNOCENT KIDS!
INNOCENT?! YOU KNOW WHO I SNATCH FROM? SCUM THAT SLEEPS ON OUR STREETS. DIRT THAT IGNORES OUR BORDERS. GARBAGE THAT FILLS THEIR VEINS WITH POISON.
WHY ARE WE STILL YAPPIN'? LET'S KICK THIS GUY'S ASS!
HELL YEAH. GET HIM!

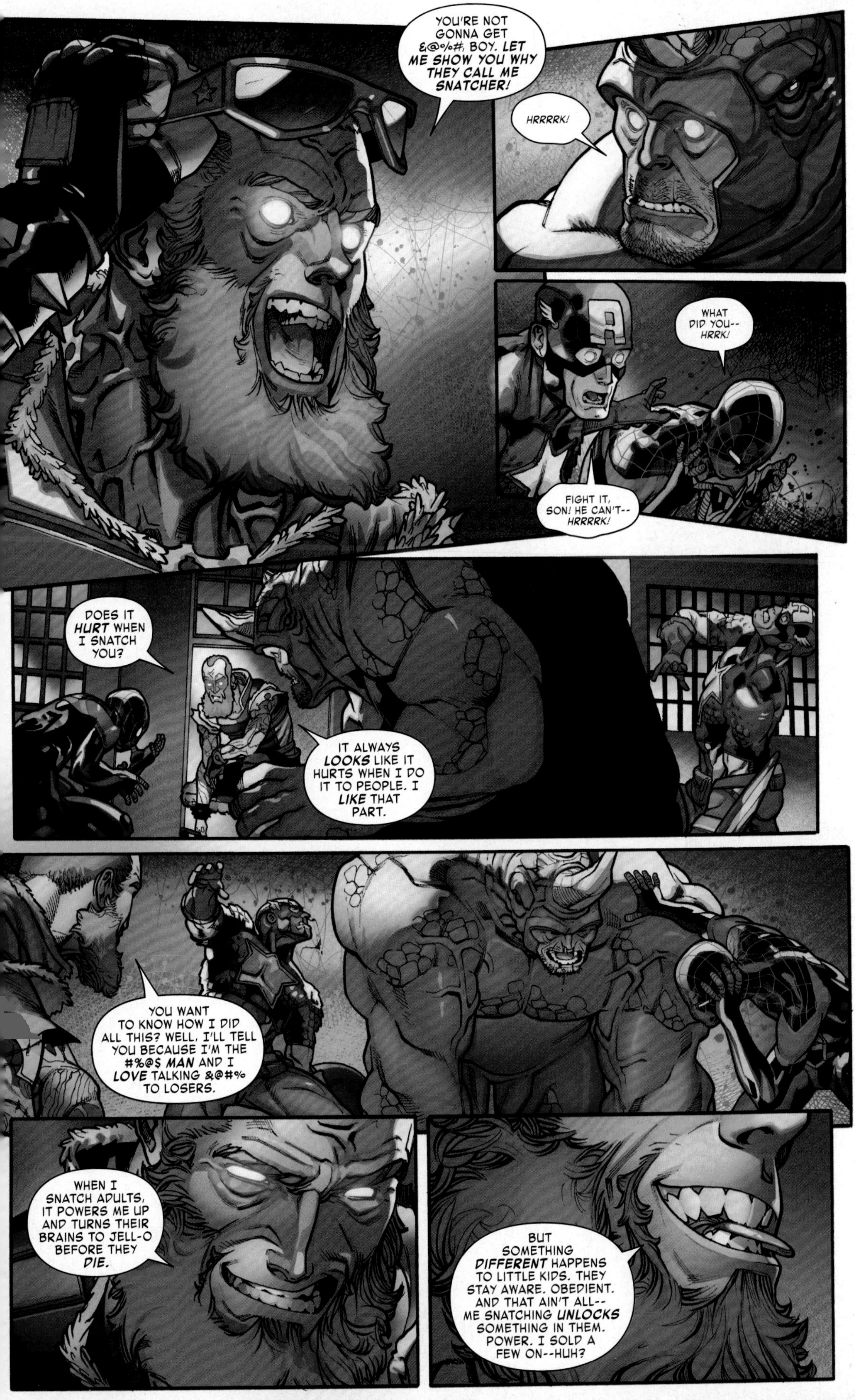

YOU'RE NOT GONNA GET &@%#, BOY. LET ME SHOW YOU WHY THEY CALL ME SNATCHER!
HRRRRK!
WHAT DID YOU-- HRRK!
FIGHT IT, SON! HE CAN'T-- HRRRRK!
DOES IT HURT WHEN I SNATCH YOU?
IT ALWAYS LOOKS LIKE IT HURTS WHEN I DO IT TO PEOPLE. I LIKE THAT PART.
YOU WANT TO KNOW HOW I DID ALL THIS? WELL, I'LL TELL YOU BECAUSE I'M THE #%@$ MAN AND I LOVE TALKING &@#% TO LOSERS.
WHEN I SNATCH ADULTS, IT POWERS ME UP AND TURNS THEIR BRAINS TO JELL-O BEFORE THEY DIE.
BUT SOMETHING DIFFERENT HAPPENS TO LITTLE KIDS. THEY STAY AWARE. OBEDIENT. AND THAT AIN'T ALL-- ME SNATCHING UNLOCKS SOMETHING IN THEM. POWER. I SOLD A FEW ON--HUH?

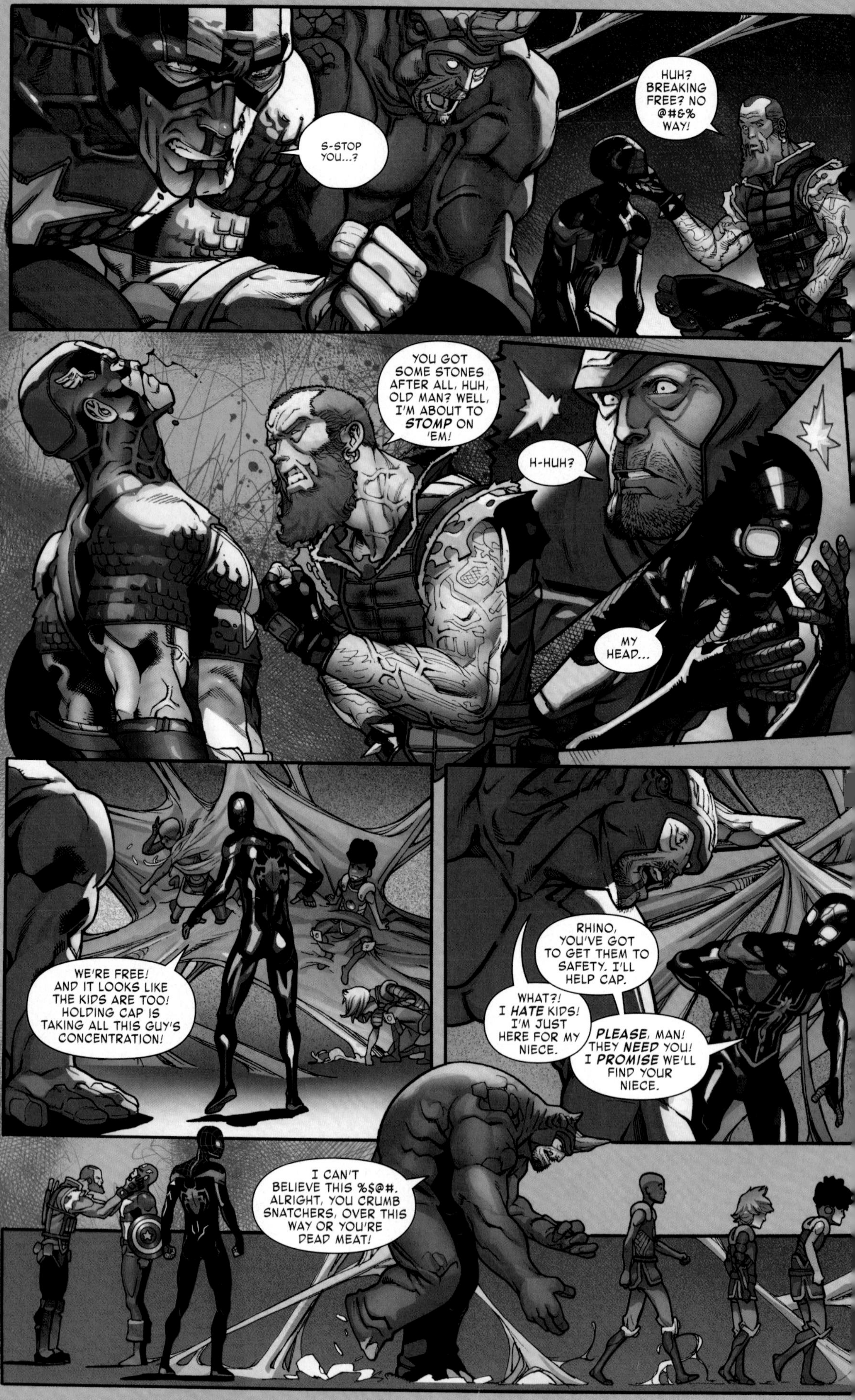
S-STOP YOU...?
HUH? BREAKING FREE? NO @#&% WAY!
YOU GOT SOME STONES AFTER ALL, HUH, OLD MAN? WELL, I'M ABOUT TO STOMP ON 'EM!
H-HUH?
MY HEAD...
WE'RE FREE! AND IT LOOKS LIKE THE KIDS ARE TOO! HOLDING CAP IS TAKING ALL THIS GUY'S CONCENTRATION!
RHINO, YOU'VE GOT TO GET THEM TO SAFETY. I'LL HELP CAP.
WHAT?! I HATE KIDS! I'M JUST HERE FOR MY NIECE.
PLEASE, MAN! THEY NEED YOU! I PROMISE WE'LL FIND YOUR NIECE.
I CAN'T BELIEVE THIS %$@#. ALRIGHT, YOU CRUMB SNATCHERS, OVER THIS WAY OR YOU'RE DEAD MEAT!

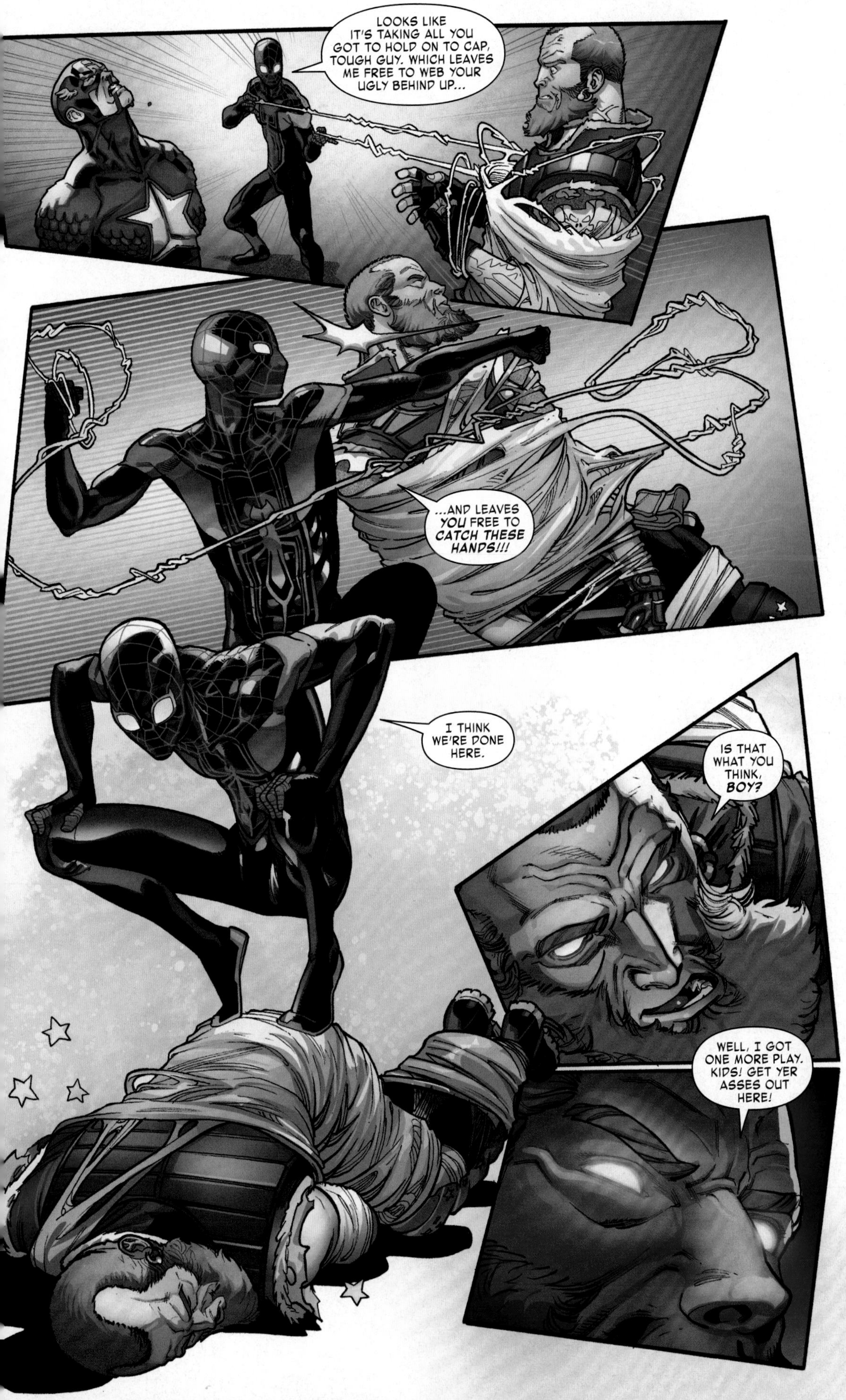
LOOKS LIKE IT'S TAKING ALL YOU GOT TO HOLD ON TO CAP, TOUGH GUY. WHICH LEAVES ME FREE TO WEB YOUR UGLY BEHIND UP...
...AND LEAVES YOU FREE TO CATCH THESE HANDS!!!
I THINK WE'RE DONE HERE.
IS THAT WHAT YOU THINK, BOY?
WELL, I GOT ONE MORE PLAY. KIDS! GET YER ASSES OUT HERE!

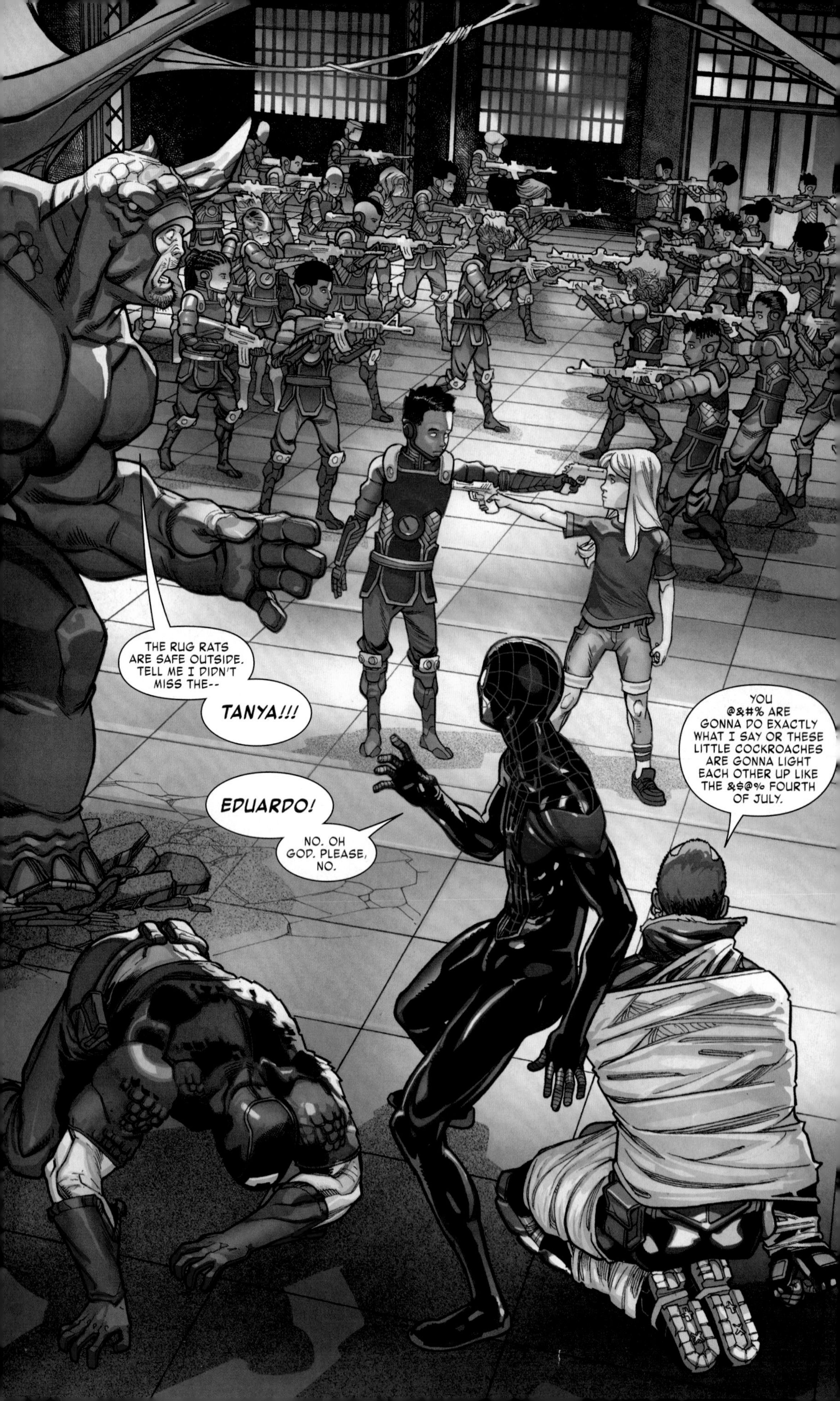
THE RUG RATS ARE SAFE OUTSIDE. TELL ME I DIDN'T MISS THE--
TANYA!!!
YOU @&#% ARE GONNA DO EXACTLY WHAT I SAY OR THESE LITTLE COCKROACHES ARE GONNA LIGHT EACH OTHER UP LIKE THE &$@% FOURTH OF JULY.
EDUARDO!
NO. OH GOD. PLEASE, NO.

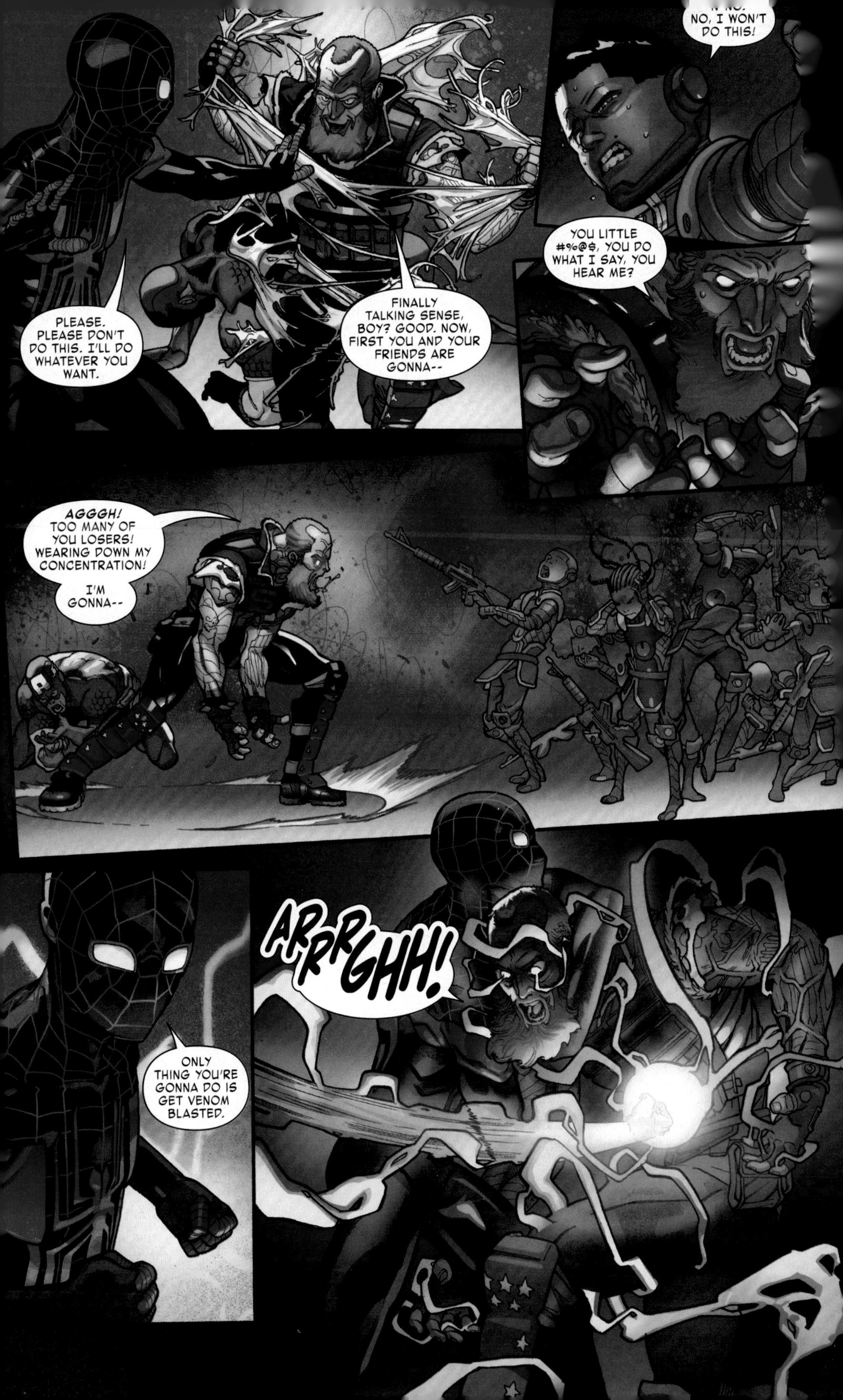
PLEASE. PLEASE DON'T DO THIS. I'LL DO WHATEVER YOU WANT.
FINALLY TALKING SENSE, BOY? GOOD. NOW, FIRST YOU AND YOUR FRIENDS ARE GONNA--
NO, I WON'T DO THIS!
YOU LITTLE #%@$, YOU DO WHAT I SAY, YOU HEAR ME?
AGGGH! TOO MANY OF YOU LOSERS! WEARING DOWN MY CONCENTRATION!
I'M GONNA--
ONLY THING YOU'RE GONNA DO IS GET VENOM BLASTED.
ARRRGHH!

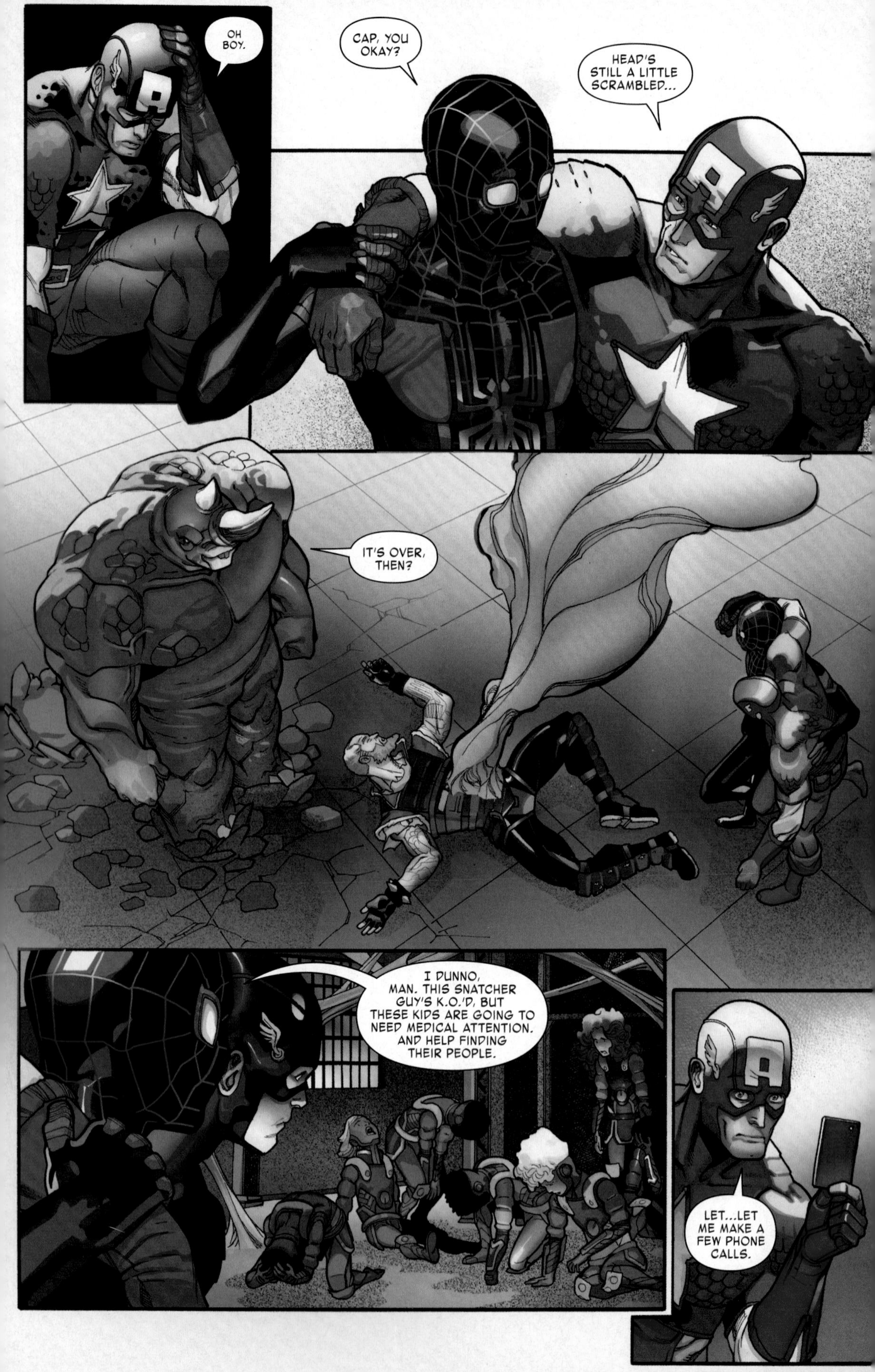
OH BOY.
CAP, YOU OKAY?
HEAD'S STILL A LITTLE SCRAMBLED...
IT'S OVER, THEN?
I DUNNO, MAN. THIS SNATCHER GUY'S K.O.'D, BUT THESE KIDS ARE GOING TO NEED MEDICAL ATTENTION. AND HELP FINDING THEIR PEOPLE.
LET...LET ME MAKE A FEW PHONE CALLS.

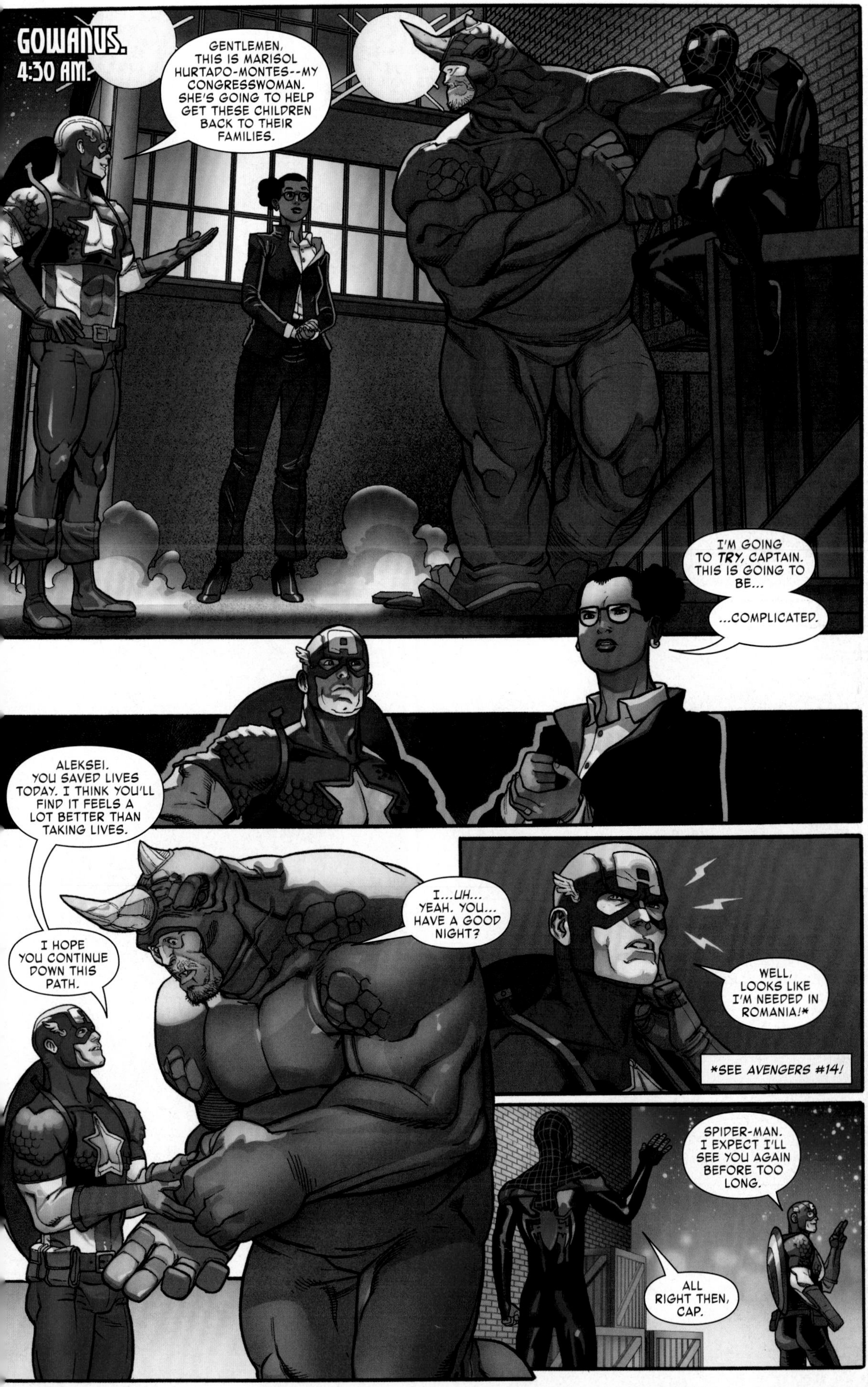
GOWANUS.
4:30 AM.
GENTLEMEN, THIS IS MARISOL HURTADO-MONTES--MY CONGRESSWOMAN. SHE'S GOING TO HELP GET THESE CHILDREN BACK TO THEIR FAMILIES.
I'M GOING TO TRY, CAPTAIN. THIS IS GOING TO BE...
...COMPLICATED.
ALEKSEI. YOU SAVED LIVES TODAY. I THINK YOU'LL FIND IT FEELS A LOT BETTER THAN TAKING LIVES.
I HOPE YOU CONTINUE DOWN THIS PATH.
I...UH... YEAH. YOU... HAVE A GOOD NIGHT?
WELL, LOOKS LIKE I'M NEEDED IN ROMANIA!*
*SEE AVENGERS #14!
SPIDER-MAN. I EXPECT I'LL SEE YOU AGAIN BEFORE TOO LONG.
ALL RIGHT THEN, CAP.

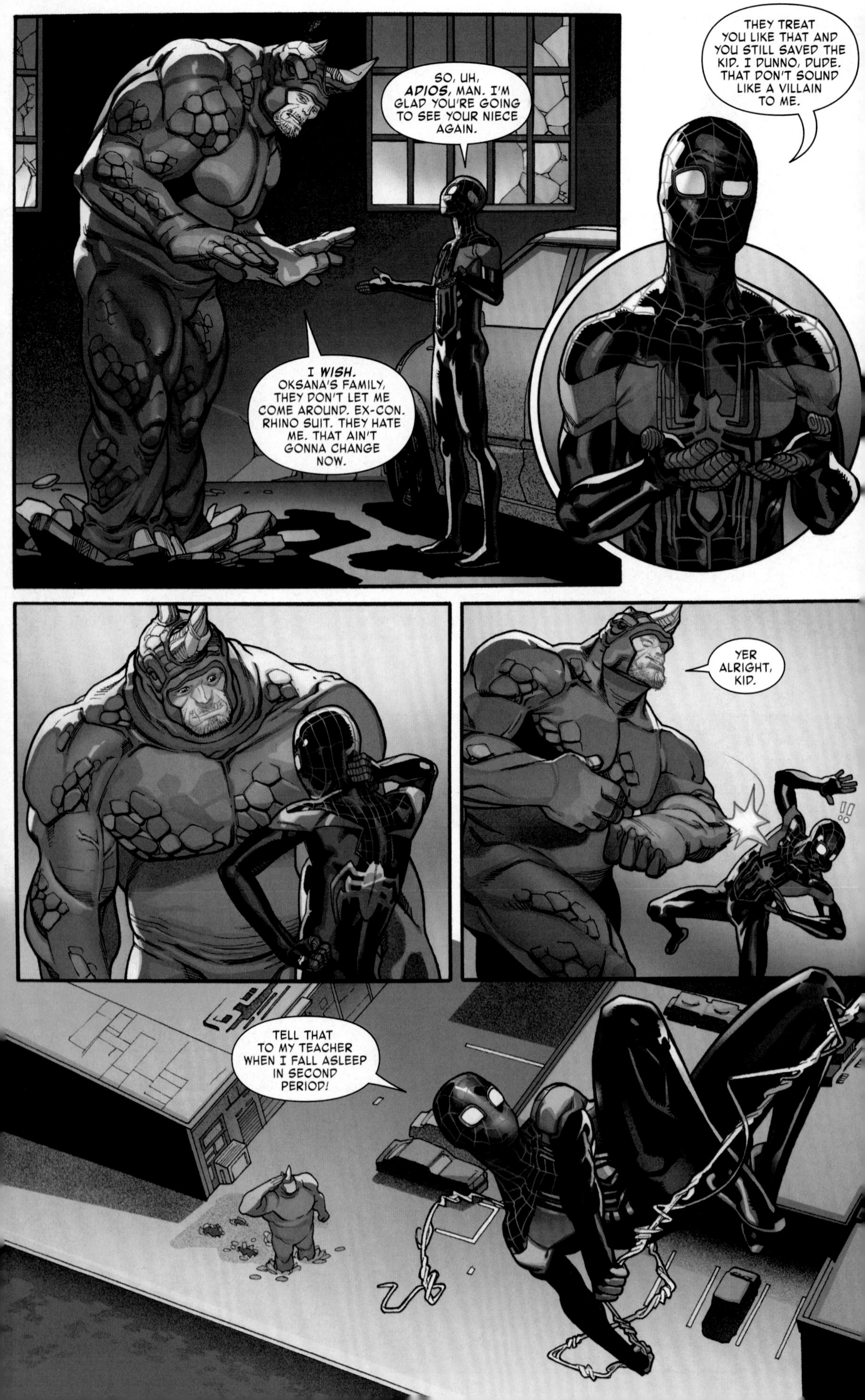
SO, UH, ADIOS, MAN. I'M GLAD YOU'RE GOING TO SEE YOUR NIECE AGAIN.
I WISH. OKSANA'S FAMILY, THEY DON'T LET ME COME AROUND. EX-CON. RHINO SUIT. THEY HATE ME. THAT AIN'T GONNA CHANGE NOW.
THEY TREAT YOU LIKE THAT AND YOU STILL SAVED THE KID. I DUNNO, DUDE. THAT DON'T SOUND LIKE A VILLAIN TO ME.
YER ALRIGHT, KID.
!!
TELL THAT TO MY TEACHER WHEN I FALL ASLEEP IN SECOND PERIOD!

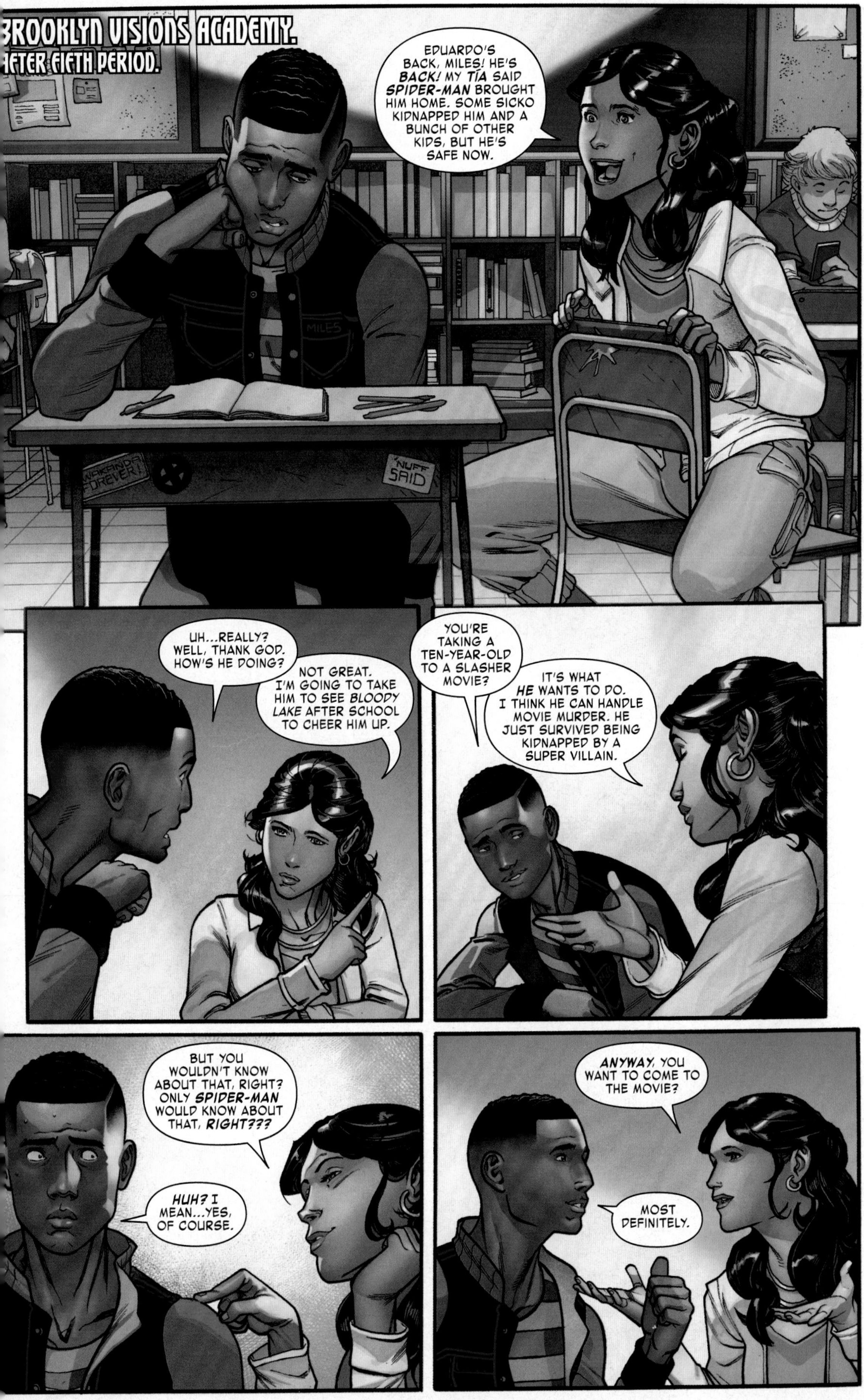
BROOKLYN VISIONS ACADEMY.
AFTER FIFTH PERIOD.
EDUARDO'S BACK, MILES! HE'S BACK! MY TÍA SAID SPIDER-MAN BROUGHT HIM HOME. SOME SICKO KIDNAPPED HIM AND A BUNCH OF OTHER KIDS, BUT HE'S SAFE NOW.
MILES
WAKANDA FOREVER!
'NUFF SAID
UH...REALLY? WELL, THANK GOD. HOW'S HE DOING?
NOT GREAT. I'M GOING TO TAKE HIM TO SEE BLOODY LAKE AFTER SCHOOL TO CHEER HIM UP.
YOU'RE TAKING A TEN-YEAR-OLD TO A SLASHER MOVIE?
IT'S WHAT HE WANTS TO DO. I THINK HE CAN HANDLE MOVIE MURDER. HE JUST SURVIVED BEING KIDNAPPED BY A SUPER VILLAIN.
BUT YOU WOULDN'T KNOW ABOUT THAT, RIGHT? ONLY SPIDER-MAN WOULD KNOW ABOUT THAT, RIGHT???
HUH? I MEAN...YES, OF COURSE.
ANYWAY, YOU WANT TO COME TO THE MOVIE?
MOST DEFINITELY.

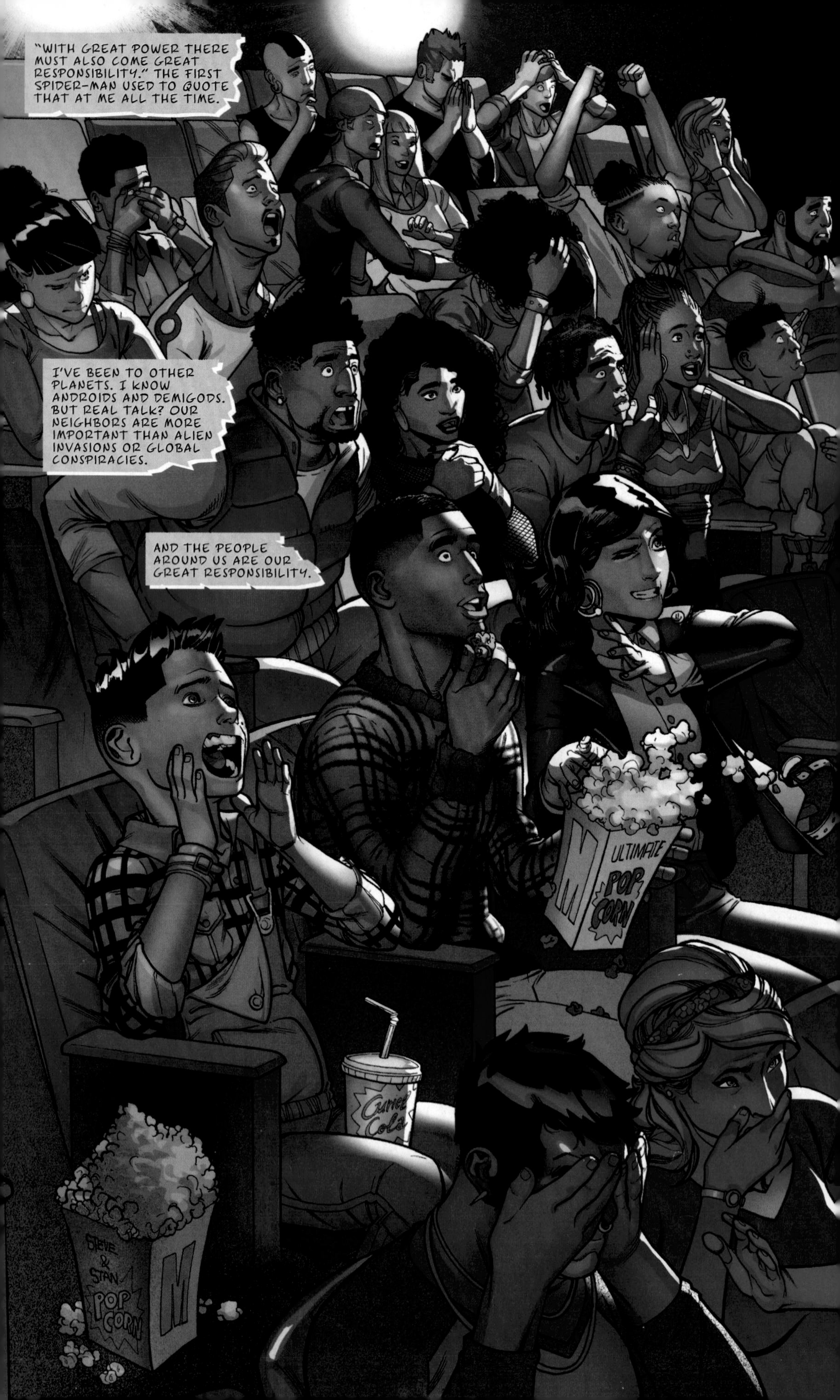
"WITH GREAT POWER THERE MUST ALSO COME GREAT RESPONSIBILITY." THE FIRST SPIDER-MAN USED TO QUOTE THAT AT ME ALL THE TIME.
I'VE BEEN TO OTHER PLANETS. I KNOW ANDROIDS AND DEMIGODS. BUT REAL TALK? OUR NEIGHBORS ARE MORE IMPORTANT THAN ALIEN INVASIONS OR GLOBAL CONSPIRACIES.
AND THE PEOPLE AROUND US ARE OUR GREAT RESPONSIBILITY.
ULTIMATE POP CORN
Curiel Cola
STEVE & STAN POP CORN

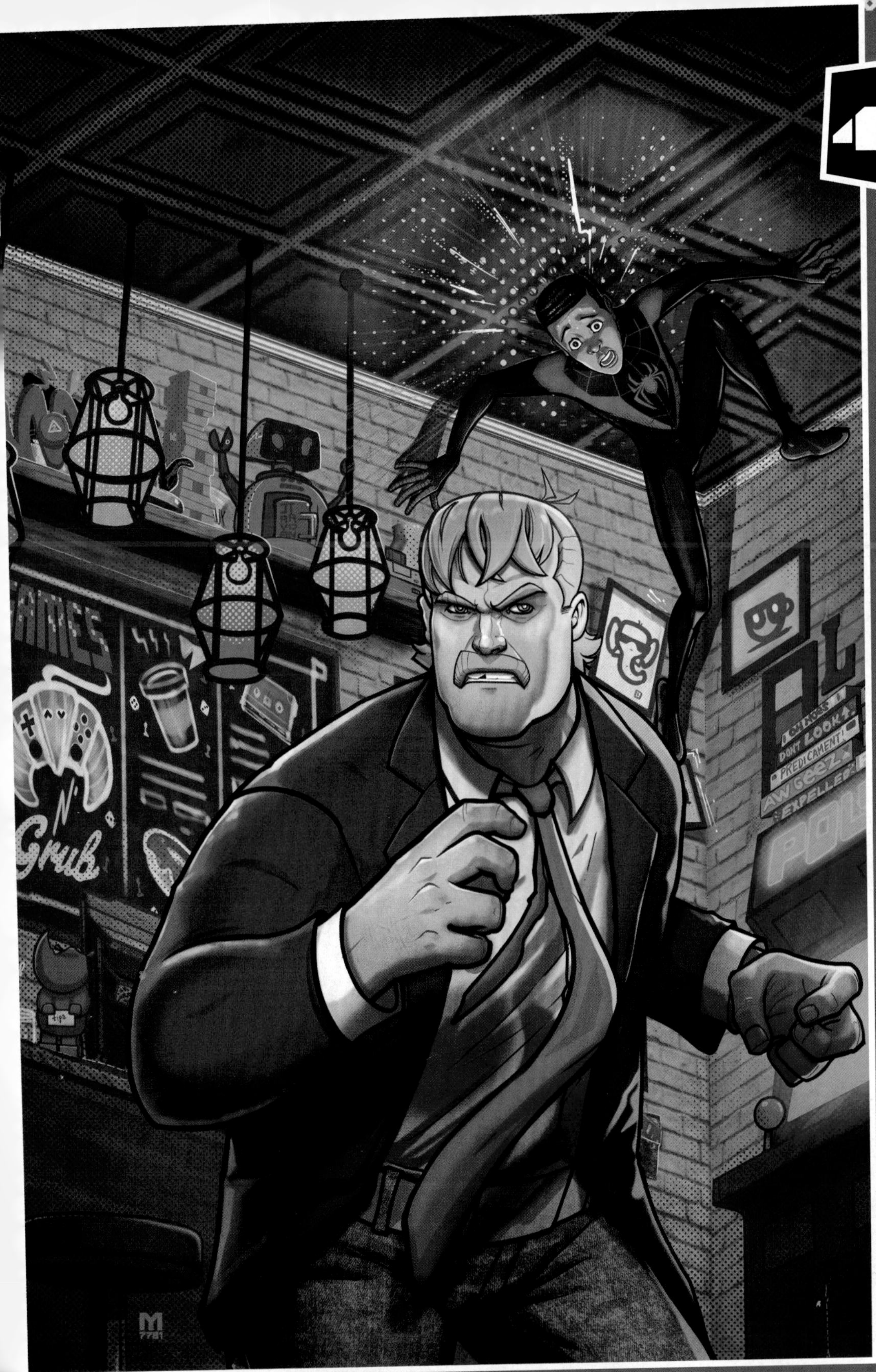
GAMES
Grub
OH NOES
DONT LOOK
PREDICAMENT!
AW GEEZ
EXPELLE
tips

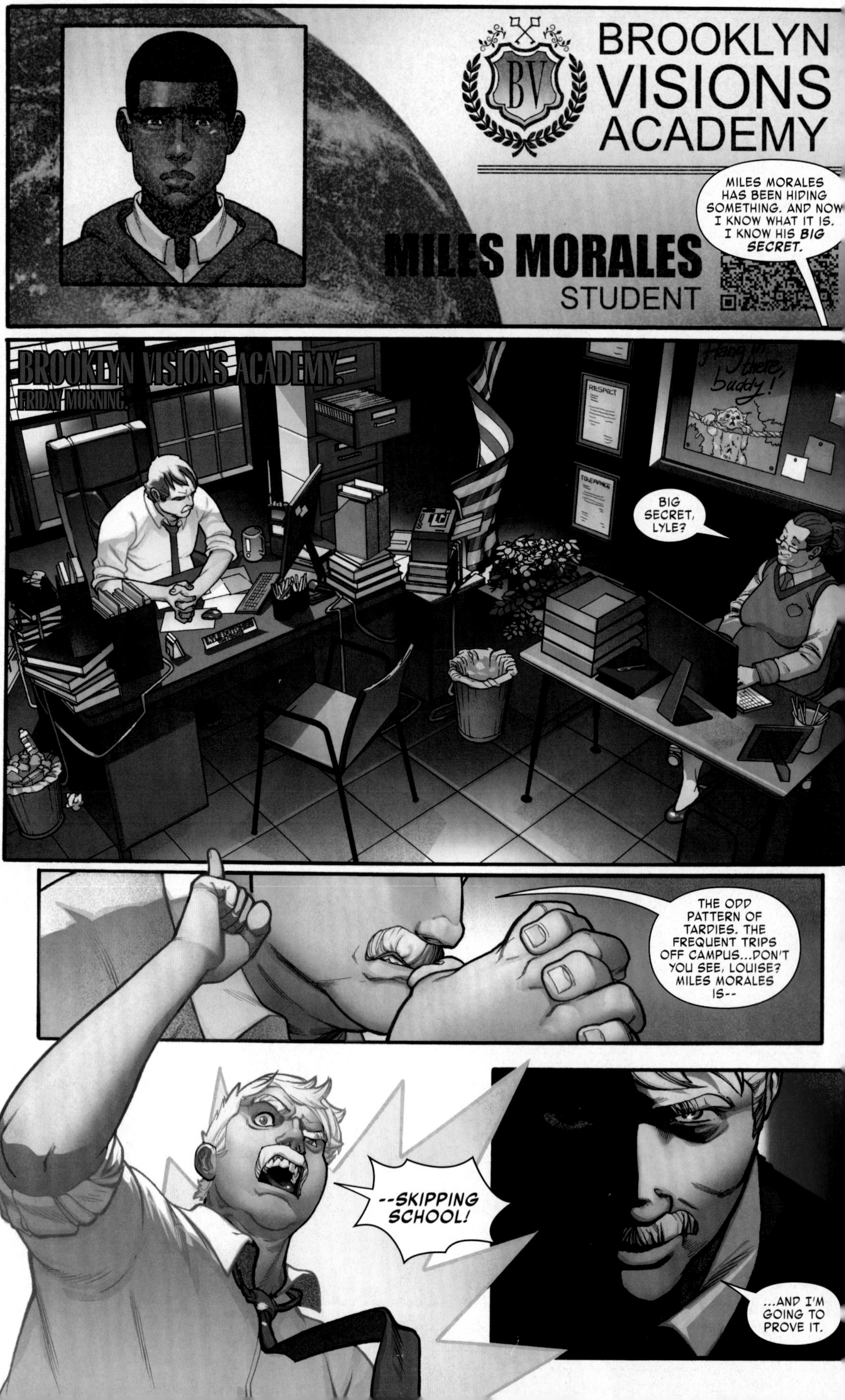
BROOKLYN VISIONS ACADEMY
MILES MORALES
STUDENT
MILES MORALES HAS BEEN HIDING SOMETHING. AND NOW I KNOW WHAT IT IS. I KNOW HIS BIG SECRET.
BROOKLYN VISIONS ACADEMY. FRIDAY MORNING.
RESPECT
TOLERANCE
Hang in there, buddy!
BIG SECRET, LYLE?
THE ODD PATTERN OF TARDIES. THE FREQUENT TRIPS OFF CAMPUS...DON'T YOU SEE, LOUISE? MILES MORALES IS--
--SKIPPING SCHOOL!
...AND I'M GOING TO PROVE IT.

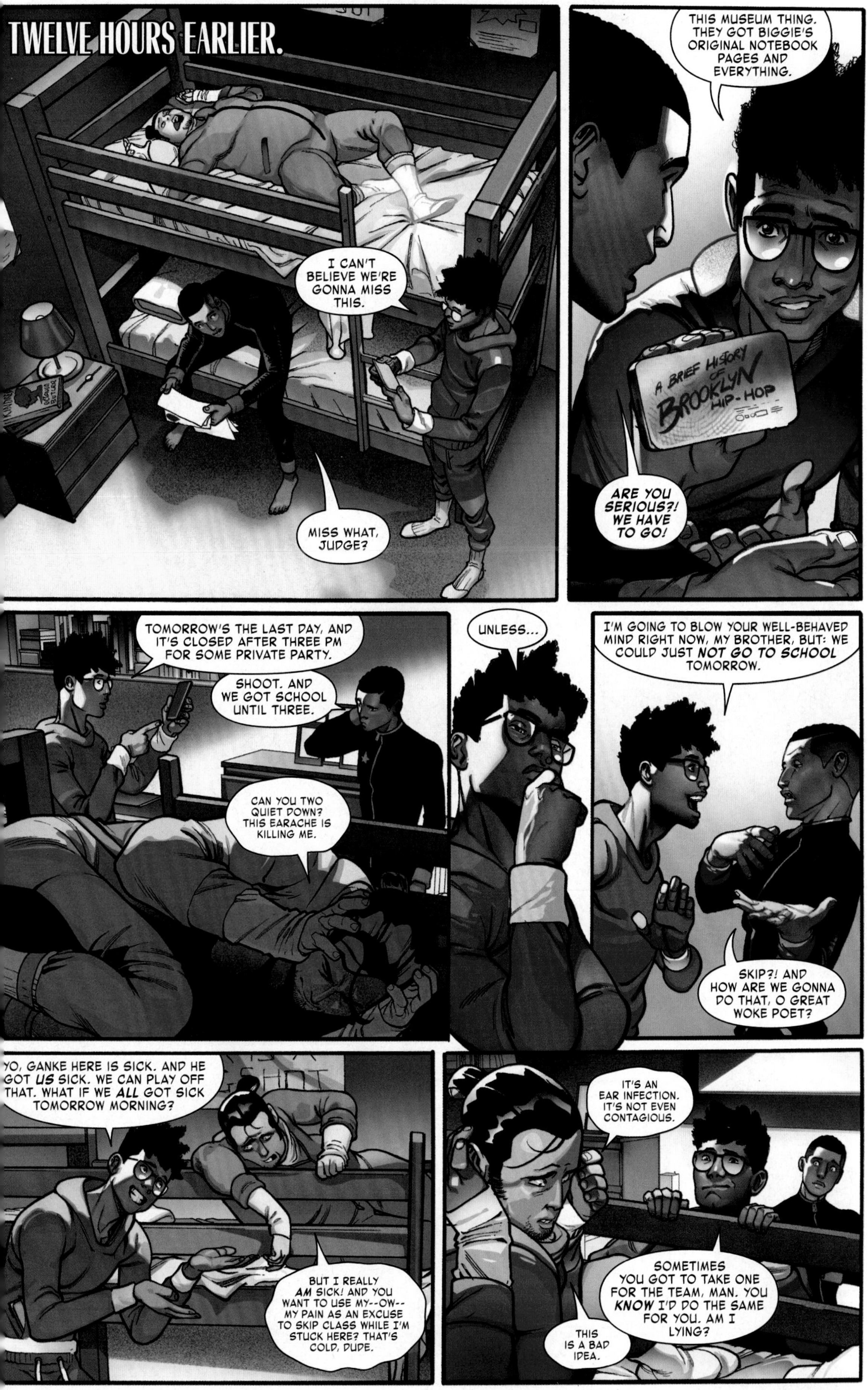
TWELVE HOURS EARLIER.
I CAN'T BELIEVE WE'RE GONNA MISS THIS.
MISS WHAT, JUDGE?
THIS MUSEUM THING. THEY GOT BIGGIE'S ORIGINAL NOTEBOOK PAGES AND EVERYTHING.
A BRIEF HISTORY OF BROOKLYN HIP-HOP
ARE YOU SERIOUS?! WE HAVE TO GO!
TOMORROW'S THE LAST DAY, AND IT'S CLOSED AFTER THREE PM FOR SOME PRIVATE PARTY.
SHOOT. AND WE GOT SCHOOL UNTIL THREE.
CAN YOU TWO QUIET DOWN? THIS EARACHE IS KILLING ME.
UNLESS...
I'M GOING TO BLOW YOUR WELL-BEHAVED MIND RIGHT NOW, MY BROTHER, BUT: WE COULD JUST NOT GO TO SCHOOL TOMORROW.
SKIP?! AND HOW ARE WE GONNA DO THAT, O GREAT WOKE POET?
YO, GANKE HERE IS SICK. AND HE GOT US SICK. WE CAN PLAY OFF THAT. WHAT IF WE ALL GOT SICK TOMORROW MORNING?
BUT I REALLY AM SICK! AND YOU WANT TO USE MY--OW-- MY PAIN AS AN EXCUSE TO SKIP CLASS WHILE I'M STUCK HERE? THAT'S COLD, DUDE.
IT'S AN EAR INFECTION. IT'S NOT EVEN CONTAGIOUS.
SOMETIMES YOU GOT TO TAKE ONE FOR THE TEAM, MAN. YOU KNOW I'D DO THE SAME FOR YOU. AM I LYING?
THIS IS A BAD IDEA.

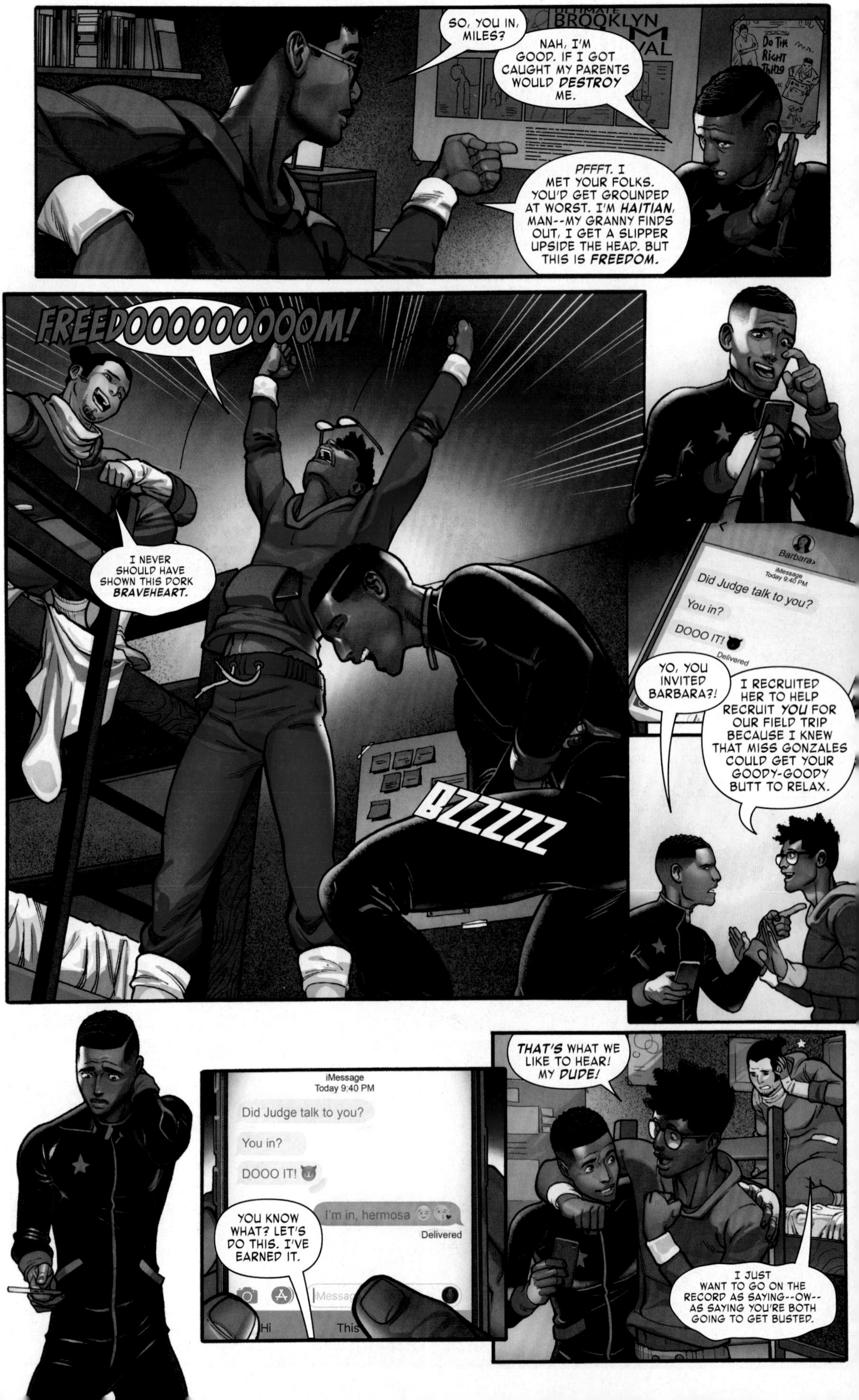
ULTIMATE BROOKLYN M VAL
DO THE RIGHT THING
SO, YOU IN, MILES?
NAH, I'M GOOD. IF I GOT CAUGHT MY PARENTS WOULD DESTROY ME.
PFFFT. I MET YOUR FOLKS. YOU'D GET GROUNDED AT WORST. I'M HAITIAN, MAN--MY GRANNY FINDS OUT, I GET A SLIPPER UPSIDE THE HEAD. BUT THIS IS FREEDOM.
FREEDOOOOOOOOOM!
I NEVER SHOULD HAVE SHOWN THIS DORK BRAVEHEART.
BZZZZZ
Barbara
iMessage
Today 9:40 PM
Did Judge talk to you?
You in?
DOOO IT!
Delivered
YO, YOU INVITED BARBARA?!
I RECRUITED HER TO HELP RECRUIT YOU FOR OUR FIELD TRIP BECAUSE I KNEW THAT MISS GONZALES COULD GET YOUR GOODY-GOODY BUTT TO RELAX.
iMessage
Today 9:40 PM
Did Judge talk to you?
You in?
DOOO IT!
I'm in, hermosa
Delivered
YOU KNOW WHAT? LET'S DO THIS. I'VE EARNED IT.
THAT'S WHAT WE LIKE TO HEAR! MY DUDE!
I JUST WANT TO GO ON THE RECORD AS SAYING--OW--AS SAYING YOU'RE BOTH GOING TO GET BUSTED.

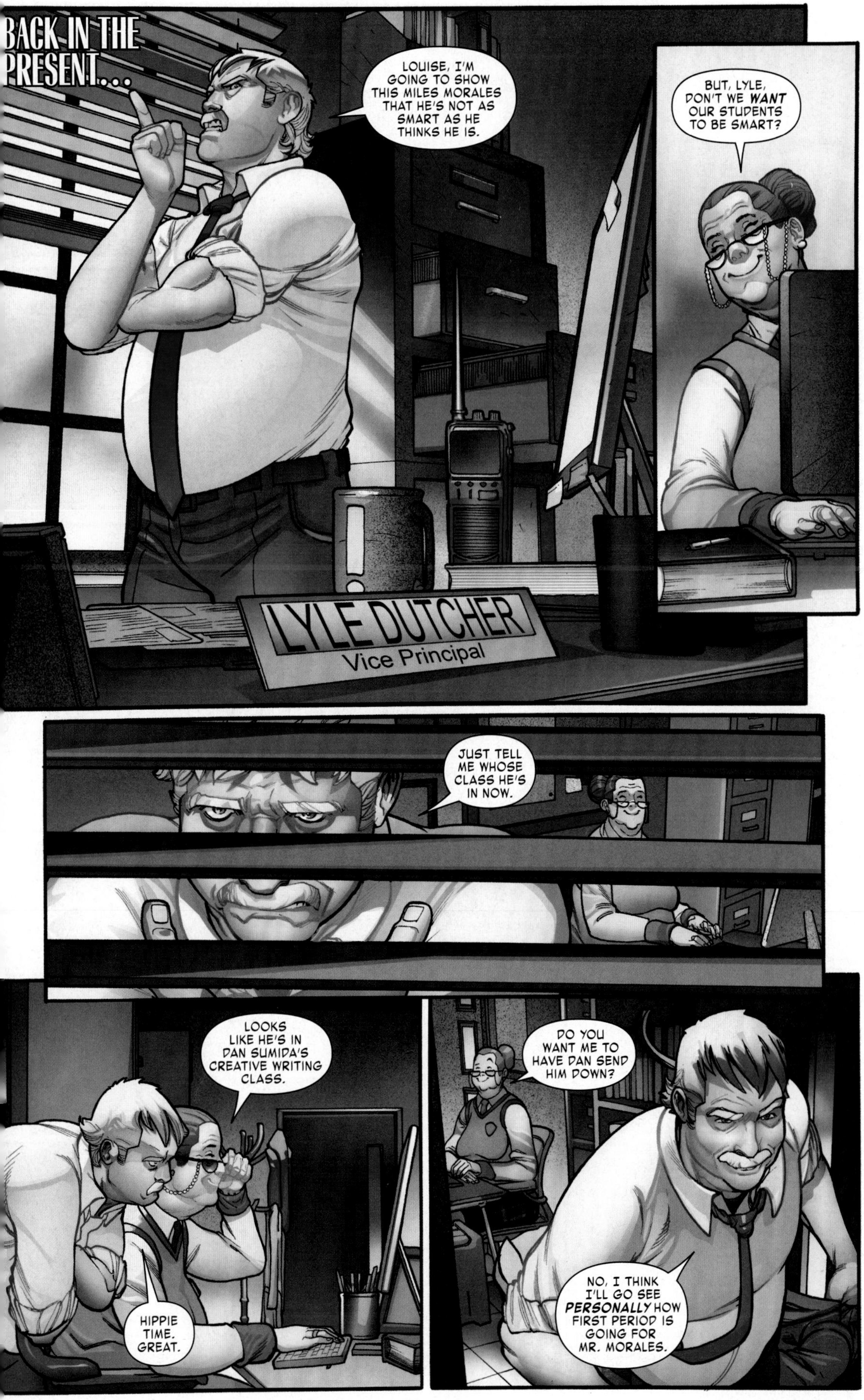
BACK IN THE PRESENT...
LOUISE, I'M GOING TO SHOW THIS MILES MORALES THAT HE'S NOT AS SMART AS HE THINKS HE IS.
BUT, LYLE, DON'T WE WANT OUR STUDENTS TO BE SMART?
LYLE DUTCHER
Vice Principal
JUST TELL ME WHOSE CLASS HE'S IN NOW.
LOOKS LIKE HE'S IN DAN SUMIDA'S CREATIVE WRITING CLASS.
HIPPIE TIME. GREAT.
DO YOU WANT ME TO HAVE DAN SEND HIM DOWN?
NO, I THINK I'LL GO SEE PERSONALLY HOW FIRST PERIOD IS GOING FOR MR. MORALES.

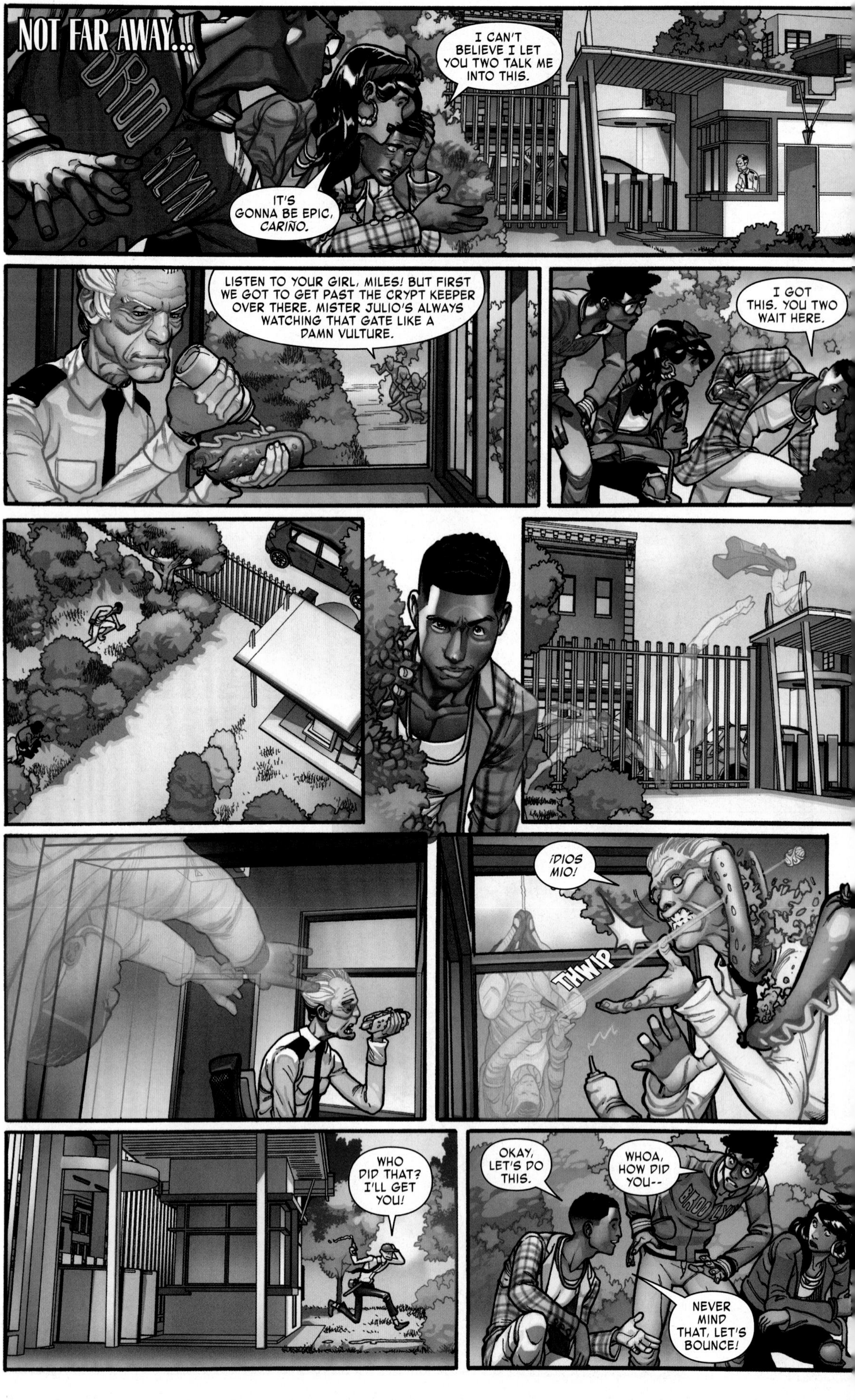
NOT FAR AWAY...
I CAN'T BELIEVE I LET YOU TWO TALK ME INTO THIS.
IT'S GONNA BE EPIC, *CARIÑO.*
LISTEN TO YOUR GIRL, MILES! BUT FIRST WE GOT TO GET PAST THE CRYPT KEEPER OVER THERE. MISTER JULIO'S ALWAYS WATCHING THAT GATE LIKE A DAMN VULTURE.
I GOT THIS. YOU TWO WAIT HERE.
¡DIOS MIO!
THWIP
WHO DID THAT? I'LL GET YOU!
OKAY, LET'S DO THIS.
WHOA, HOW DID YOU--
NEVER MIND THAT, LET'S BOUNCE!

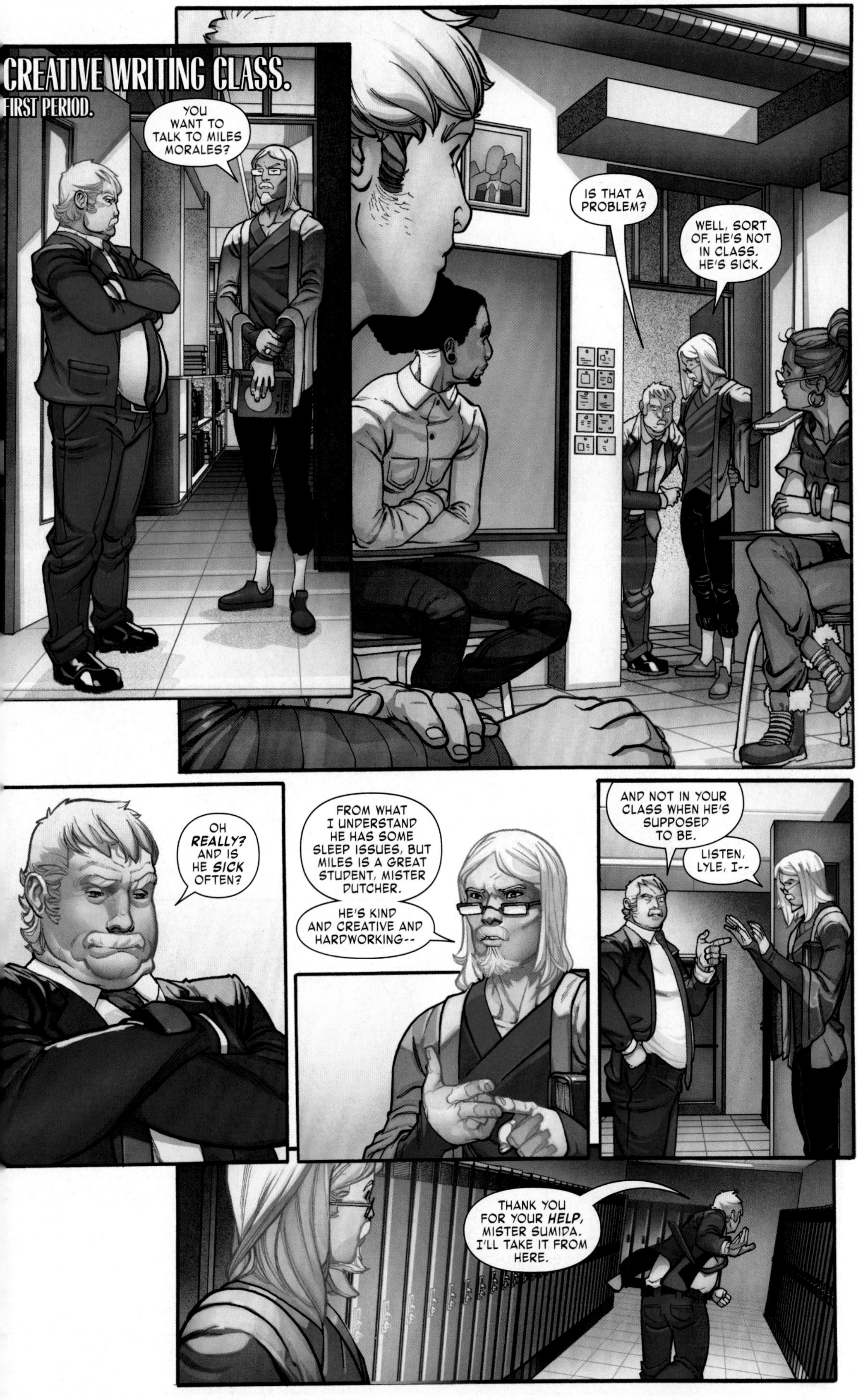
CREATIVE WRITING CLASS.
FIRST PERIOD.
YOU WANT TO TALK TO MILES MORALES?
IS THAT A PROBLEM?
WELL, SORT OF. HE'S NOT IN CLASS. HE'S SICK.
OH REALLY? AND IS HE SICK OFTEN?
FROM WHAT I UNDERSTAND HE HAS SOME SLEEP ISSUES, BUT MILES IS A GREAT STUDENT, MISTER DUTCHER.
HE'S KIND AND CREATIVE AND HARDWORKING--
AND NOT IN YOUR CLASS WHEN HE'S SUPPOSED TO BE.
LISTEN, LYLE, I--
THANK YOU FOR YOUR HELP, MISTER SUMIDA. I'LL TAKE IT FROM HERE.

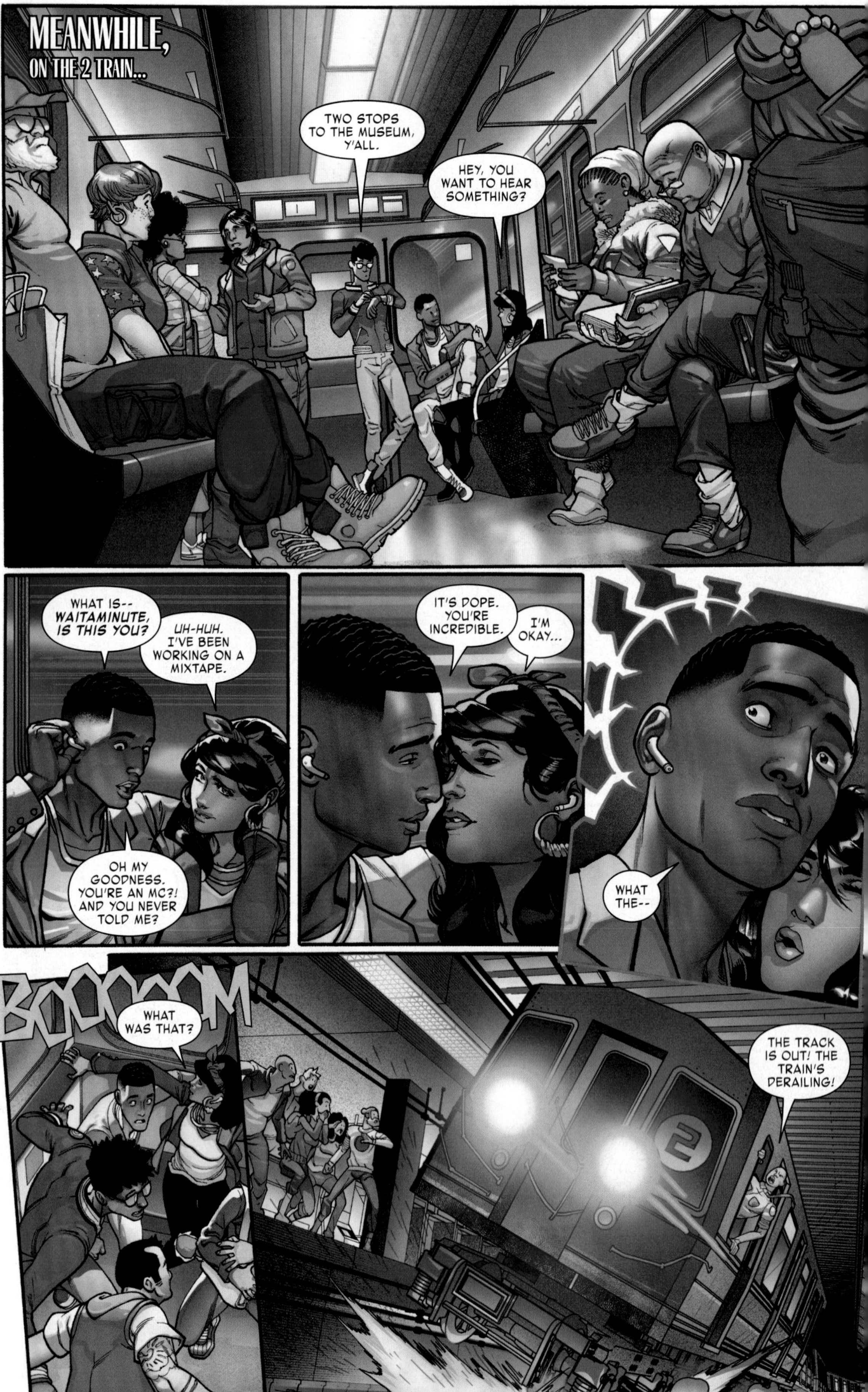
MEANWHILE,
ON THE 2 TRAIN...
TWO STOPS TO THE MUSEUM, Y'ALL.
HEY, YOU WANT TO HEAR SOMETHING?
WHAT IS-- WAITAMINUTE, IS THIS YOU?
UH-HUH. I'VE BEEN WORKING ON A MIXTAPE.
OH MY GOODNESS. YOU'RE AN MC?! AND YOU NEVER TOLD ME?
IT'S DOPE. YOU'RE INCREDIBLE.
I'M OKAY...
WHAT THE--
BOOOOOM
WHAT WAS THAT?
THE TRACK IS OUT! THE TRAIN'S DERAILING!

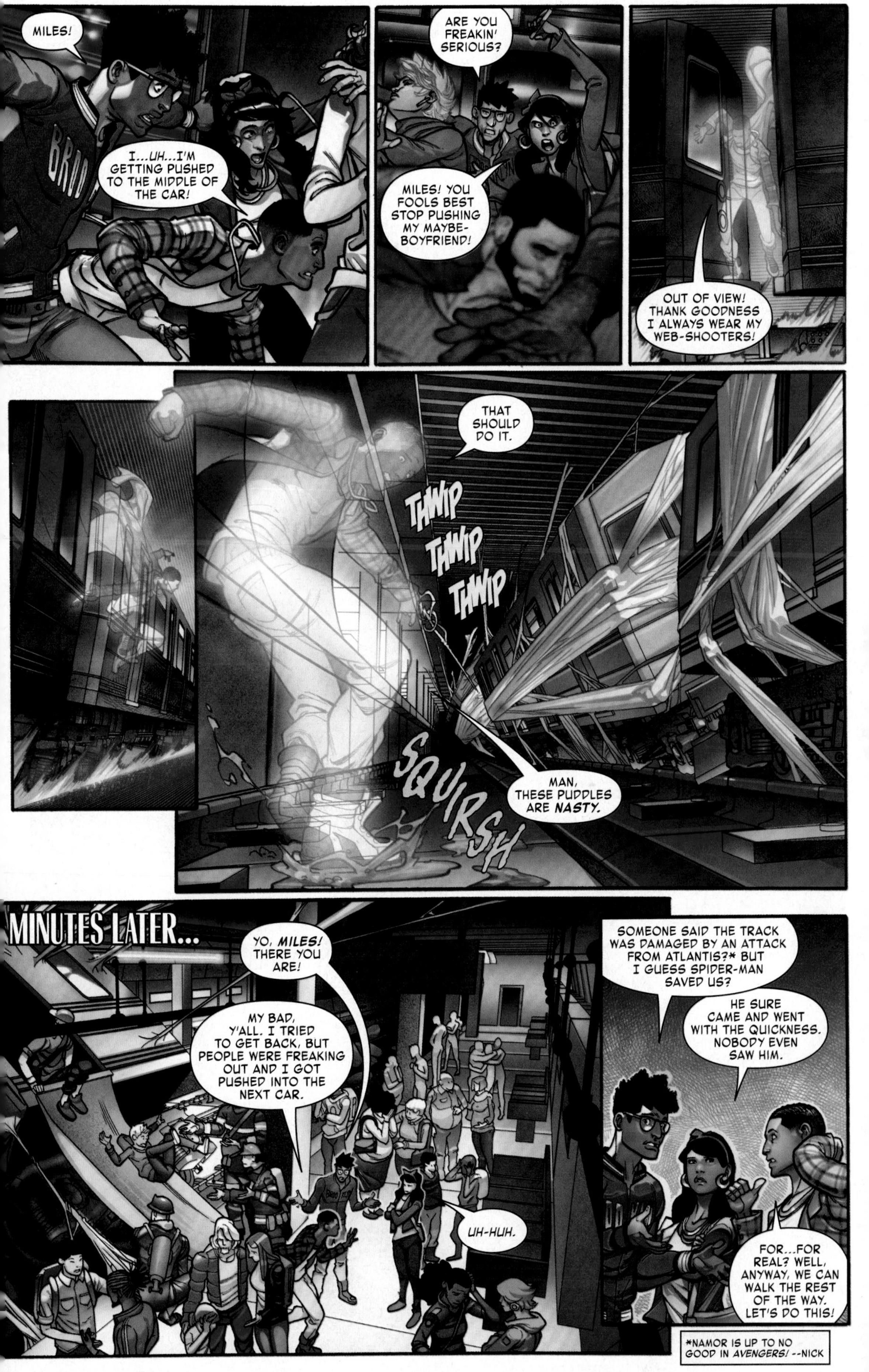
MILES!
I...UH...I'M GETTING PUSHED TO THE MIDDLE OF THE CAR!
ARE YOU FREAKIN' SERIOUS?
MILES! YOU FOOLS BEST STOP PUSHING MY MAYBE-BOYFRIEND!
OUT OF VIEW! THANK GOODNESS I ALWAYS WEAR MY WEB-SHOOTERS!
THAT SHOULD DO IT.
THWIP
THWIP
THWIP
SQUIRSH
MAN, THESE PUDDLES ARE NASTY.
MINUTES LATER...
YO, MILES! THERE YOU ARE!
MY BAD, Y'ALL. I TRIED TO GET BACK, BUT PEOPLE WERE FREAKING OUT AND I GOT PUSHED INTO THE NEXT CAR.
UH-HUH.
SOMEONE SAID THE TRACK WAS DAMAGED BY AN ATTACK FROM ATLANTIS?* BUT I GUESS SPIDER-MAN SAVED US?
HE SURE CAME AND WENT WITH THE QUICKNESS. NOBODY EVEN SAW HIM.
FOR...FOR REAL? WELL, ANYWAY, WE CAN WALK THE REST OF THE WAY. LET'S DO THIS!
*NAMOR IS UP TO NO GOOD IN AVENGERS! --NICK

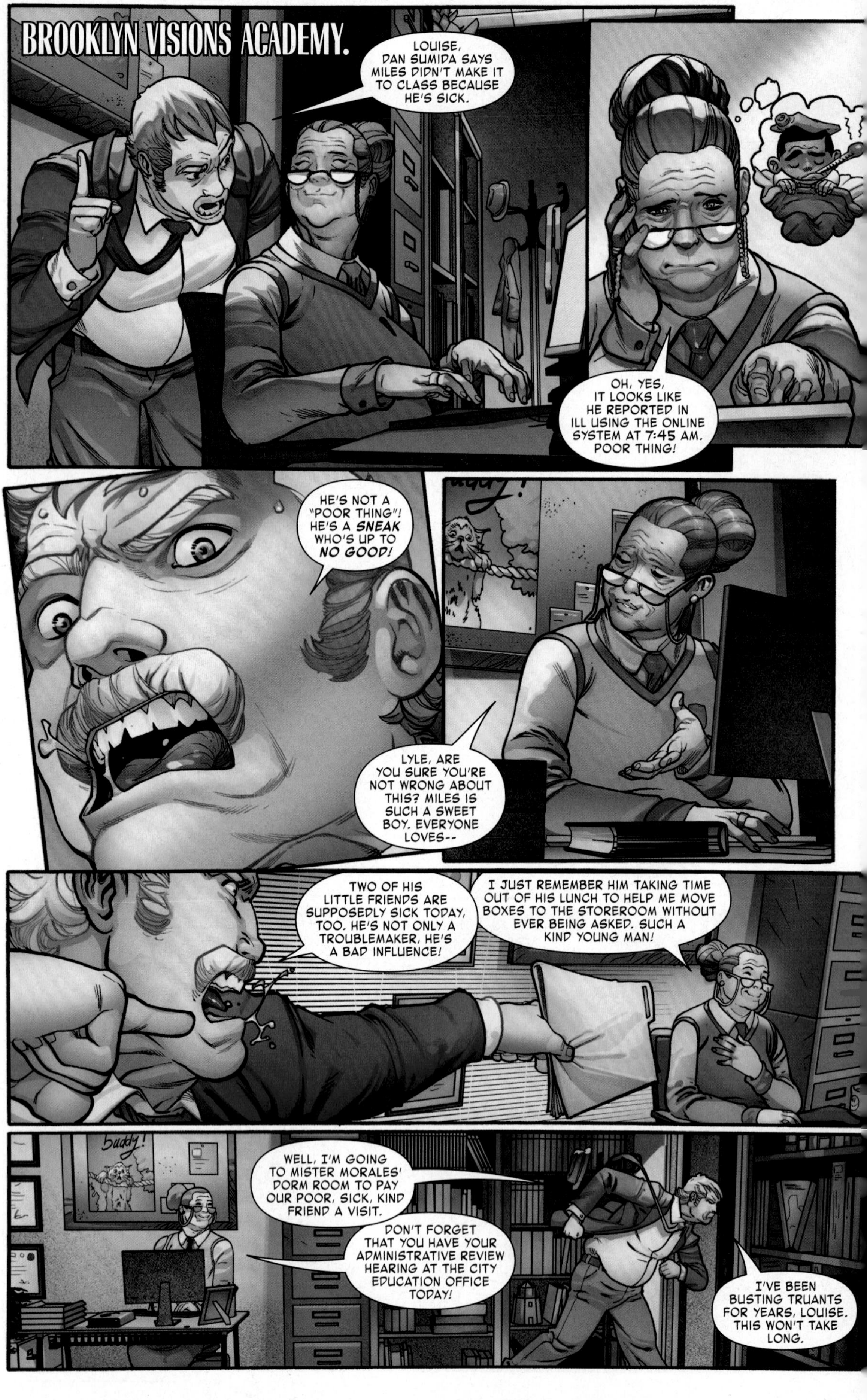
BROOKLYN VISIONS ACADEMY.
LOUISE, DAN SUMIDA SAYS MILES DIDN'T MAKE IT TO CLASS BECAUSE HE'S SICK.
OH, YES, IT LOOKS LIKE HE REPORTED IN ILL USING THE ONLINE SYSTEM AT 7:45 AM. POOR THING!
HE'S NOT A "POOR THING"! HE'S A SNEAK WHO'S UP TO NO GOOD!
LYLE, ARE YOU SURE YOU'RE NOT WRONG ABOUT THIS? MILES IS SUCH A SWEET BOY. EVERYONE LOVES--
TWO OF HIS LITTLE FRIENDS ARE SUPPOSEDLY SICK TODAY, TOO. HE'S NOT ONLY A TROUBLEMAKER, HE'S A BAD INFLUENCE!
I JUST REMEMBER HIM TAKING TIME OUT OF HIS LUNCH TO HELP ME MOVE BOXES TO THE STOREROOM WITHOUT EVER BEING ASKED. SUCH A KIND YOUNG MAN!
WELL, I'M GOING TO MISTER MORALES' DORM ROOM TO PAY OUR POOR, SICK, KIND FRIEND A VISIT.
DON'T FORGET THAT YOU HAVE YOUR ADMINISTRATIVE REVIEW HEARING AT THE CITY EDUCATION OFFICE TODAY!
I'VE BEEN BUSTING TRUANTS FOR YEARS, LOUISE. THIS WON'T TAKE LONG.

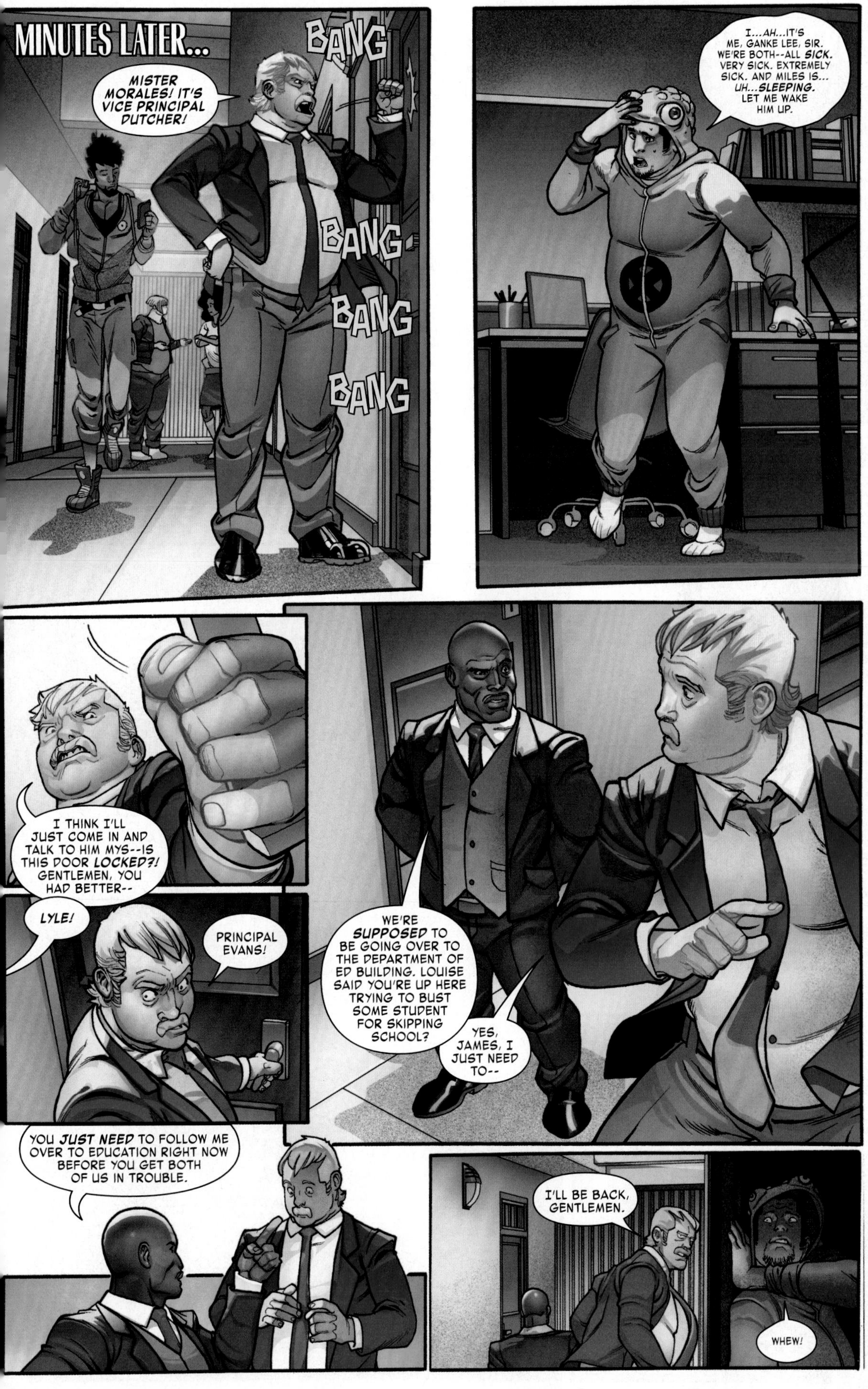
MINUTES LATER...
BANG
MISTER MORALES! IT'S VICE PRINCIPAL DUTCHER!
BANG
BANG
BANG
I...AH...IT'S ME, GANKE LEE, SIR. WE'RE BOTH--ALL SICK. VERY SICK. EXTREMELY SICK. AND MILES IS... UH...SLEEPING. LET ME WAKE HIM UP.
I THINK I'LL JUST COME IN AND TALK TO HIM MYS--IS THIS DOOR LOCKED?! GENTLEMEN, YOU HAD BETTER--
LYLE!
PRINCIPAL EVANS!
WE'RE SUPPOSED TO BE GOING OVER TO THE DEPARTMENT OF ED BUILDING. LOUISE SAID YOU'RE UP HERE TRYING TO BUST SOME STUDENT FOR SKIPPING SCHOOL?
YES, JAMES, I JUST NEED TO--
YOU JUST NEED TO FOLLOW ME OVER TO EDUCATION RIGHT NOW BEFORE YOU GET BOTH OF US IN TROUBLE.
I'LL BE BACK, GENTLEMEN.
WHEW!

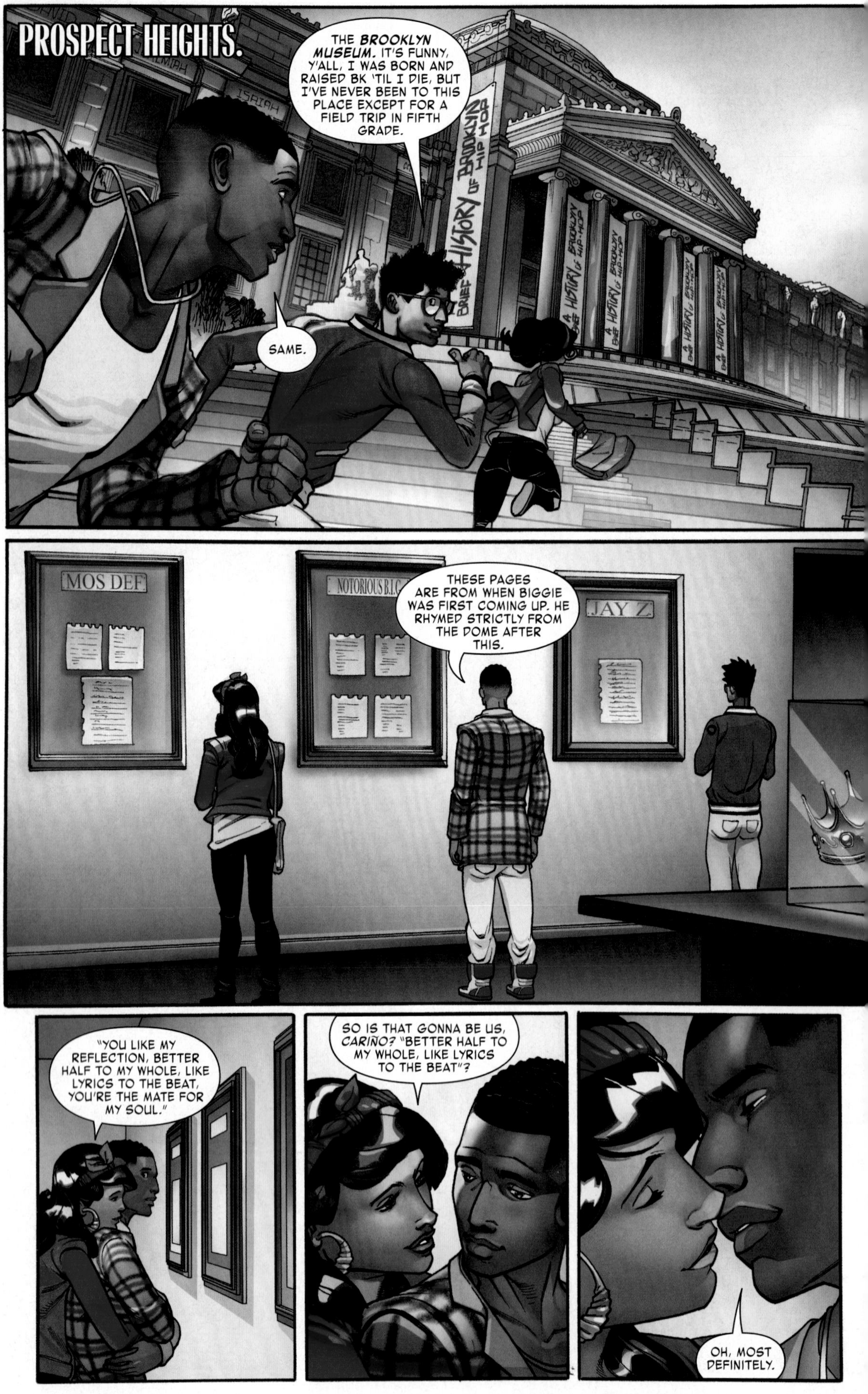
PROSPECT HEIGHTS.
THE BROOKLYN MUSEUM. IT'S FUNNY, Y'ALL, I WAS BORN AND RAISED BK 'TIL I DIE, BUT I'VE NEVER BEEN TO THIS PLACE EXCEPT FOR A FIELD TRIP IN FIFTH GRADE.
SAME.
BRIEF HISTORY OF BROOKLYN HIP HOP
A BRIEF HISTORY OF BROOKLYN HIP-HOP
MOS DEF
NOTORIOUS B.I.G.
JAY Z
THESE PAGES ARE FROM WHEN BIGGIE WAS FIRST COMING UP. HE RHYMED STRICTLY FROM THE DOME AFTER THIS.
"YOU LIKE MY REFLECTION, BETTER HALF TO MY WHOLE, LIKE LYRICS TO THE BEAT, YOU'RE THE MATE FOR MY SOUL."
SO IS THAT GONNA BE US, CARIÑO? "BETTER HALF TO MY WHOLE, LIKE LYRICS TO THE BEAT"?
OH, MOST DEFINITELY.

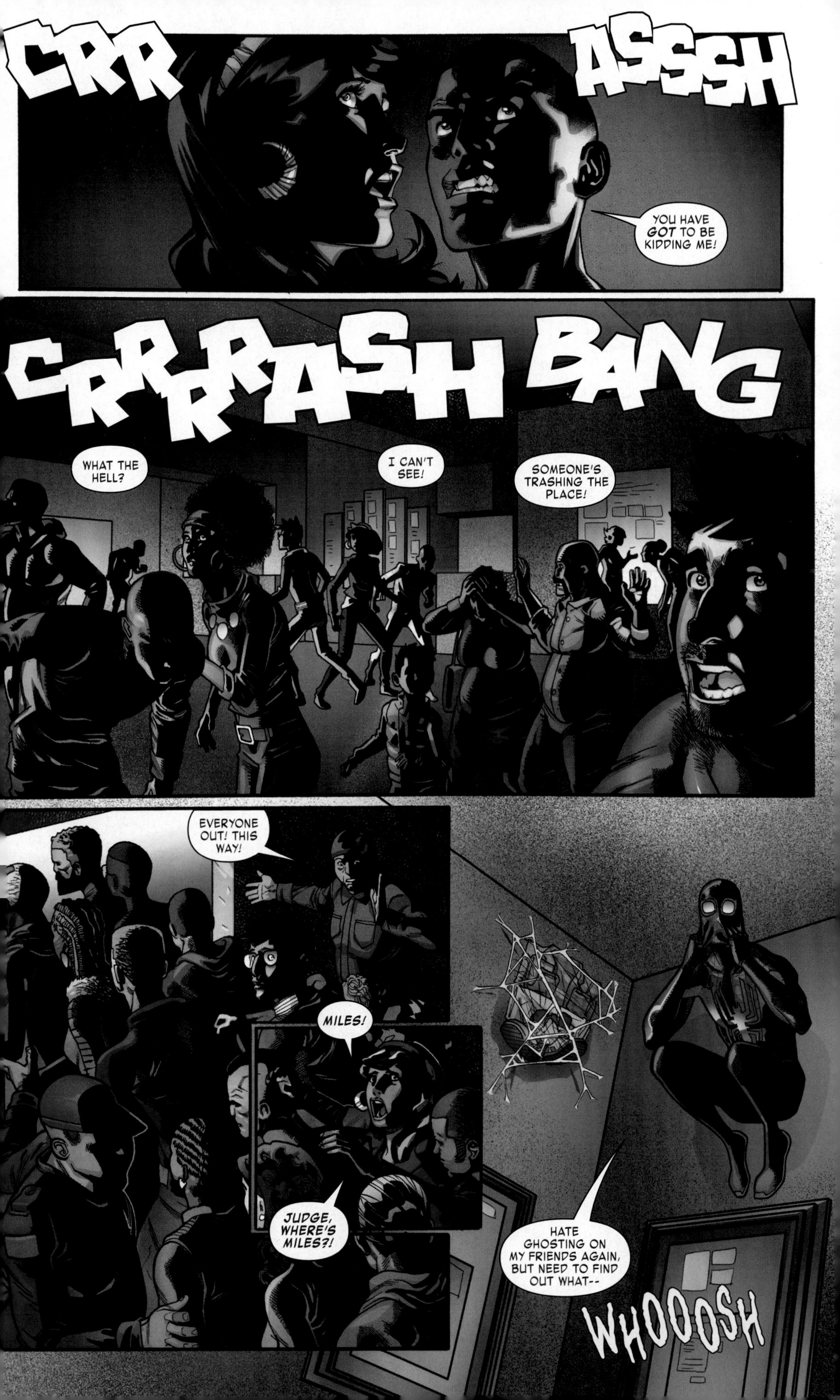

CRR
ASSSH
YOU HAVE GOT TO BE KIDDING ME!
CRRRRASH BANG
WHAT THE HELL?
I CAN'T SEE!
SOMEONE'S TRASHING THE PLACE!
EVERYONE OUT! THIS WAY!
MILES!
JUDGE, WHERE'S MILES?!
HATE GHOSTING ON MY FRIENDS AGAIN, BUT NEED TO FIND OUT WHAT--
WHOOOSH

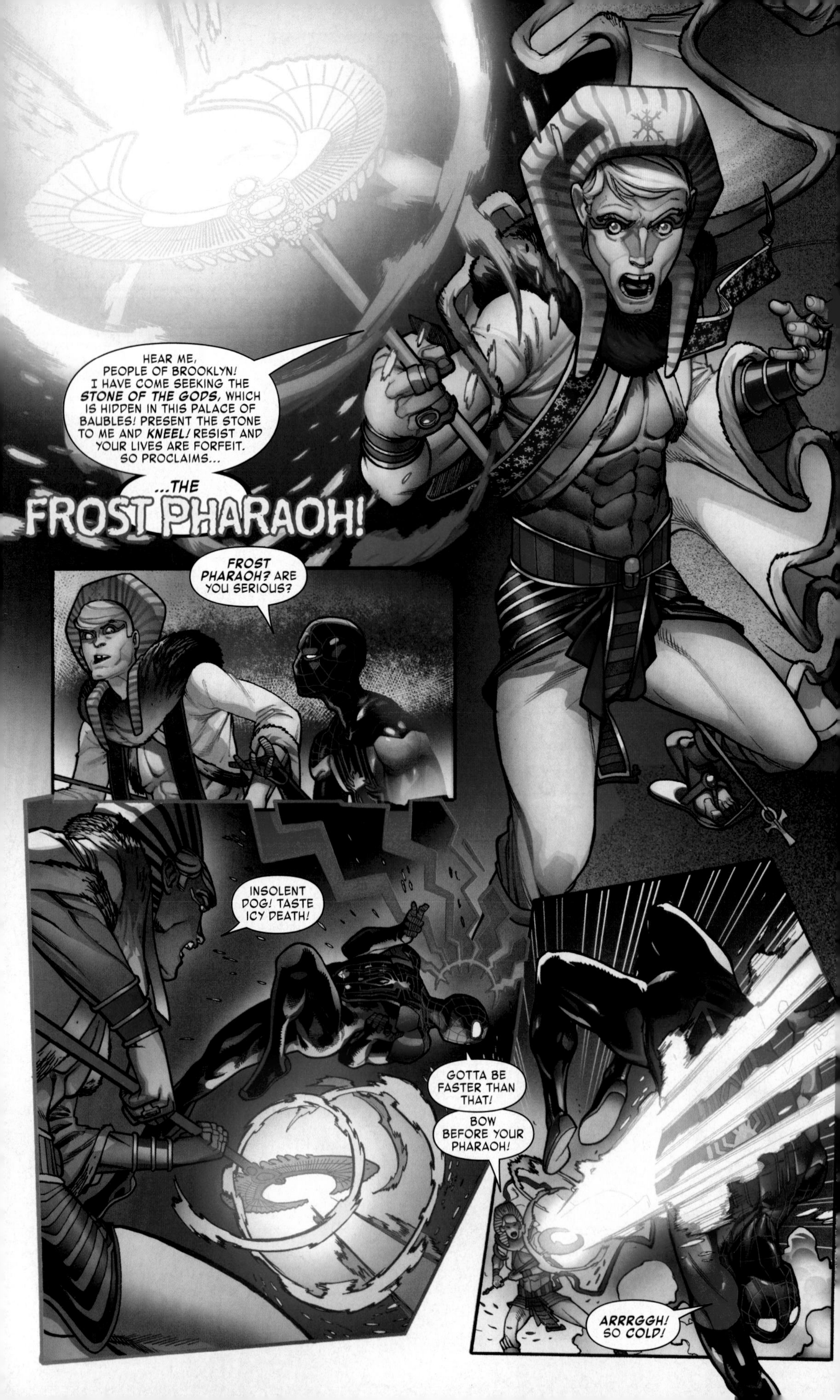

HEAR ME, PEOPLE OF BROOKLYN! I HAVE COME SEEKING THE STONE OF THE GODS, WHICH IS HIDDEN IN THIS PALACE OF BAUBLES! PRESENT THE STONE TO ME AND KNEEL! RESIST AND YOUR LIVES ARE FORFEIT. SO PROCLAIMS...
...THE FROST PHARAOH!
FROST PHARAOH? ARE YOU SERIOUS?
INSOLENT DOG! TASTE ICY DEATH!
GOTTA BE FASTER THAN THAT!
BOW BEFORE YOUR PHARAOH!
ARRRGGH! SO COLD!

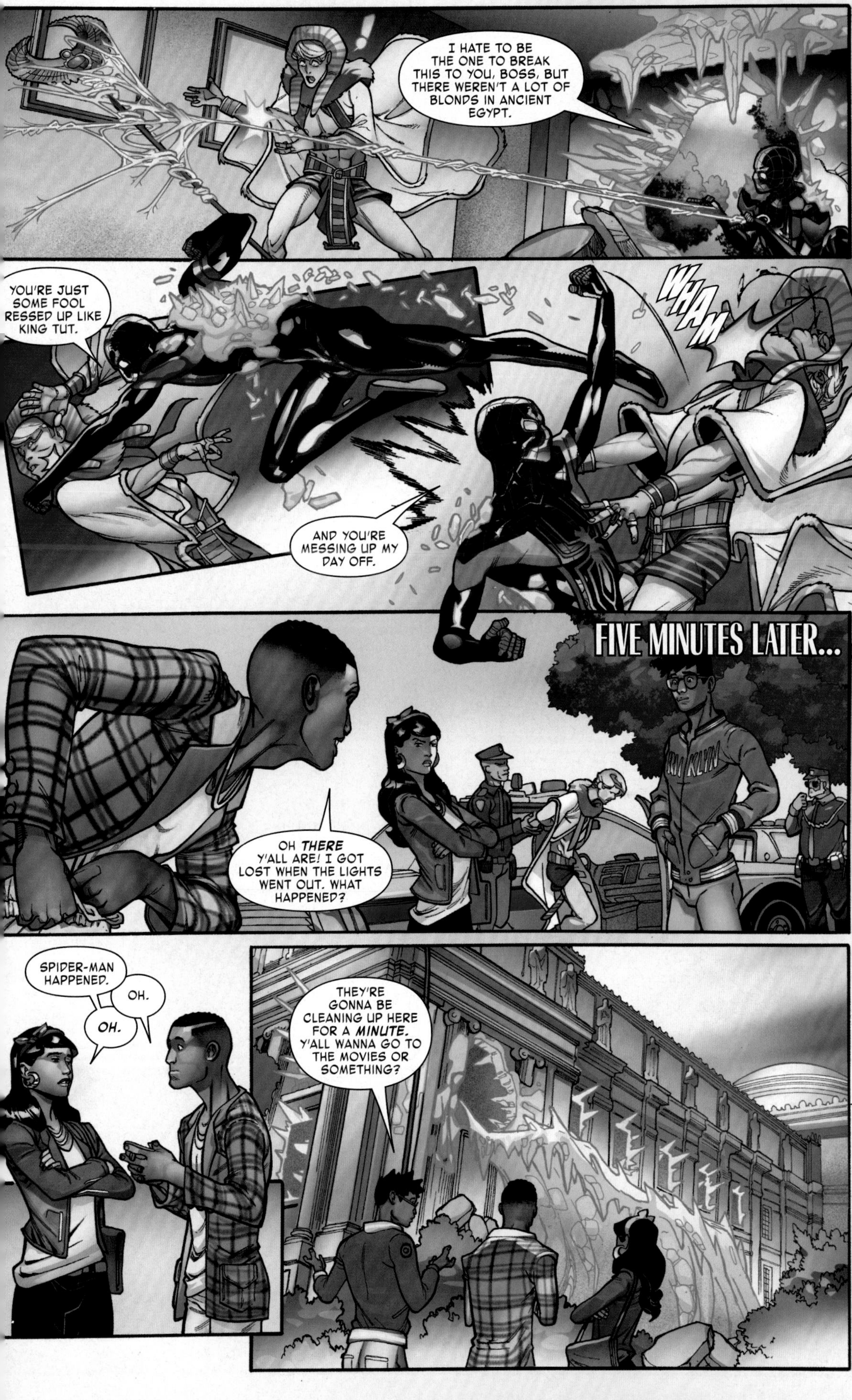
I HATE TO BE THE ONE TO BREAK THIS TO YOU, BOSS, BUT THERE WEREN'T A LOT OF BLONDS IN ANCIENT EGYPT.
YOU'RE JUST SOME FOOL RESSED UP LIKE KING TUT.
WHAM
AND YOU'RE MESSING UP MY DAY OFF.
FIVE MINUTES LATER...
OH THERE Y'ALL ARE! I GOT LOST WHEN THE LIGHTS WENT OUT. WHAT HAPPENED?
SPIDER-MAN HAPPENED.
OH.
OH.
THEY'RE GONNA BE CLEANING UP HERE FOR A MINUTE. Y'ALL WANNA GO TO THE MOVIES OR SOMETHING?

NEARBY...

THAT WHOLE MEETING WAS *RIDICULOUS.* PENCIL PUSHERS TELLING ME HOW TO DO MY JOB.

"PENCIL PUSHERS"? YOU'RE A VICE PRINCIPAL, LYLE, NOT A NAVY SEAL. YOU'VE GOT TO LEARN TO CALM DOWN.

I'LL CALM DOWN WHEN I'M BACK AT--HEY, WHAT'S TAKING SO LONG, ANYWAY? WE'VE BEEN SITTING AT THIS LIGHT FOR TWENTY MINUTES!

SOME BIG THING AT THE MUSEUM. NEWS SAYS SPIDER-MAN SAVED A BUNCH OF PEOPLE.

SPIDER-MAN! NOW *THERE'S* A MAN WITH A SENSE OF *RESPONSIBILITY.* BRAVERY. TRADITION.

I ONLY WISH OUR STUDENTS WOULD LEARN SOME OF THOSE LESSONS.

SPIDER-MAN COULD TEACH A BAD APPLE LIKE MILES MORALES A THING OR TWO.

WHY DID YOU EVEN BECOME AN EDUCATOR? DO YOU EVEN *LIKE* KIDS?

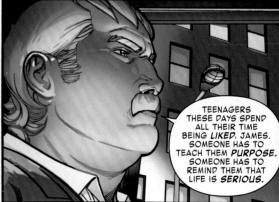

TEENAGERS THESE DAYS SPEND ALL THEIR TIME BEING *LIKED,* JAMES. SOMEONE HAS TO TEACH THEM *PURPOSE.* SOMEONE HAS TO REMIND THEM THAT LIFE IS *SERIOUS.*

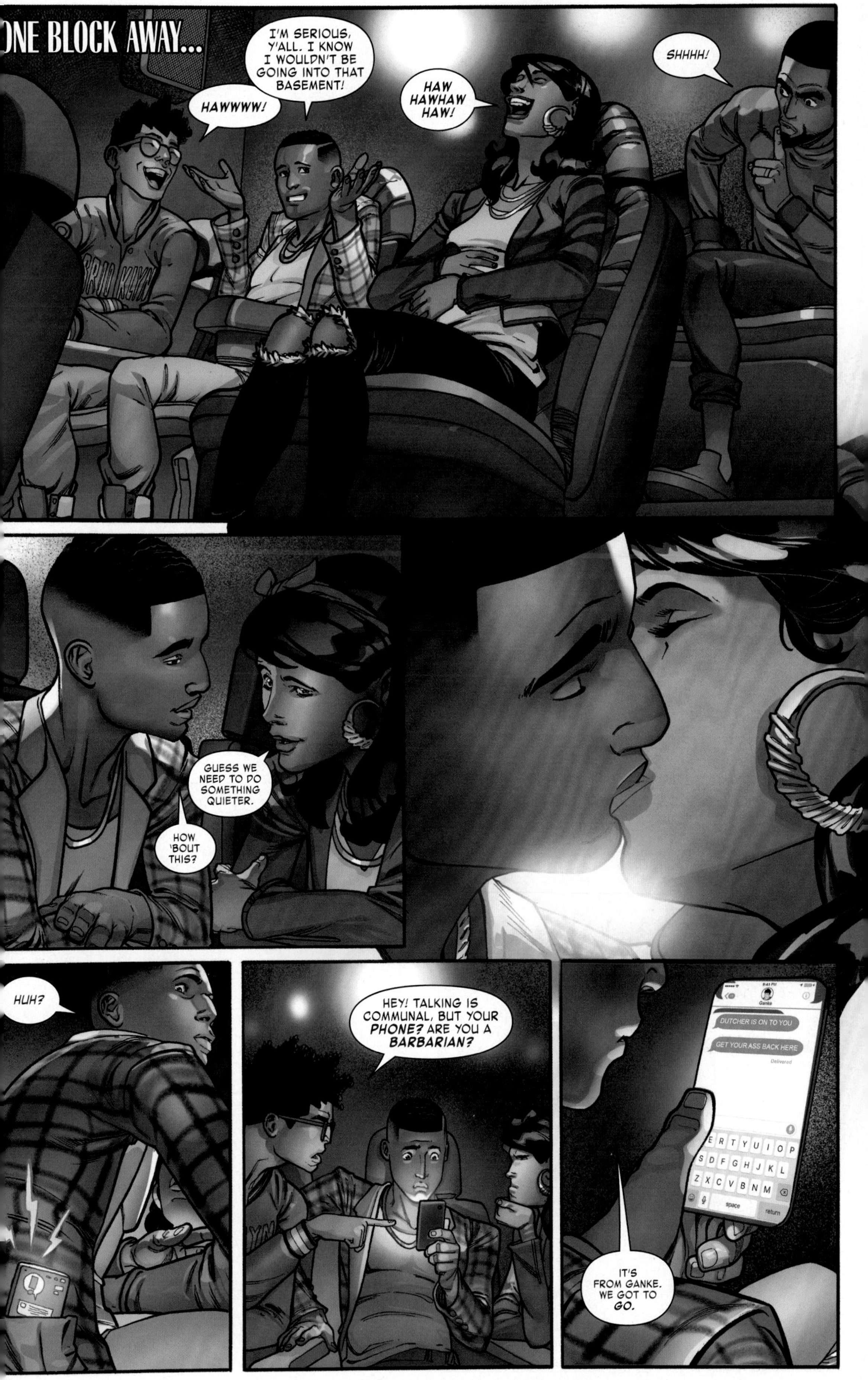
ONE BLOCK AWAY...
I'M SERIOUS, Y'ALL. I KNOW I WOULDN'T BE GOING INTO THAT BASEMENT!
HAWWWW!
HAW HAWHAW HAW!
SHHHH!
GUESS WE NEED TO DO SOMETHING QUIETER.
HOW 'BOUT THIS?
HUH?
HEY! TALKING IS COMMUNAL, BUT YOUR PHONE? ARE YOU A BARBARIAN?
DUTCHER IS ON TO YOU
GET YOUR ASS BACK HERE
Delivered
IT'S FROM GANKE. WE GOT TO GO.

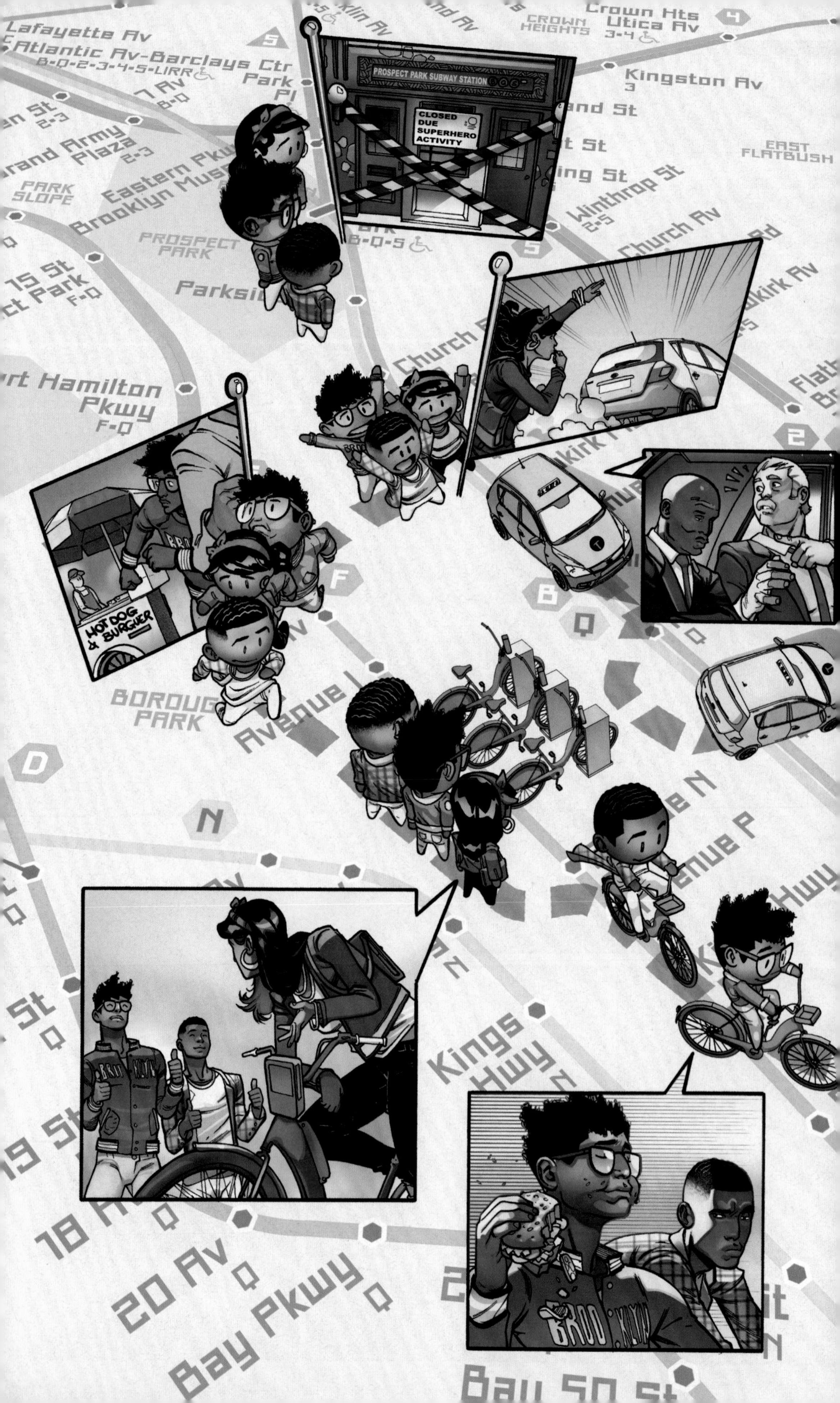

Lafayette Av
Atlantic Av-Barclays Ctr
B-Q-2-3-4-5-LIRR
Park Pl
7 Av
B-Q
Crown Hts Utica Av
3-4
CROWN HEIGHTS
Kingston Av
3
PROSPECT PARK SUBWAY STATION
CLOSED DUE SUPERHERO ACTIVITY
Grand Army Plaza
2-3
Eastern Pkwy Brooklyn Museum
PARK SLOPE
PROSPECT PARK
EAST FLATBUSH
Winthrop St
2-5
Church Av
B-Q-5
15 St
F-Q
Parkside
Fort Hamilton Pkwy
F-Q
HOT DOG & BURGUER
BOROUGH PARK
Avenue I
Avenue N
Avenue P
Kings Hwy
N
18 Av
Q
20 Av
Q
Bay Pkwy
Q
19 St
Bay 50 St

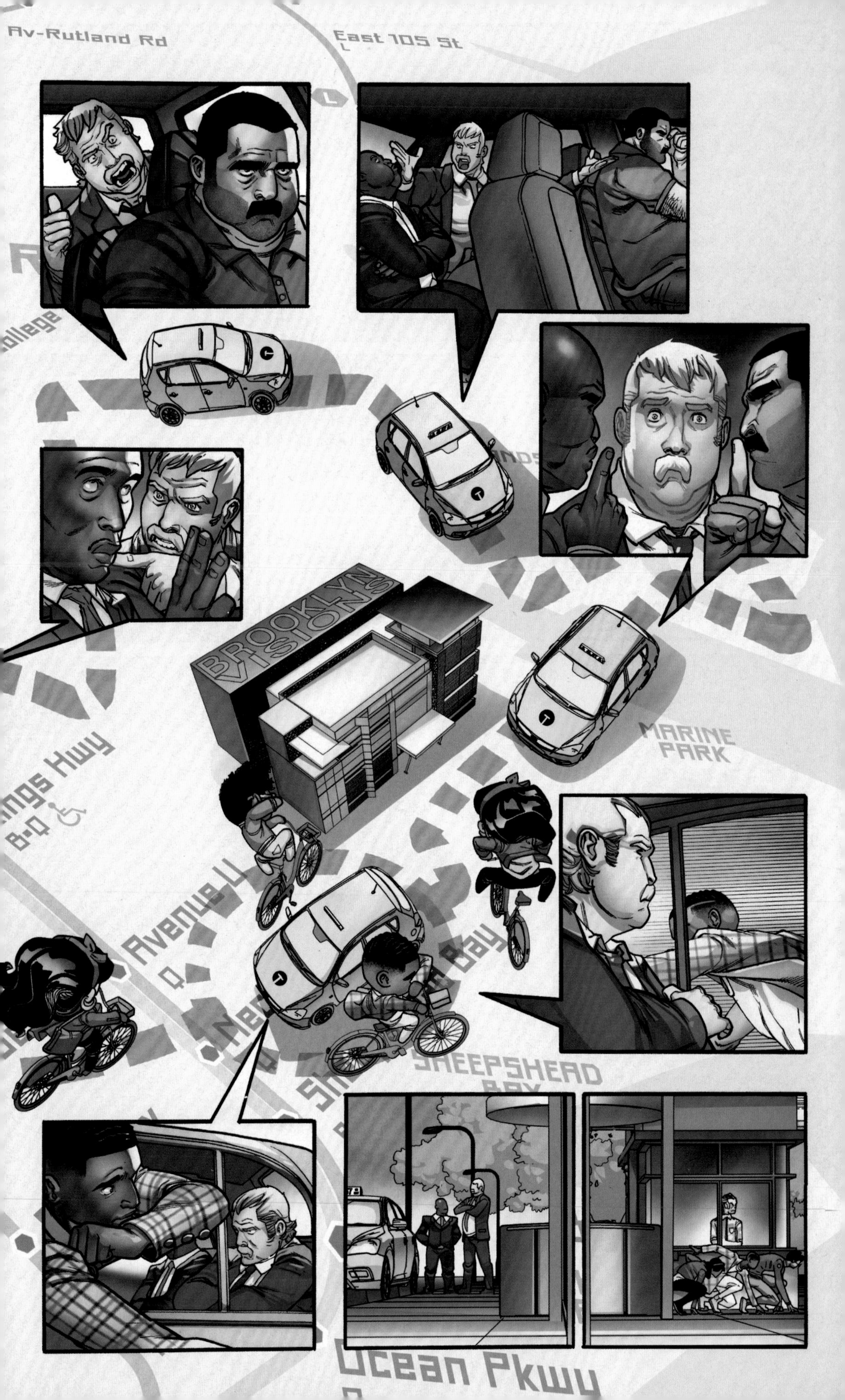

Av-Rutland Rd
East 105 St
L
BROOKLYN VISIONS
MARINE PARK
Avenue U
Q
SHEEPSHEAD
Ocean Pkwy

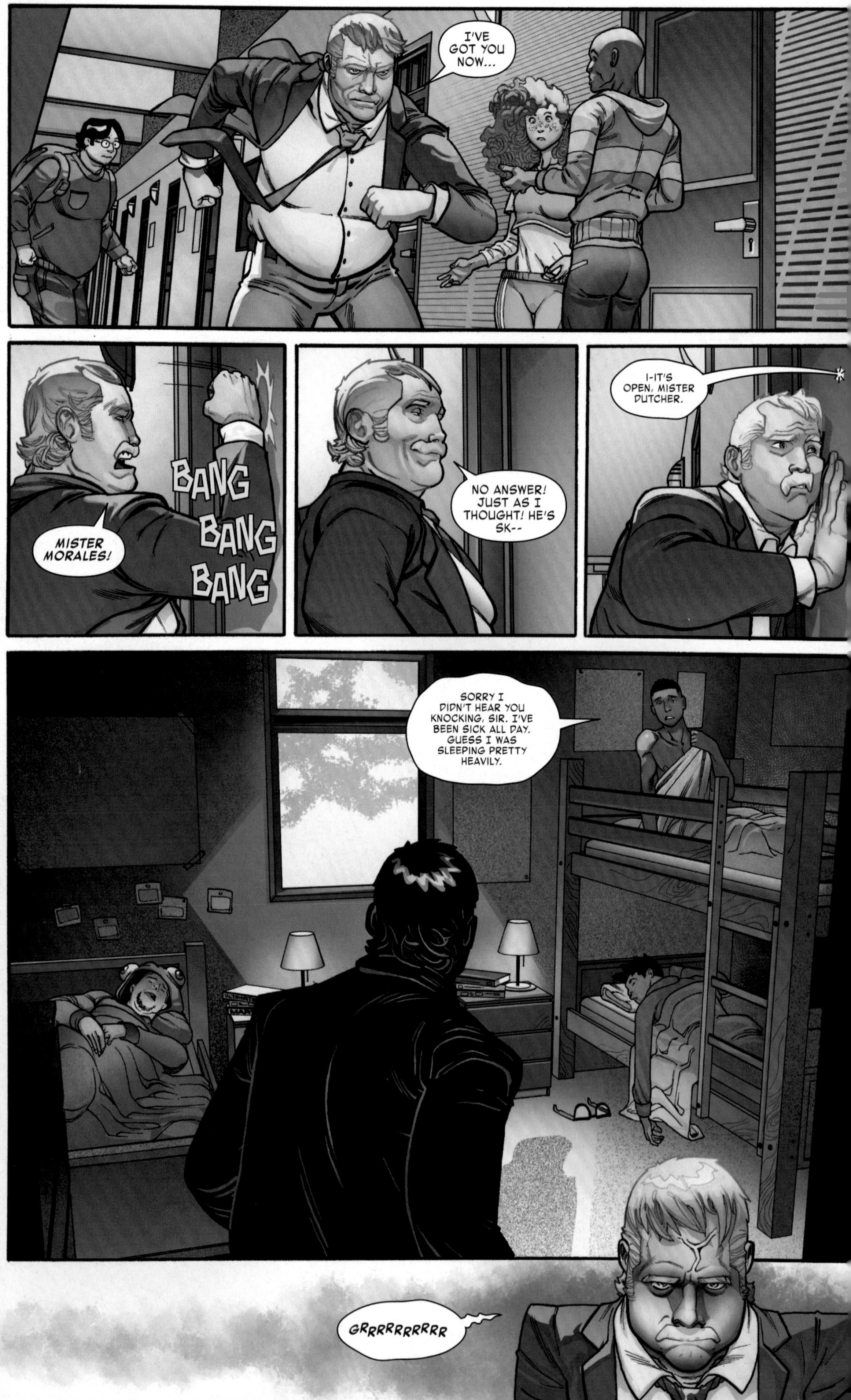
I'VE GOT YOU NOW...
MISTER MORALES!
BANG BANG BANG
NO ANSWER! JUST AS I THOUGHT! HE'S SK--
I-IT'S OPEN, MISTER DUTCHER.
SORRY I DIDN'T HEAR YOU KNOCKING, SIR. I'VE BEEN SICK ALL DAY. GUESS I WAS SLEEPING PRETTY HEAVILY.
GRRRRRRRRRR

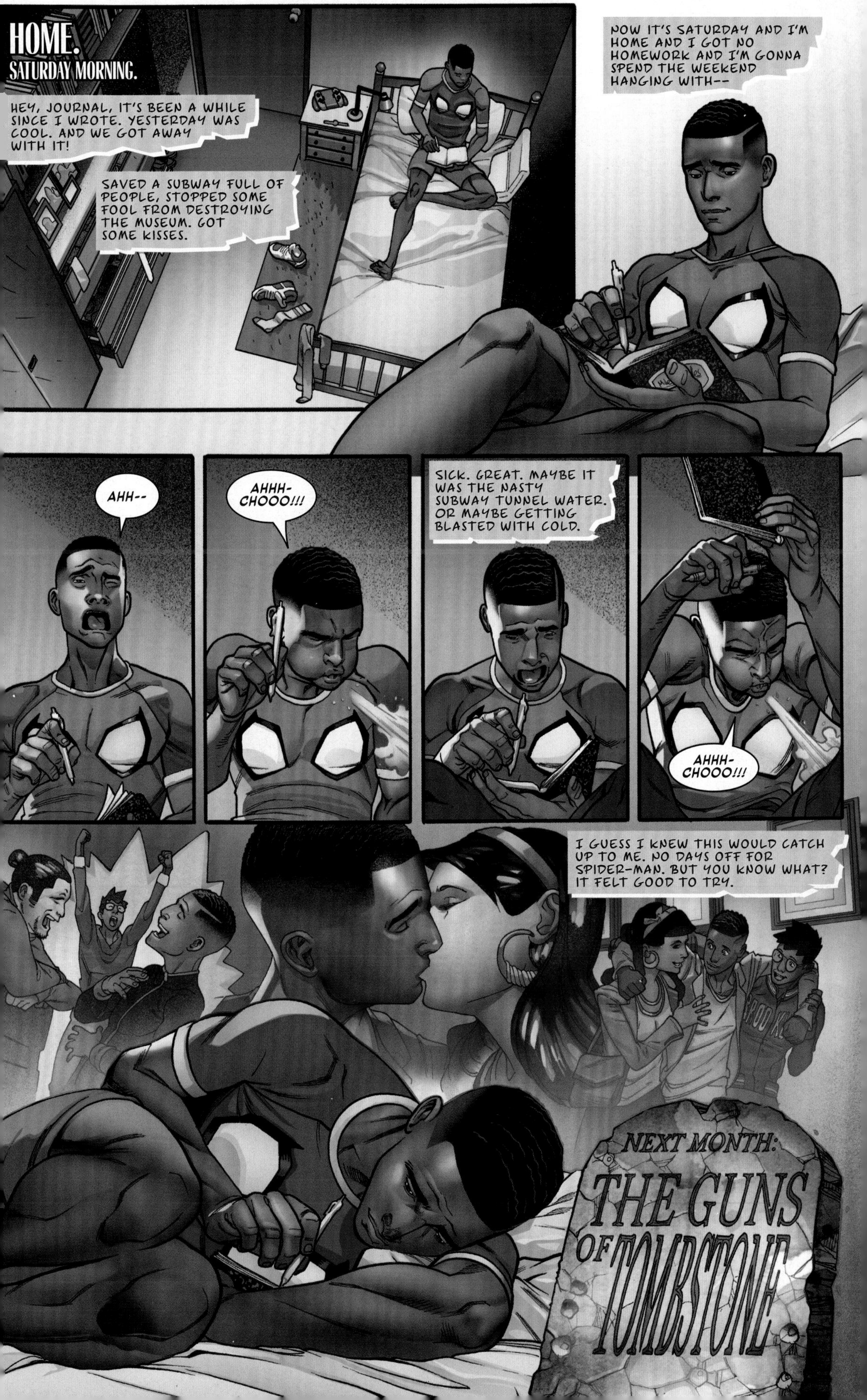
HOME.
SATURDAY MORNING.
HEY, JOURNAL, IT'S BEEN A WHILE SINCE I WROTE. YESTERDAY WAS COOL. AND WE GOT AWAY WITH IT!
SAVED A SUBWAY FULL OF PEOPLE, STOPPED SOME FOOL FROM DESTROYING THE MUSEUM. GOT SOME KISSES.
NOW IT'S SATURDAY AND I'M HOME AND I GOT NO HOMEWORK AND I'M GONNA SPEND THE WEEKEND HANGING WITH--
AHH--
AHHH-CHOOO!!!
SICK. GREAT. MAYBE IT WAS THE NASTY SUBWAY TUNNEL WATER. OR MAYBE GETTING BLASTED WITH COLD.
AHHH-CHOOO!!!
I GUESS I KNEW THIS WOULD CATCH UP TO ME. NO DAYS OFF FOR SPIDER-MAN. BUT YOU KNOW WHAT? IT FELT GOOD TO TRY.
NEXT MONTH:
THE GUNS OF TOMBSTONE

5

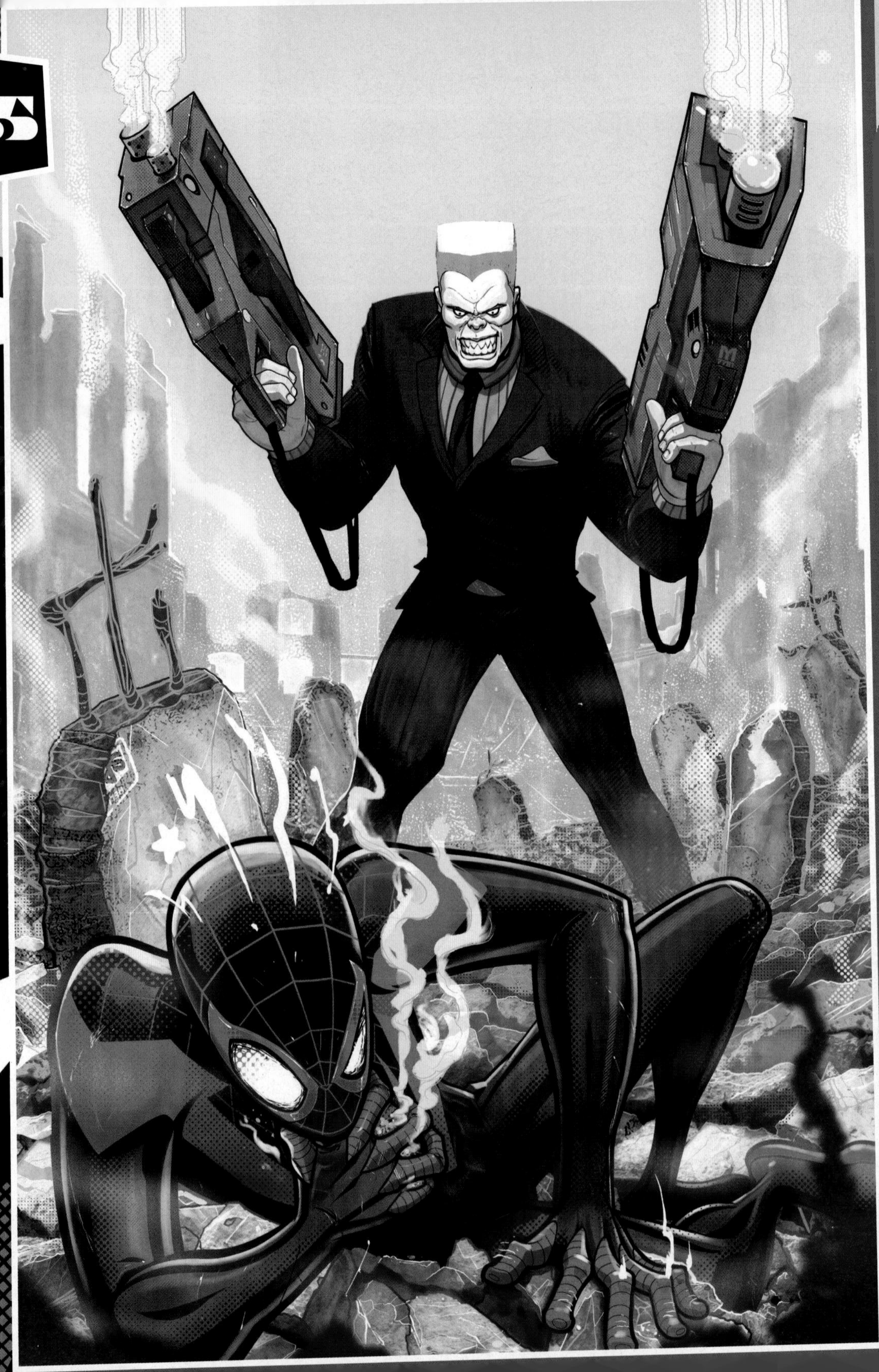

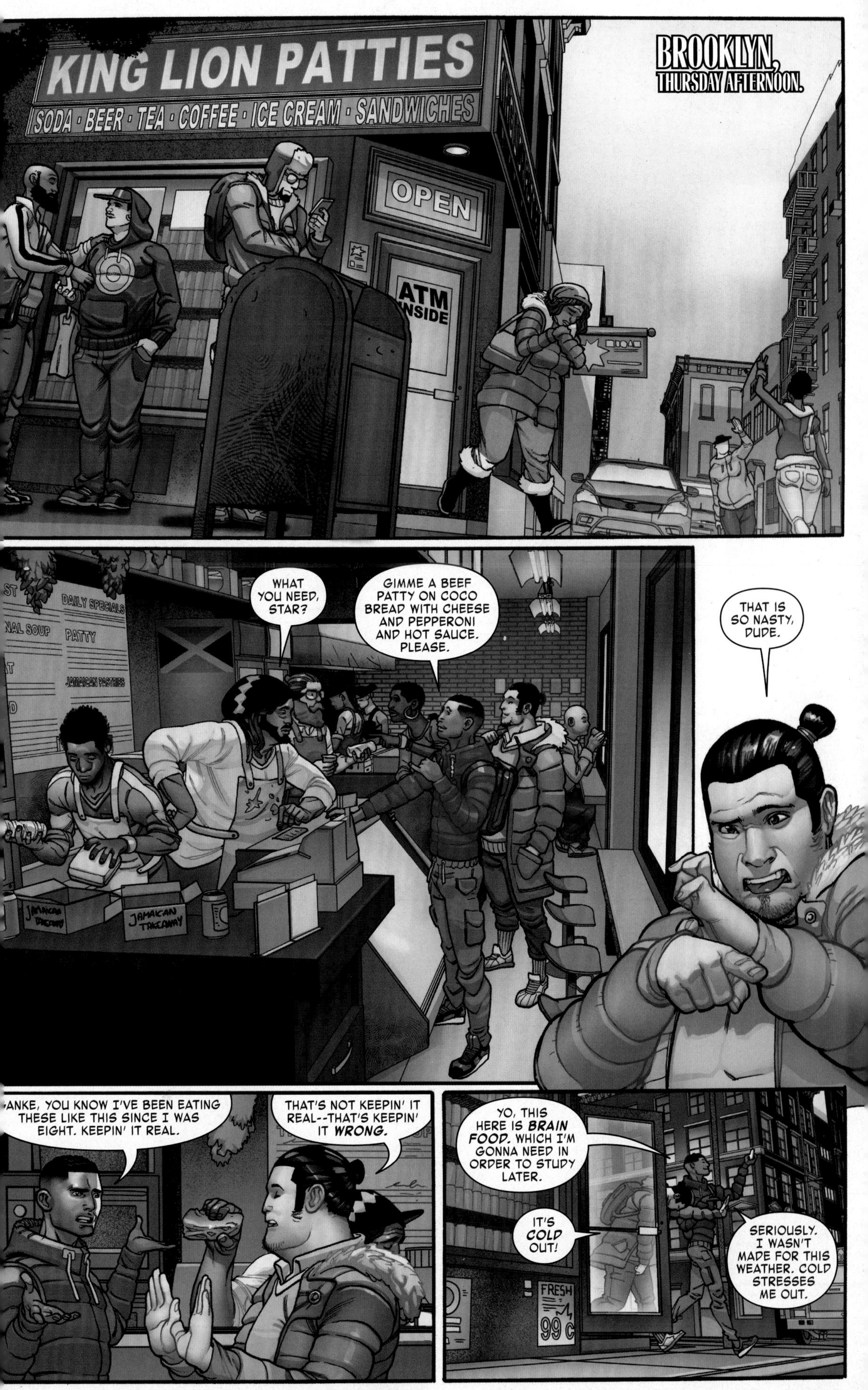
KING LION PATTIES
SODA · BEER · TEA · COFFEE · ICE CREAM · SANDWICHES
OPEN
ATM INSIDE
BROOKLYN, THURSDAY AFTERNOON.
DAILY SPECIALS
PATTY
JAMAICAN PASTRIES
WHAT YOU NEED, STAR?
GIMME A BEEF PATTY ON COCO BREAD WITH CHEESE AND PEPPERONI AND HOT SAUCE. PLEASE.
THAT IS SO NASTY, DUDE.
JAMAICAN TAKEAWAY
ANKE, YOU KNOW I'VE BEEN EATING THESE LIKE THIS SINCE I WAS EIGHT. KEEPIN' IT REAL.
THAT'S NOT KEEPIN' IT REAL--THAT'S KEEPIN' IT WRONG.
YO, THIS HERE IS BRAIN FOOD. WHICH I'M GONNA NEED IN ORDER TO STUDY LATER.
IT'S COLD OUT!
SERIOUSLY. I WASN'T MADE FOR THIS WEATHER. COLD STRESSES ME OUT.
FRESH 99 C

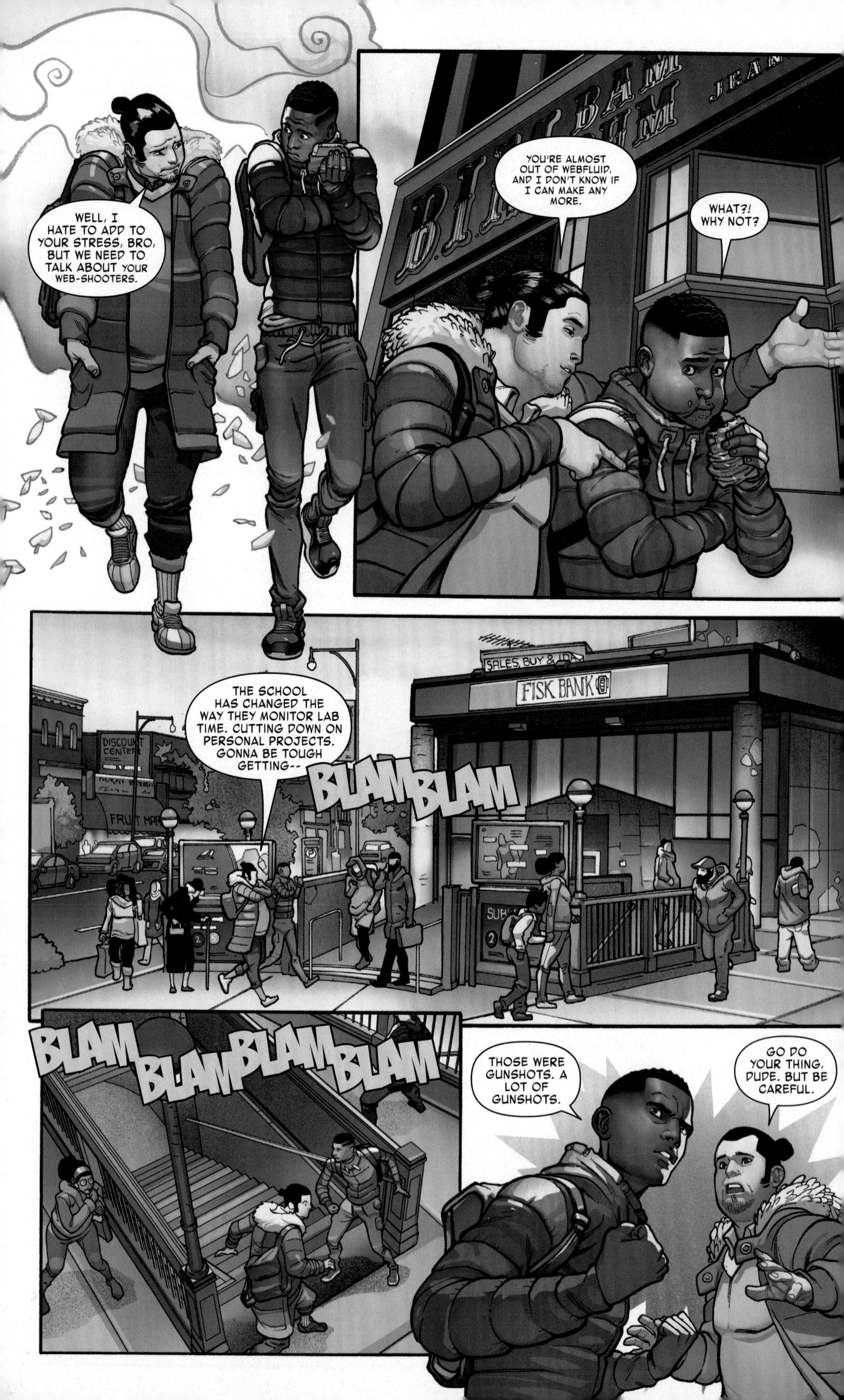

WELL, I HATE TO ADD TO YOUR STRESS, BRO, BUT WE NEED TO TALK ABOUT YOUR WEB-SHOOTERS.
YOU'RE ALMOST OUT OF WEBFLUID, AND I DON'T KNOW IF I CAN MAKE ANY MORE.
WHAT?! WHY NOT?
SALES, BUY & LOA
FISK BANK
DISCOUNT CENTER
FRUIT MA
THE SCHOOL HAS CHANGED THE WAY THEY MONITOR LAB TIME. CUTTING DOWN ON PERSONAL PROJECTS. GONNA BE TOUGH GETTING--
BLAMBLAM
BLAM BLAMBLAMBLAM
THOSE WERE GUNSHOTS. A LOT OF GUNSHOTS.
GO DO YOUR THING, DUDE. BUT BE CAREFUL.

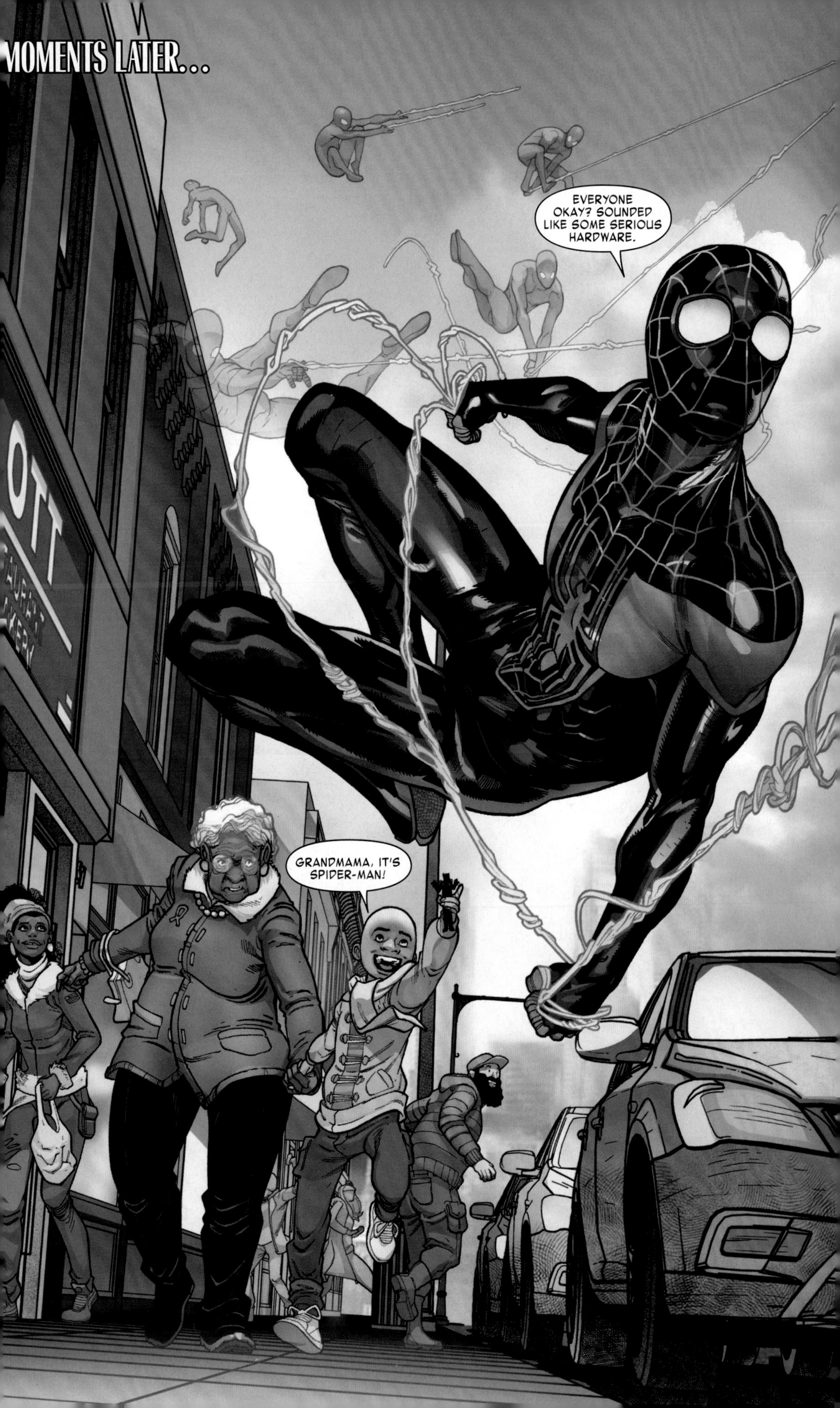
MOMENTS LATER...
EVERYONE OKAY? SOUNDED LIKE SOME SERIOUS HARDWARE.
GRANDMAMA, IT'S SPIDER-MAN!

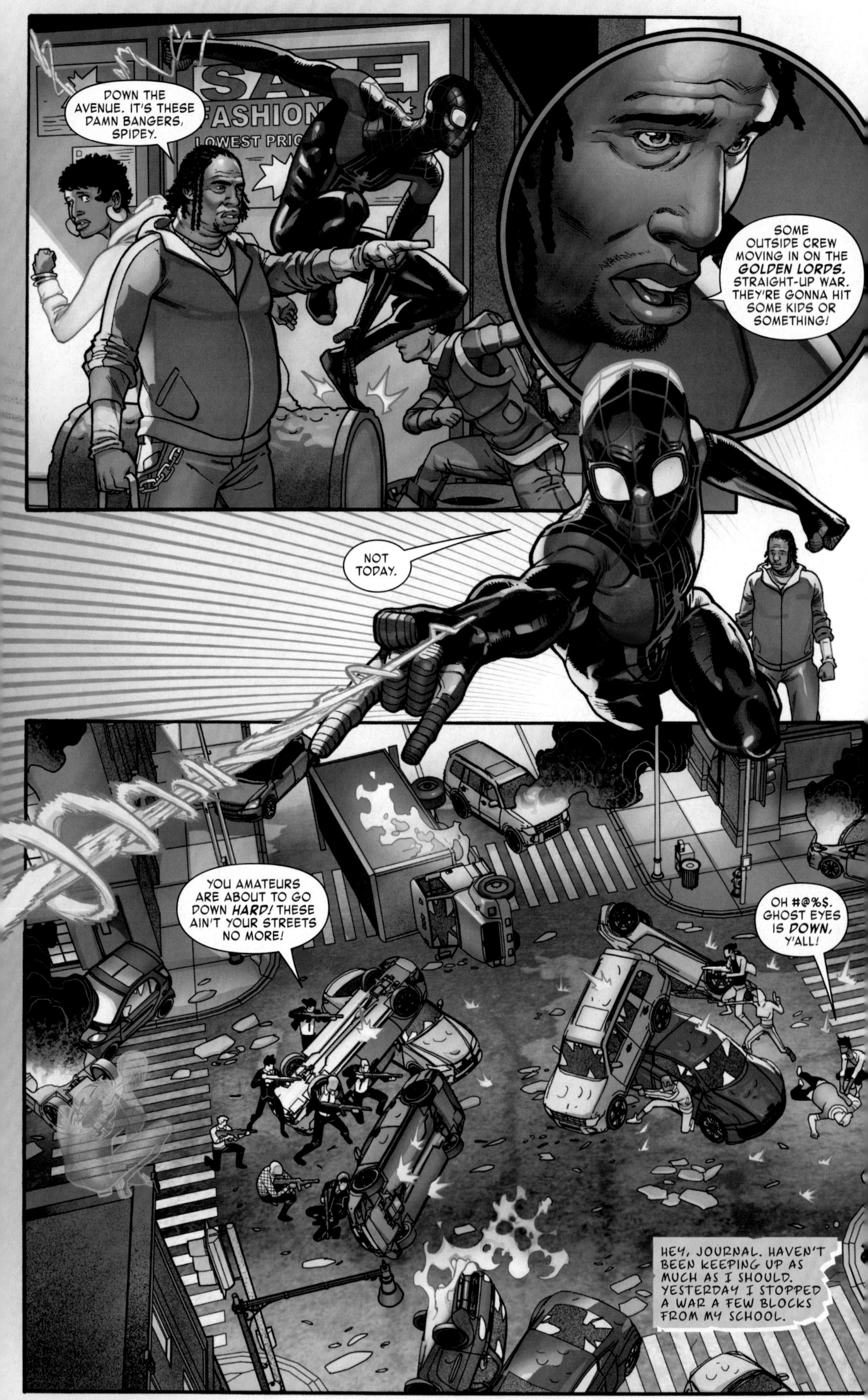
SALE
FASHION
LOWEST PRIC
DOWN THE AVENUE. IT'S THESE DAMN BANGERS, SPIDEY.
SOME OUTSIDE CREW MOVING IN ON THE GOLDEN LORDS. STRAIGHT-UP WAR. THEY'RE GONNA HIT SOME KIDS OR SOMETHING!
NOT TODAY.
YOU AMATEURS ARE ABOUT TO GO DOWN HARD! THESE AIN'T YOUR STREETS NO MORE!
OH #@%$. GHOST EYES IS DOWN, Y'ALL!
HEY, JOURNAL. HAVEN'T BEEN KEEPING UP AS MUCH AS I SHOULD. YESTERDAY I STOPPED A WAR A FEW BLOCKS FROM MY SCHOOL.

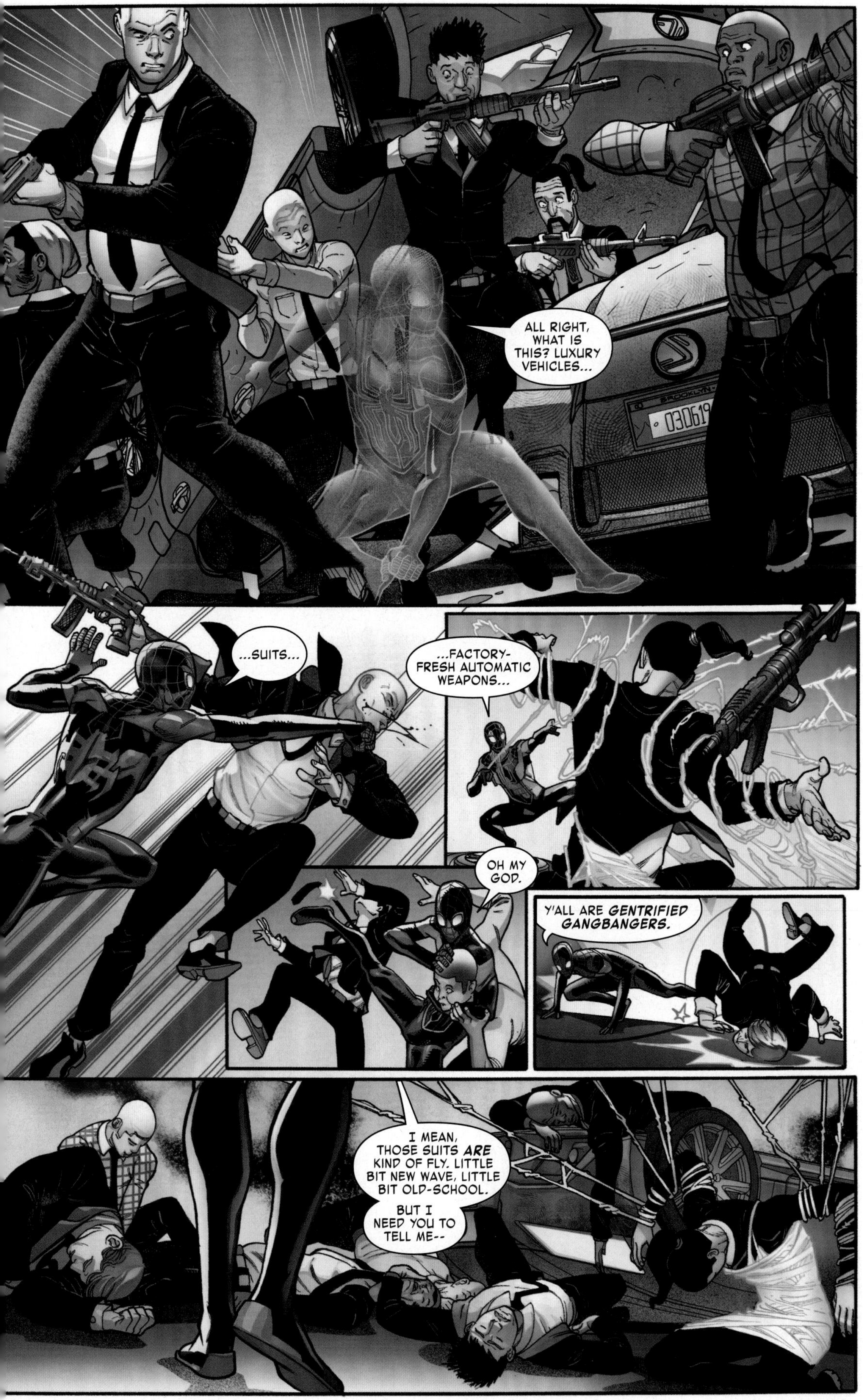
ALL RIGHT, WHAT IS THIS? LUXURY VEHICLES...
BROOKLYN
030619
...SUITS...
...FACTORY-FRESH AUTOMATIC WEAPONS...
OH MY GOD.
Y'ALL ARE *GENTRIFIED GANGBANGERS.*
I MEAN, THOSE SUITS *ARE* KIND OF FLY. LITTLE BIT NEW WAVE, LITTLE BIT OLD-SCHOOL.
BUT I NEED YOU TO TELL ME--

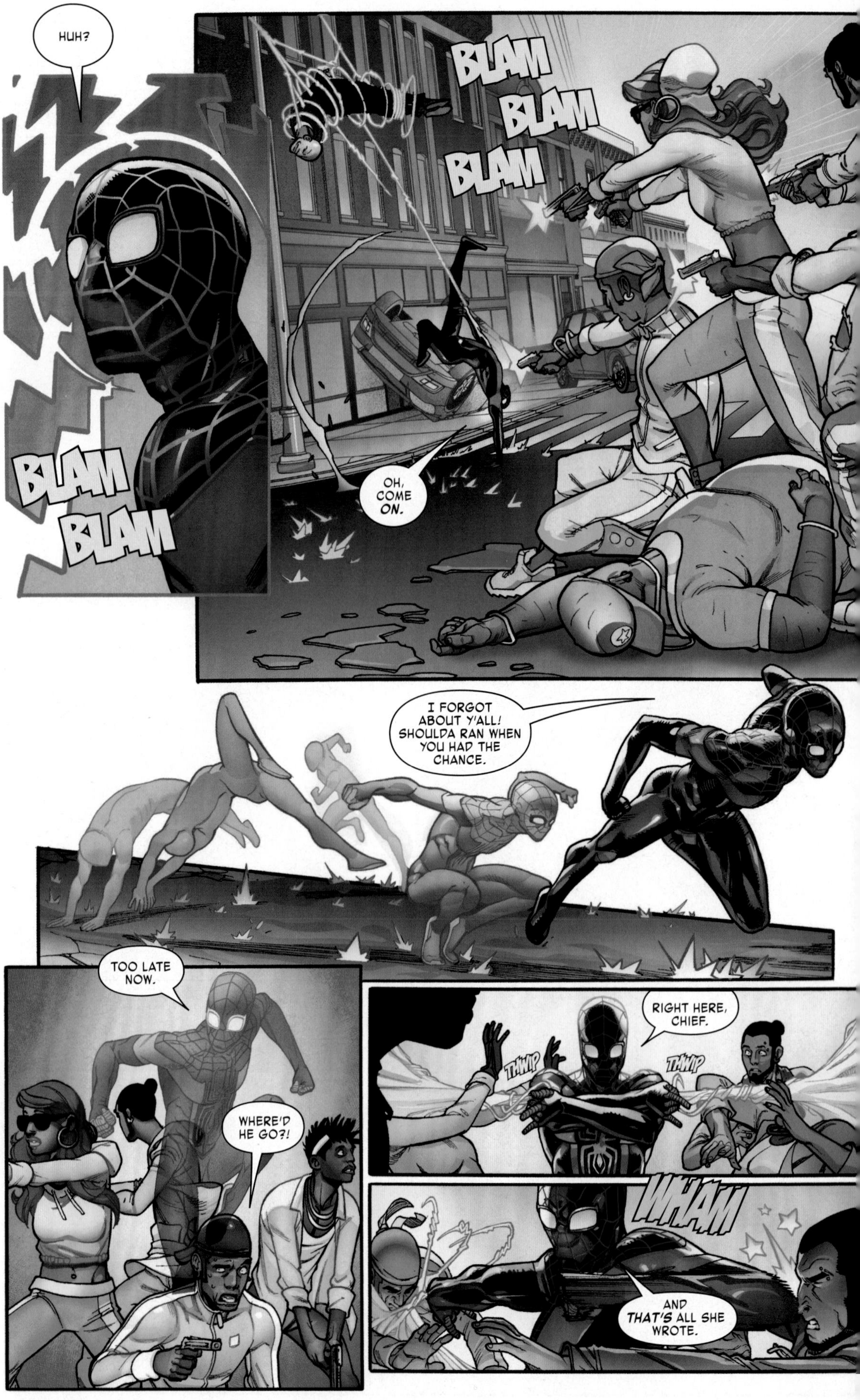
HUH?
BLAM
BLAM
BLAM
BLAM
BLAM
OH, COME ON.
I FORGOT ABOUT Y'ALL! SHOULDA RAN WHEN YOU HAD THE CHANCE.
TOO LATE NOW.
WHERE'D HE GO?!
RIGHT HERE, CHIEF.
THWIP
THWIP
WHAM
AND THAT'S ALL SHE WROTE.

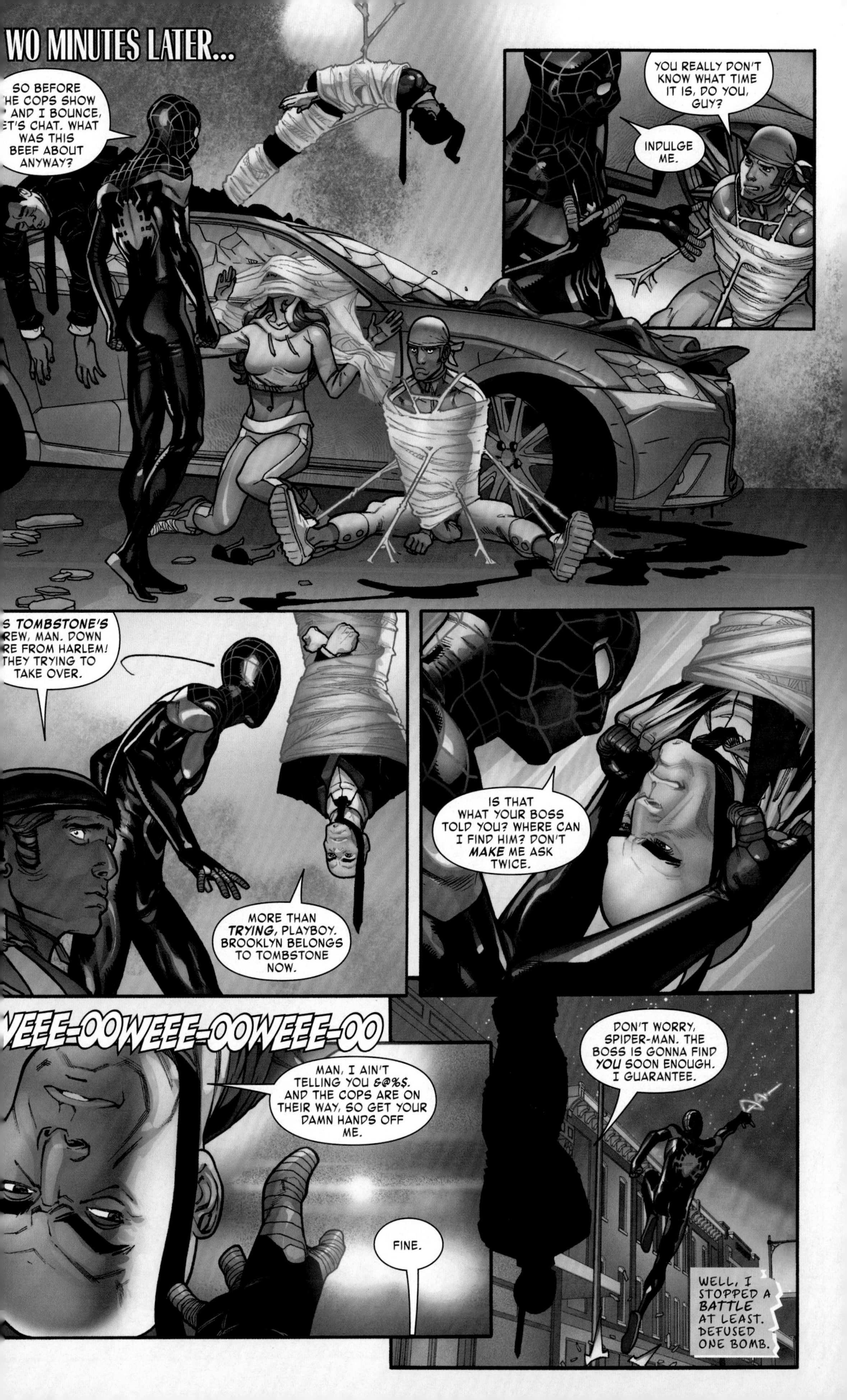

WO MINUTES LATER...
SO BEFORE HE COPS SHOW AND I BOUNCE, ET'S CHAT. WHAT WAS THIS BEEF ABOUT ANYWAY?
YOU REALLY DON'T KNOW WHAT TIME IT IS, DO YOU, GUY?
INDULGE ME.
S TOMBSTONE'S REW, MAN. DOWN RE FROM HARLEM! THEY TRYING TO TAKE OVER.
MORE THAN TRYING, PLAYBOY. BROOKLYN BELONGS TO TOMBSTONE NOW.
IS THAT WHAT YOUR BOSS TOLD YOU? WHERE CAN I FIND HIM? DON'T MAKE ME ASK TWICE.
VEEE-OOWEEE-OOWEEE-OO
MAN, I AIN'T TELLING YOU &@%$. AND THE COPS ARE ON THEIR WAY, SO GET YOUR DAMN HANDS OFF ME.
FINE.
DON'T WORRY, SPIDER-MAN. THE BOSS IS GONNA FIND YOU SOON ENOUGH. I GUARANTEE.
WELL, I STOPPED A BATTLE AT LEAST. DEFUSED ONE BOMB.

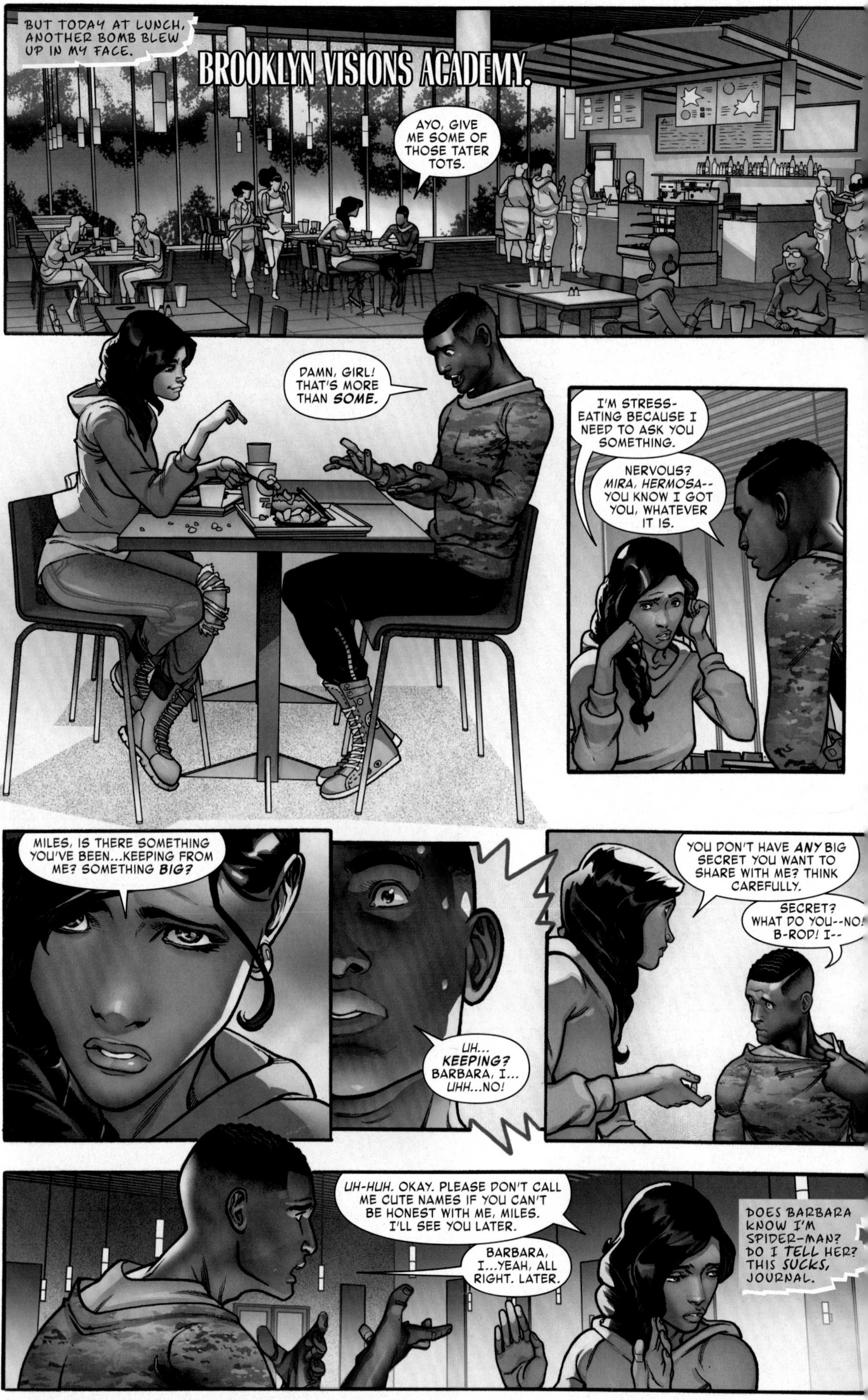

BUT TODAY AT LUNCH, ANOTHER BOMB BLEW UP IN MY FACE.
BROOKLYN VISIONS ACADEMY.
AYO, GIVE ME SOME OF THOSE TATER TOTS.
DAMN, GIRL! THAT'S MORE THAN SOME.
I'M STRESS-EATING BECAUSE I NEED TO ASK YOU SOMETHING.
NERVOUS? MIRA, HERMOSA--YOU KNOW I GOT YOU, WHATEVER IT IS.
MILES, IS THERE SOMETHING YOU'VE BEEN...KEEPING FROM ME? SOMETHING BIG?
UH... KEEPING? BARBARA, I... UHH...NO!
YOU DON'T HAVE ANY BIG SECRET YOU WANT TO SHARE WITH ME? THINK CAREFULLY.
SECRET? WHAT DO YOU--NO! B-ROD! I--
UH-HUH. OKAY. PLEASE DON'T CALL ME CUTE NAMES IF YOU CAN'T BE HONEST WITH ME, MILES. I'LL SEE YOU LATER.
BARBARA, I...YEAH, ALL RIGHT. LATER.
DOES BARBARA KNOW I'M SPIDER-MAN? DO I TELL HER? THIS SUCKS, JOURNAL.

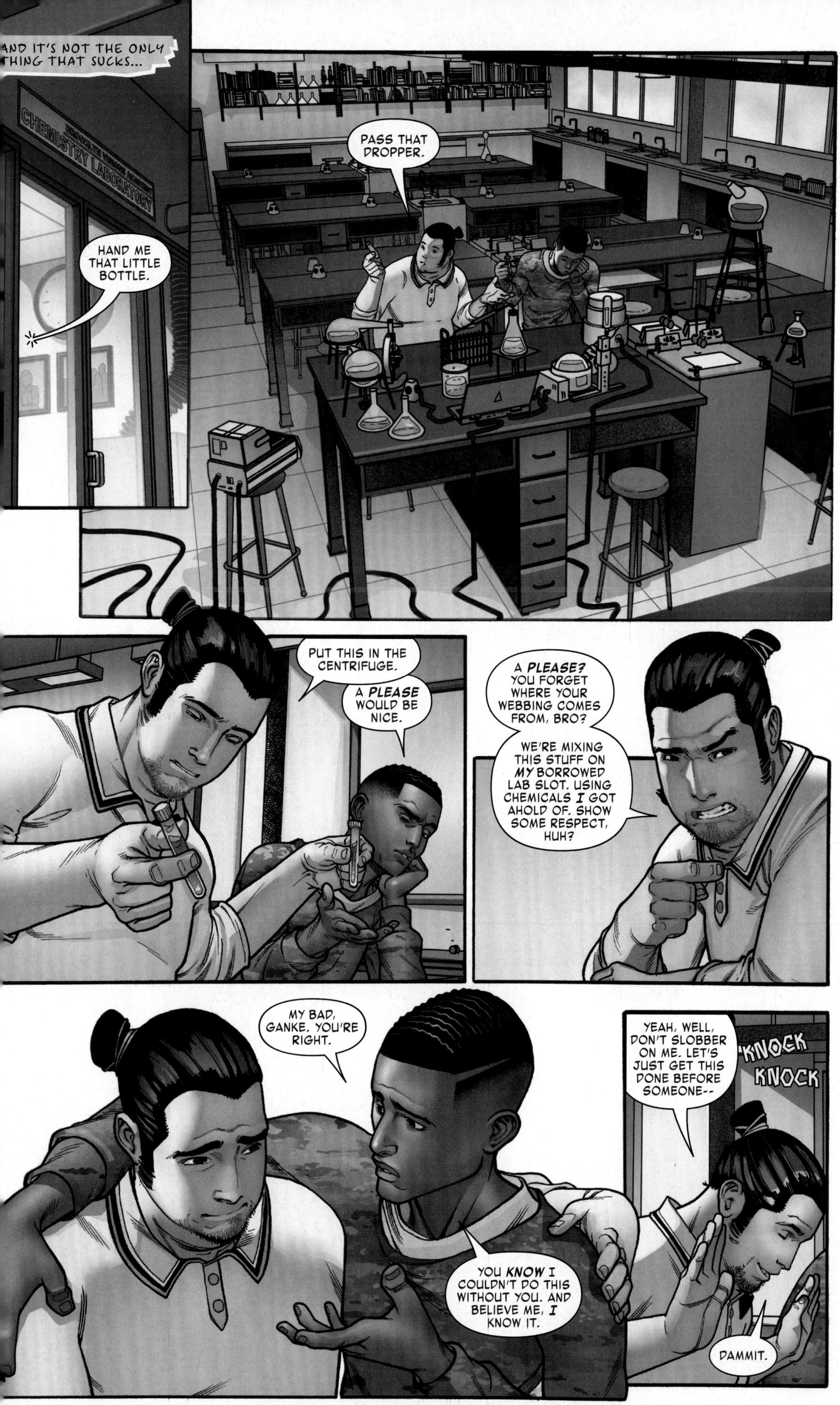
AND IT'S NOT THE ONLY THING THAT SUCKS...
CHEMISTRY LABORATORY
HAND ME THAT LITTLE BOTTLE.
PASS THAT DROPPER.
PUT THIS IN THE CENTRIFUGE.
A PLEASE WOULD BE NICE.
A PLEASE? YOU FORGET WHERE YOUR WEBBING COMES FROM, BRO?
WE'RE MIXING THIS STUFF ON MY BORROWED LAB SLOT. USING CHEMICALS I GOT AHOLD OF. SHOW SOME RESPECT, HUH?
MY BAD, GANKE. YOU'RE RIGHT.
YOU KNOW I COULDN'T DO THIS WITHOUT YOU. AND BELIEVE ME, I KNOW IT.
YEAH, WELL, DON'T SLOBBER ON ME. LET'S JUST GET THIS DONE BEFORE SOMEONE--
KNOCK KNOCK
DAMMIT.

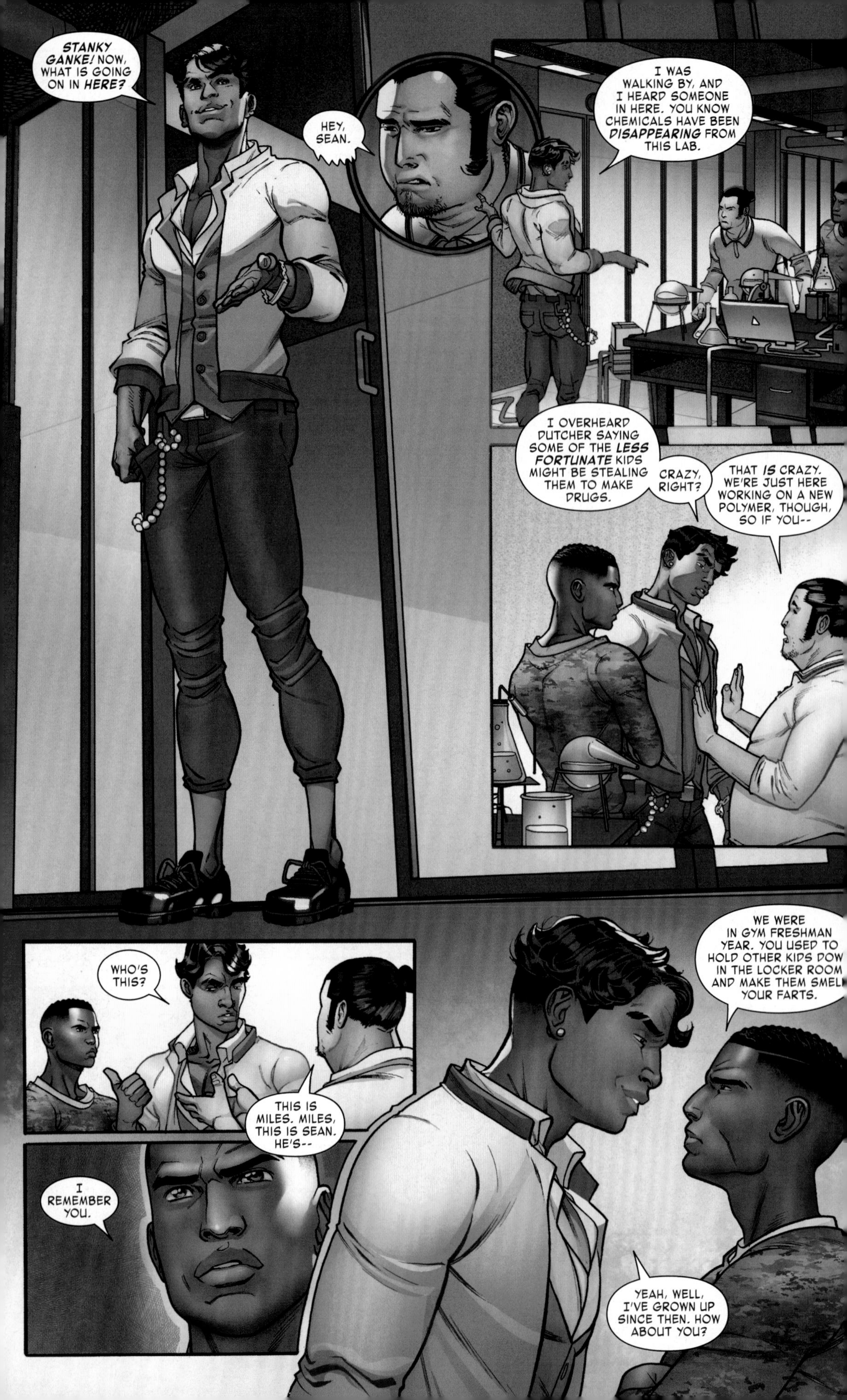
STANKY GANKE! NOW, WHAT IS GOING ON IN HERE?
HEY, SEAN.
I WAS WALKING BY, AND I HEARD SOMEONE IN HERE. YOU KNOW CHEMICALS HAVE BEEN DISAPPEARING FROM THIS LAB.
I OVERHEARD DUTCHER SAYING SOME OF THE LESS FORTUNATE KIDS MIGHT BE STEALING THEM TO MAKE DRUGS.
CRAZY, RIGHT?
THAT IS CRAZY. WE'RE JUST HERE WORKING ON A NEW POLYMER, THOUGH, SO IF YOU--
WHO'S THIS?
THIS IS MILES. MILES, THIS IS SEAN. HE'S--
I REMEMBER YOU.
WE WERE IN GYM FRESHMAN YEAR. YOU USED TO HOLD OTHER KIDS DOW IN THE LOCKER ROOM AND MAKE THEM SMEL YOUR FARTS.
YEAH, WELL, I'VE GROWN UP SINCE THEN. HOW ABOUT YOU?

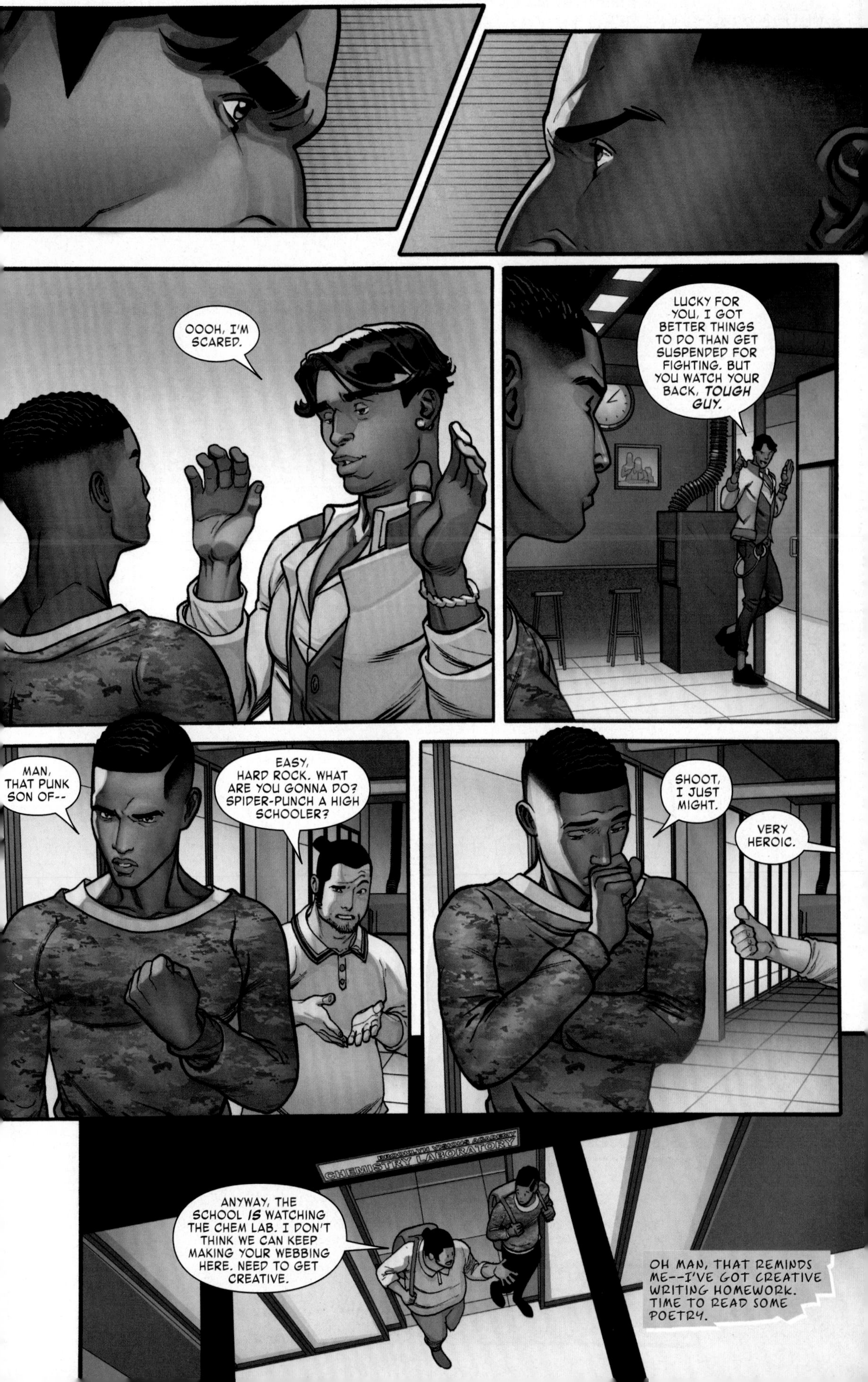
OOOH, I'M SCARED.
LUCKY FOR YOU, I GOT BETTER THINGS TO DO THAN GET SUSPENDED FOR FIGHTING. BUT YOU WATCH YOUR BACK, *TOUGH GUY.*
MAN, THAT PUNK SON OF--
EASY, HARD ROCK. WHAT ARE YOU GONNA DO? SPIDER-PUNCH A HIGH SCHOOLER?
SHOOT, I JUST MIGHT.
VERY HEROIC.
CHEMISTRY LABORATORY
ANYWAY, THE SCHOOL *IS* WATCHING THE CHEM LAB. I DON'T THINK WE CAN KEEP MAKING YOUR WEBBING HERE. NEED TO GET CREATIVE.
OH MAN, THAT REMINDS ME--I'VE GOT CREATIVE WRITING HOMEWORK. TIME TO READ SOME POETRY.

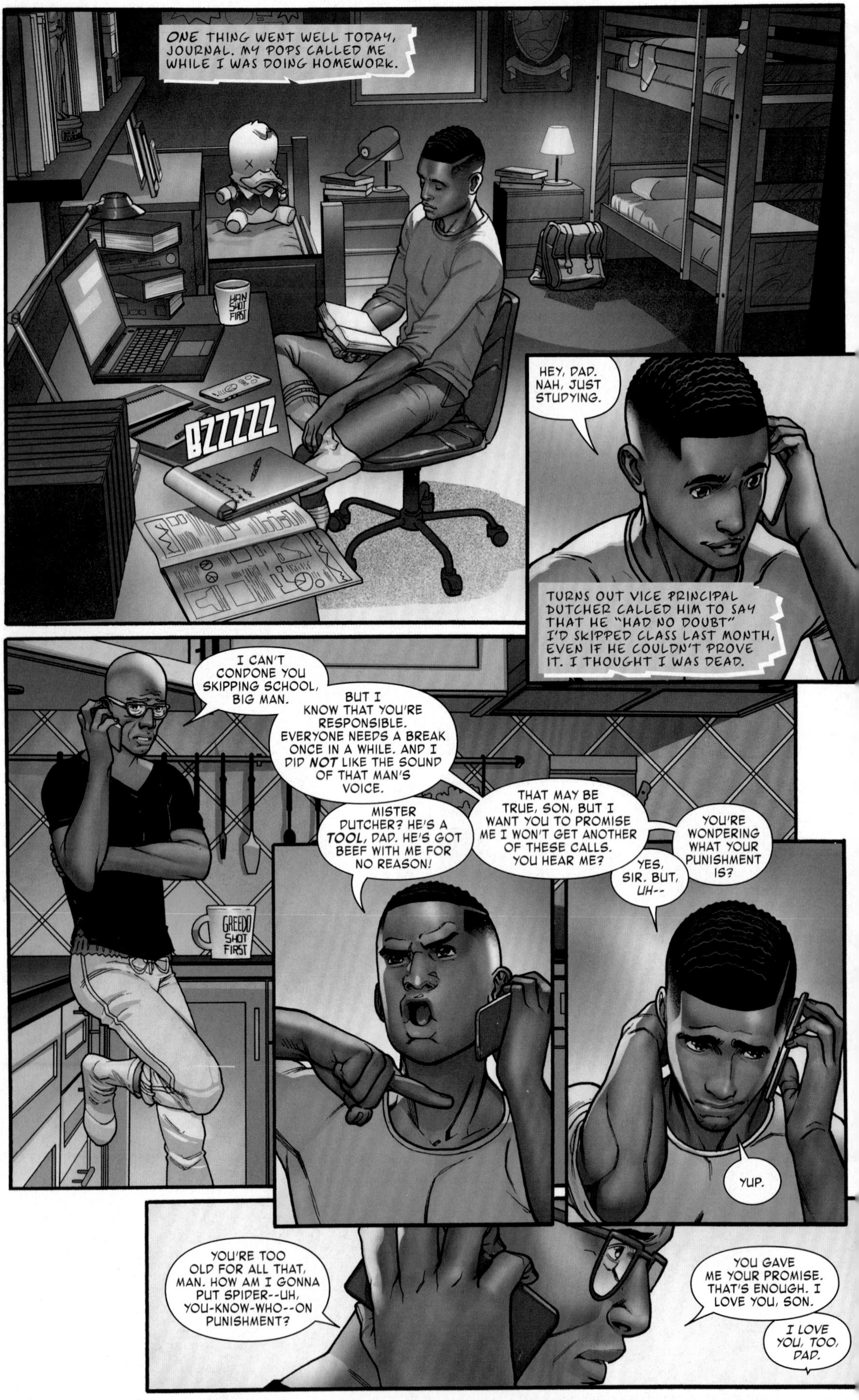
ONE THING WENT WELL TODAY, JOURNAL. MY POPS CALLED ME WHILE I WAS DOING HOMEWORK.
HAN SHOT FIRST
BZZZZZ
HEY, DAD. NAH, JUST STUDYING.
TURNS OUT VICE PRINCIPAL DUTCHER CALLED HIM TO SAY THAT HE "HAD NO DOUBT" I'D SKIPPED CLASS LAST MONTH, EVEN IF HE COULDN'T PROVE IT. I THOUGHT I WAS DEAD.
I CAN'T CONDONE YOU SKIPPING SCHOOL, BIG MAN.
BUT I KNOW THAT YOU'RE RESPONSIBLE. EVERYONE NEEDS A BREAK ONCE IN A WHILE. AND I DID NOT LIKE THE SOUND OF THAT MAN'S VOICE.
GREEDO SHOT FIRST
MISTER DUTCHER? HE'S A TOOL, DAD. HE'S GOT BEEF WITH ME FOR NO REASON!
THAT MAY BE TRUE, SON, BUT I WANT YOU TO PROMISE ME I WON'T GET ANOTHER OF THESE CALLS. YOU HEAR ME?
YES, SIR. BUT, UH--
YOU'RE WONDERING WHAT YOUR PUNISHMENT IS?
YUP.
YOU'RE TOO OLD FOR ALL THAT, MAN. HOW AM I GONNA PUT SPIDER--UH, YOU-KNOW-WHO--ON PUNISHMENT?
YOU GAVE ME YOUR PROMISE. THAT'S ENOUGH. I LOVE YOU, SON.
I LOVE YOU, TOO, DAD.

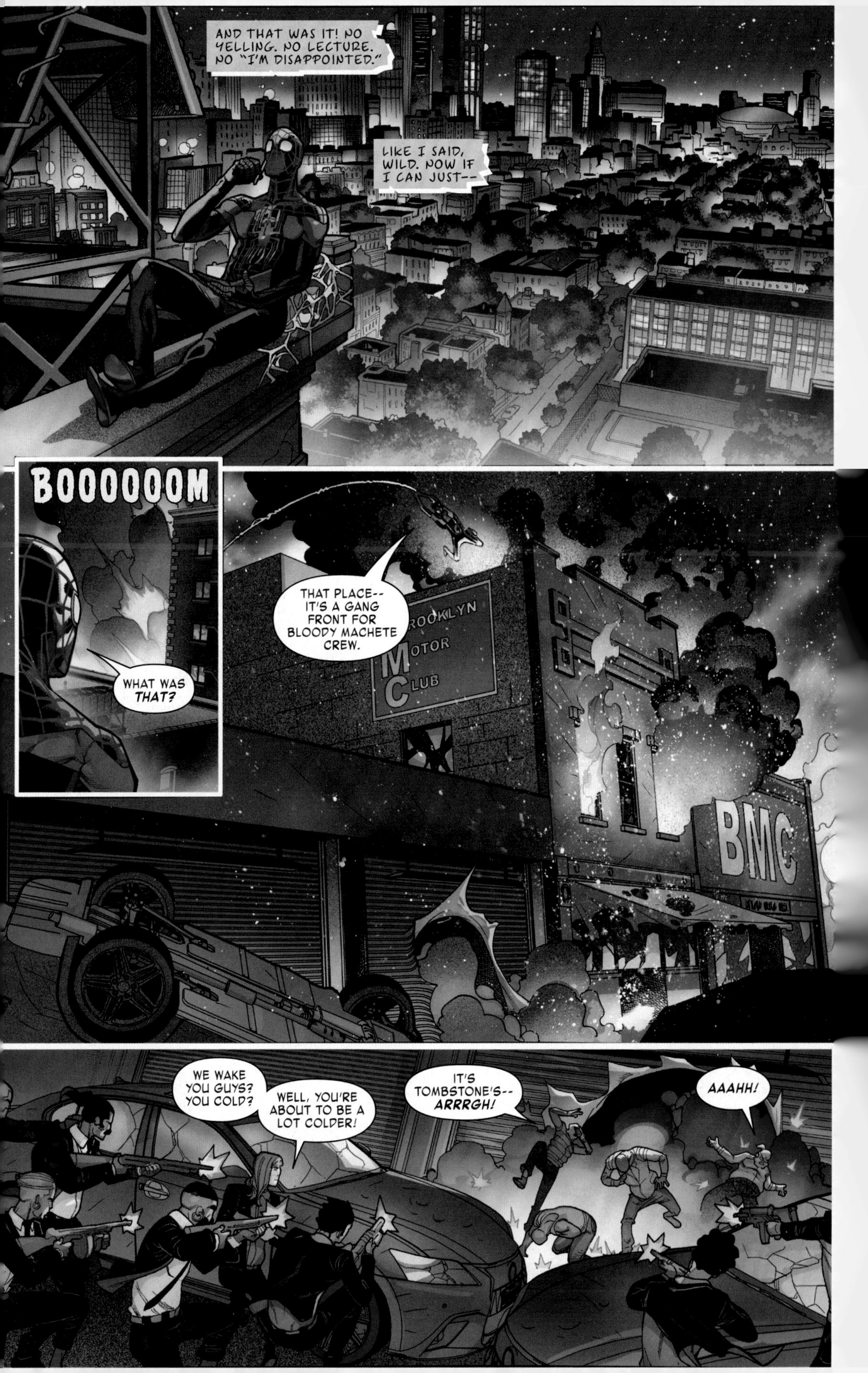
AND THAT WAS IT! NO YELLING. NO LECTURE. NO "I'M DISAPPOINTED."
LIKE I SAID, WILD. NOW IF I CAN JUST--
BOOOOOOM
WHAT WAS THAT?
THAT PLACE-- IT'S A GANG FRONT FOR BLOODY MACHETE CREW.
ROOKLYN MOTOR CLUB
BMC
WE WAKE YOU GUYS? YOU COLD?
WELL, YOU'RE ABOUT TO BE A LOT COLDER!
IT'S TOMBSTONE'S-- ARRRGH!
AAAHH!

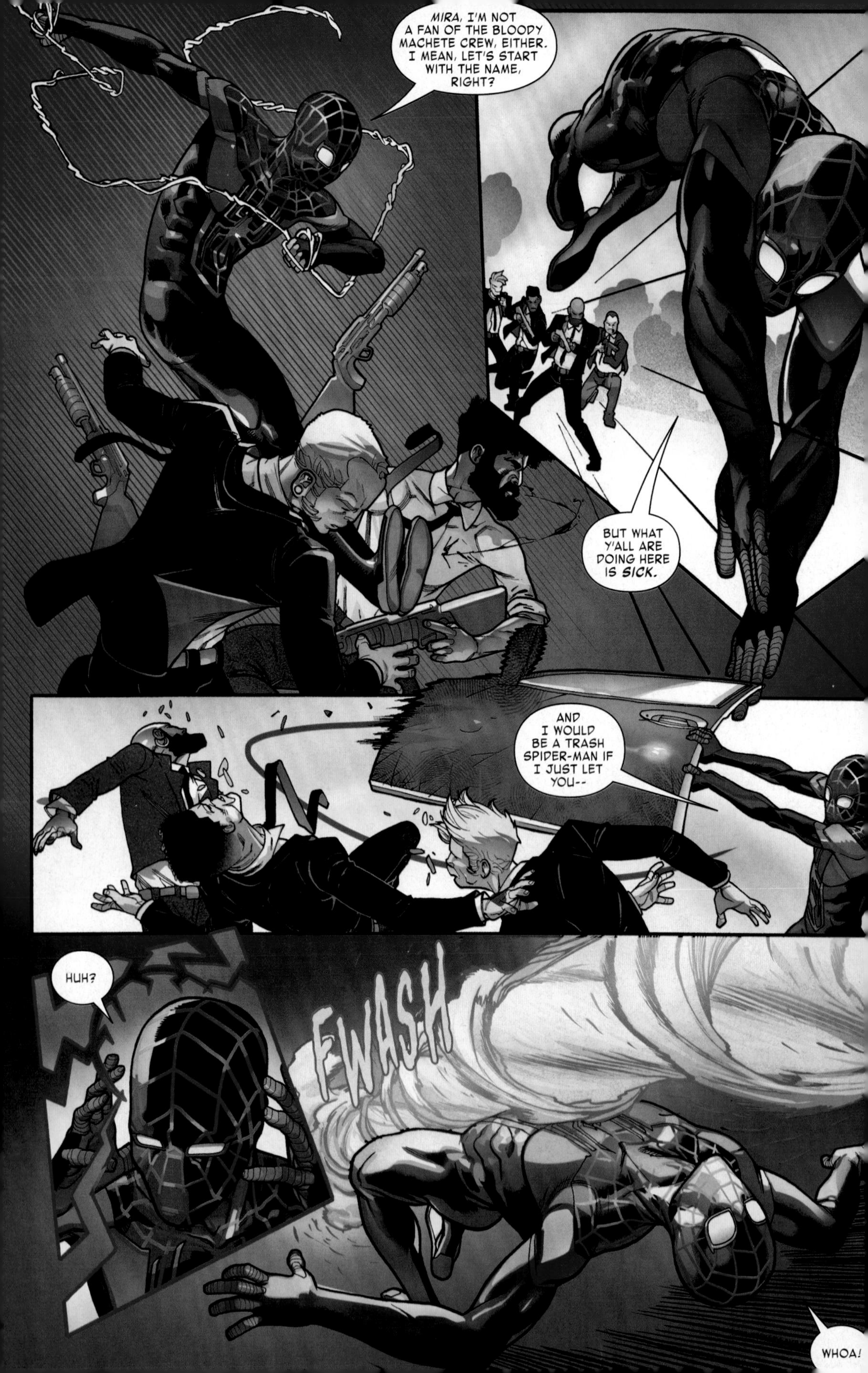
MIRA, I'M NOT A FAN OF THE BLOODY MACHETE CREW, EITHER. I MEAN, LET'S START WITH THE NAME, RIGHT?
BUT WHAT Y'ALL ARE DOING HERE IS SICK.
AND I WOULD BE A TRASH SPIDER-MAN IF I JUST LET YOU--
HUH?
FWASH
WHOA!

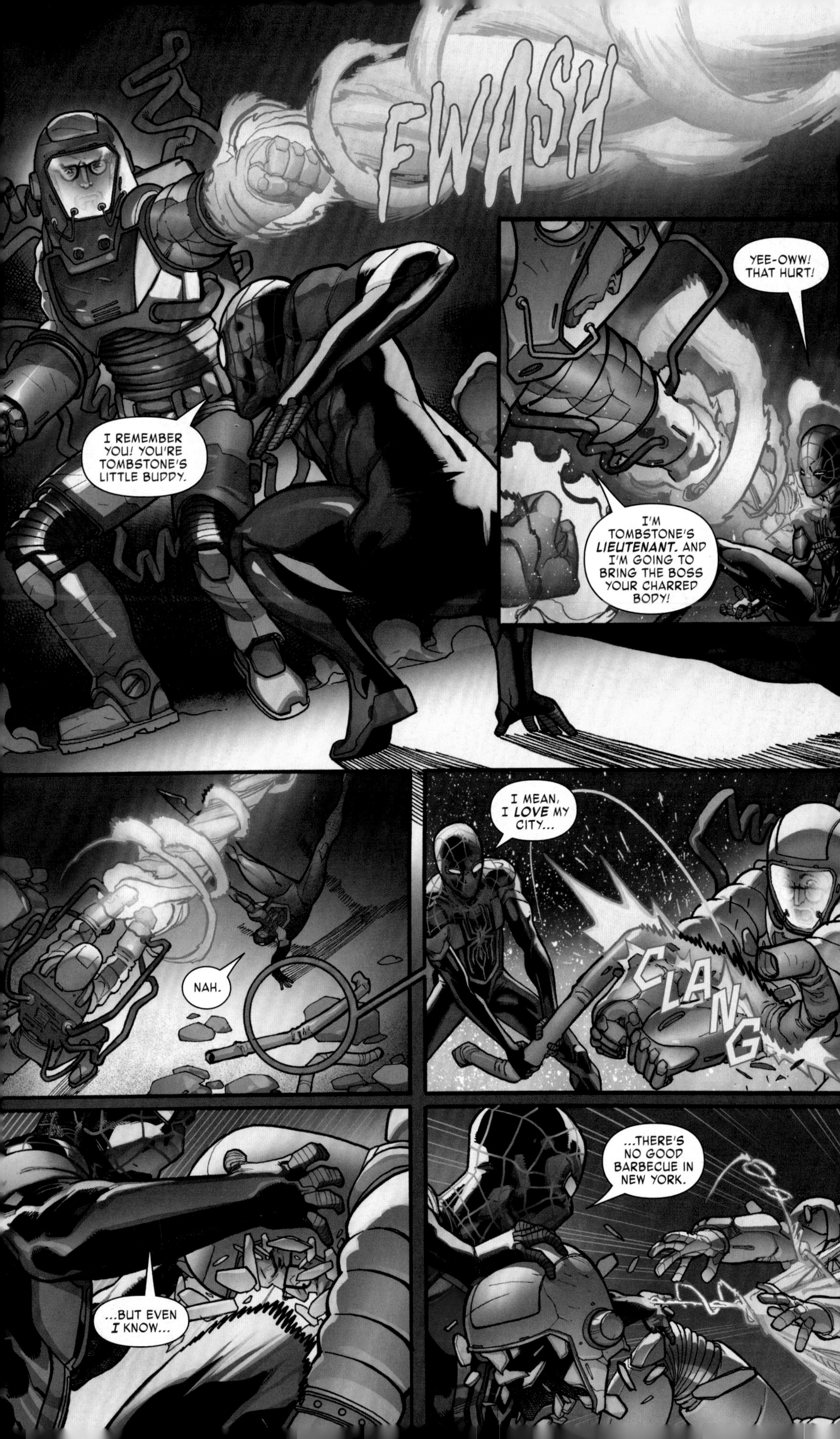
FWASH
I REMEMBER YOU! YOU'RE TOMBSTONE'S LITTLE BUDDY.
YEE-OWW! THAT HURT!
I'M TOMBSTONE'S LIEUTENANT. AND I'M GOING TO BRING THE BOSS YOUR CHARRED BODY!
NAH.
I MEAN, I LOVE MY CITY...
CLANG
...BUT EVEN I KNOW...
...THERE'S NO GOOD BARBECUE IN NEW YORK.

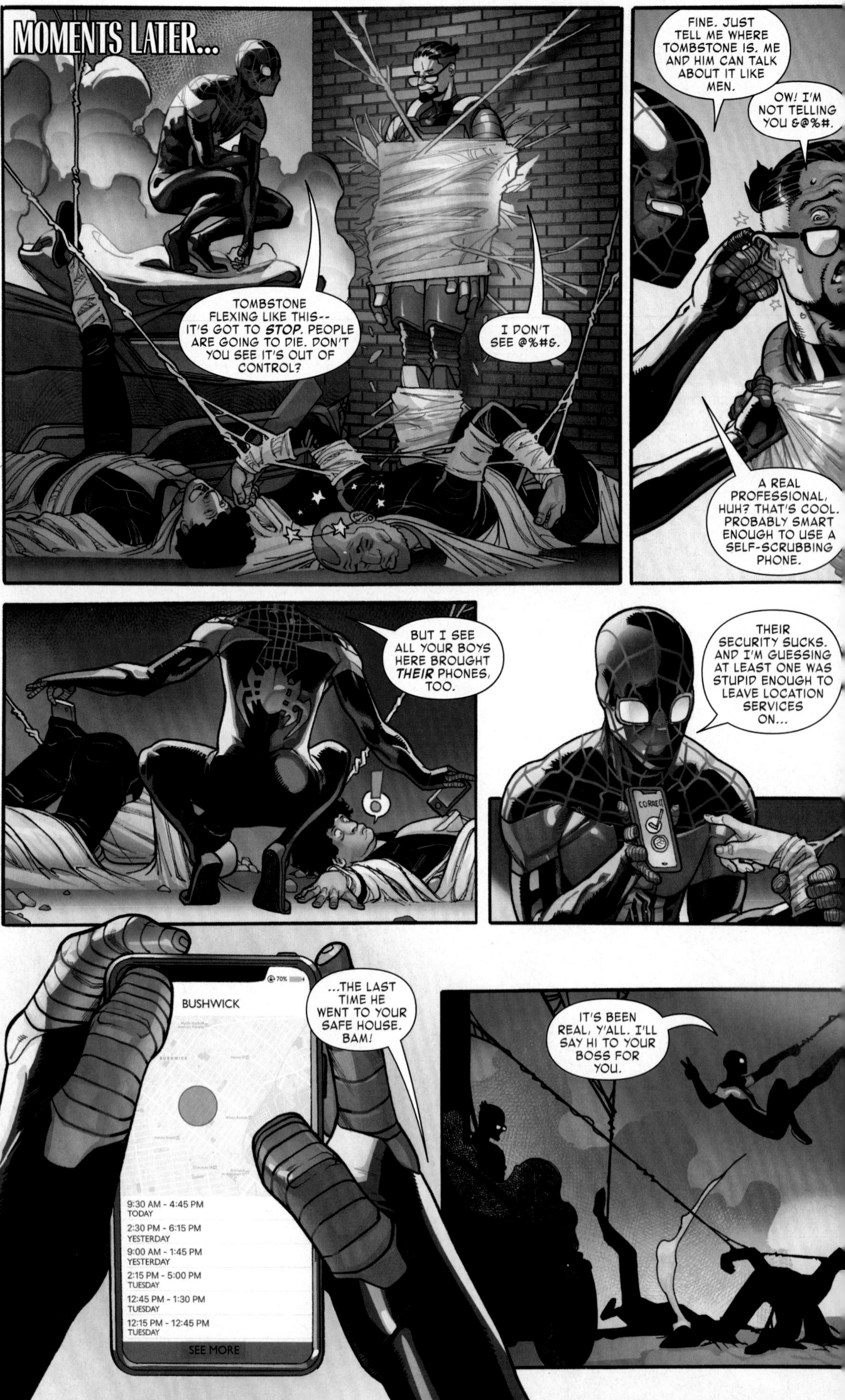
MOMENTS LATER...
TOMBSTONE FLEXING LIKE THIS-- IT'S GOT TO *STOP.* PEOPLE ARE GOING TO DIE. DON'T YOU SEE IT'S OUT OF CONTROL?
I DON'T SEE @%#&.
FINE. JUST TELL ME WHERE TOMBSTONE IS. ME AND HIM CAN TALK ABOUT IT LIKE MEN.
OW! I'M NOT TELLING YOU &@%#.
A REAL PROFESSIONAL, HUH? THAT'S COOL. PROBABLY SMART ENOUGH TO USE A SELF-SCRUBBING PHONE.
BUT I SEE ALL YOUR BOYS HERE BROUGHT *THEIR* PHONES, TOO.
THEIR SECURITY SUCKS. AND I'M GUESSING AT LEAST ONE WAS STUPID ENOUGH TO LEAVE LOCATION SERVICES ON...
BUSHWICK
9:30 AM - 4:45 PM
TODAY
2:30 PM - 6:15 PM
YESTERDAY
9:00 AM - 1:45 PM
YESTERDAY
2:15 PM - 5:00 PM
TUESDAY
12:45 PM - 1:30 PM
TUESDAY
12:15 PM - 12:45 PM
TUESDAY
SEE MORE
...THE LAST TIME HE WENT TO YOUR SAFE HOUSE. BAM!
IT'S BEEN REAL, Y'ALL. I'LL SAY HI TO YOUR BOSS FOR YOU.

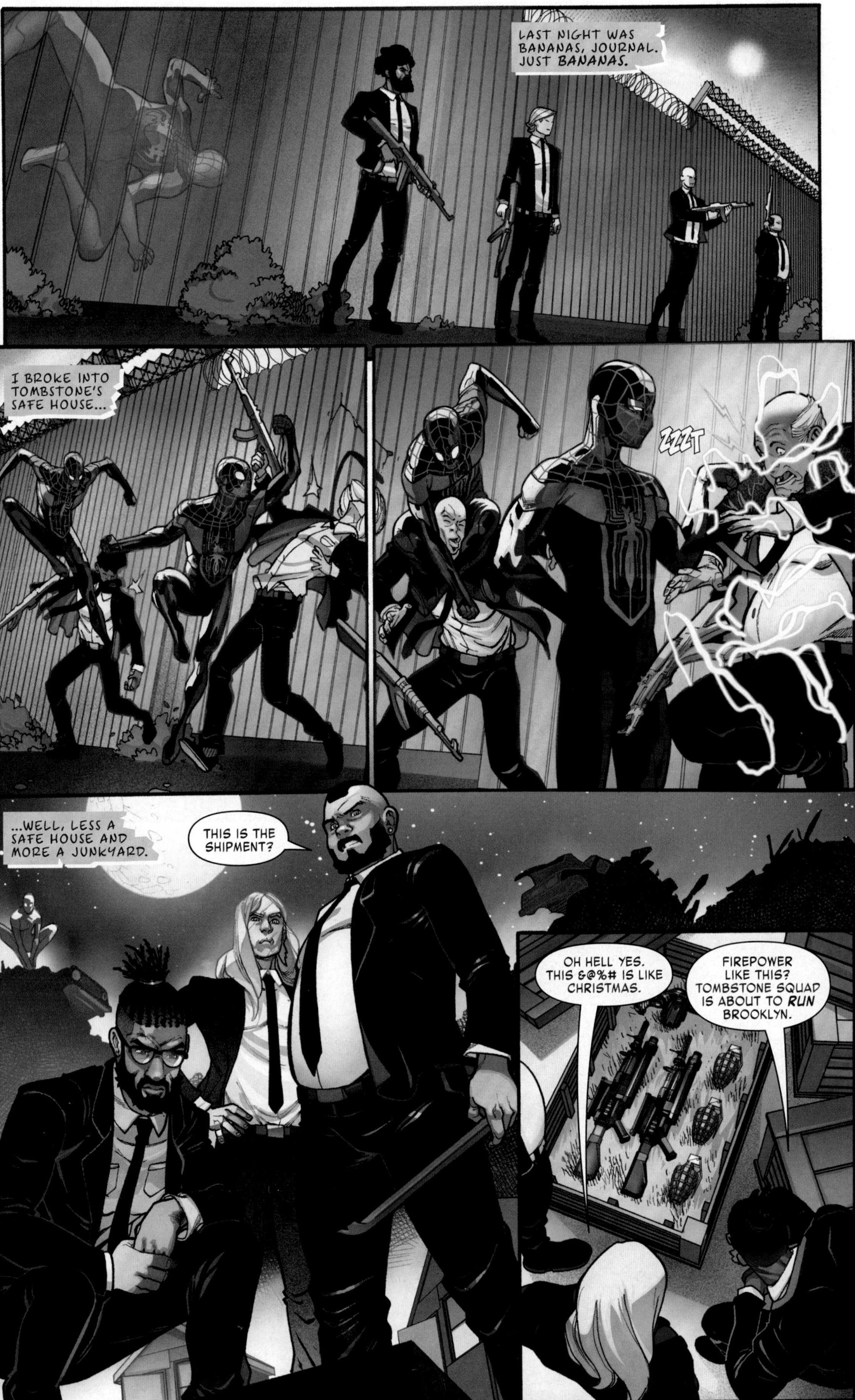
LAST NIGHT WAS BANANAS, JOURNAL. JUST BANANAS.
I BROKE INTO TOMBSTONE'S SAFE HOUSE...
ZZZT
...WELL, LESS A SAFE HOUSE AND MORE A JUNKYARD.
THIS IS THE SHIPMENT?
OH HELL YES. THIS &@%# IS LIKE CHRISTMAS.
FIREPOWER LIKE THIS? TOMBSTONE SQUAD IS ABOUT TO RUN BROOKLYN.

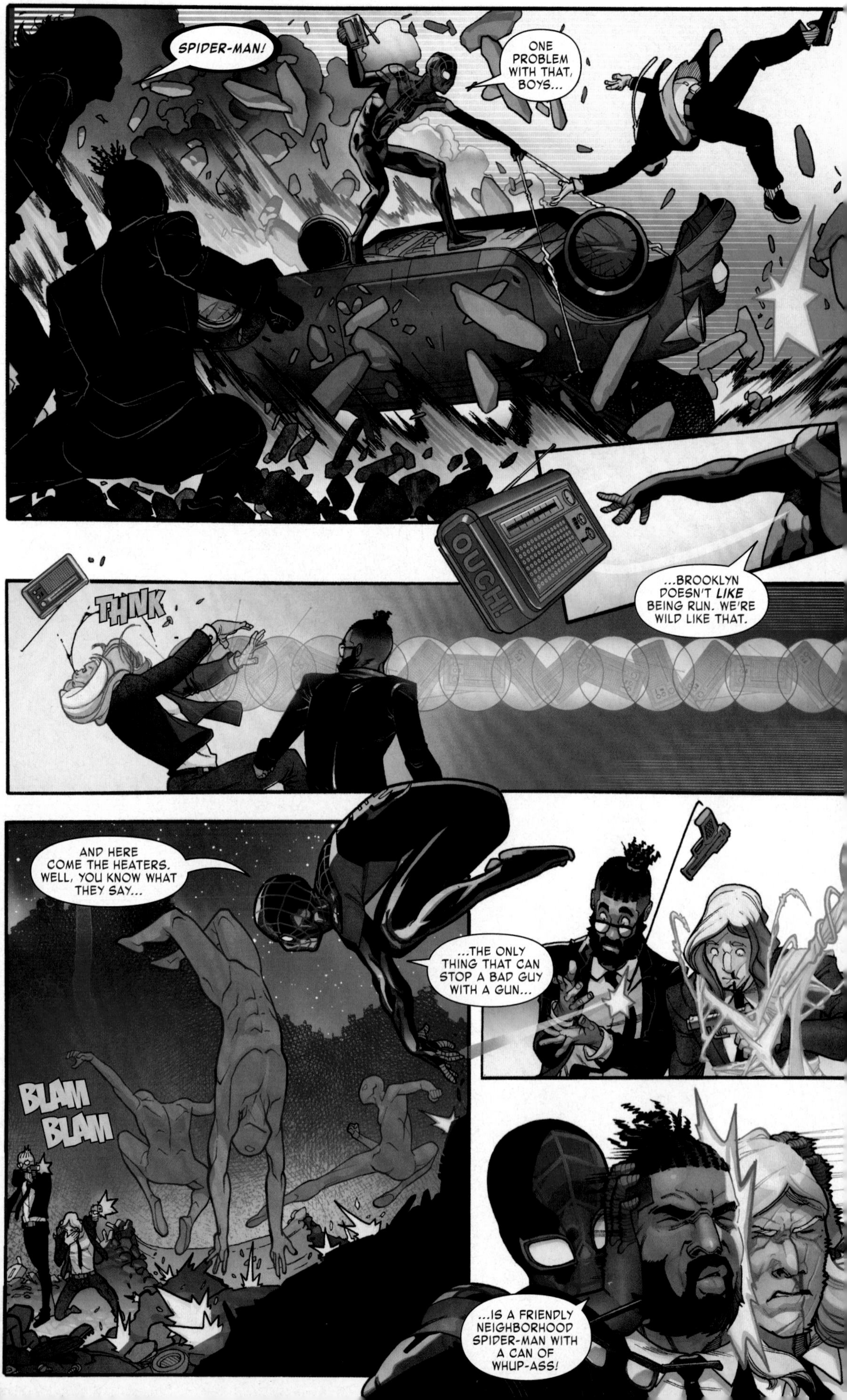

SPIDER-MAN!
ONE PROBLEM WITH THAT, BOYS...
OUCH!
...BROOKLYN DOESN'T LIKE BEING RUN. WE'RE WILD LIKE THAT.
THNK
AND HERE COME THE HEATERS. WELL, YOU KNOW WHAT THEY SAY...
...THE ONLY THING THAT CAN STOP A BAD GUY WITH A GUN...
BLAM BLAM
...IS A FRIENDLY NEIGHBORHOOD SPIDER-MAN WITH A CAN OF WHUP-ASS!

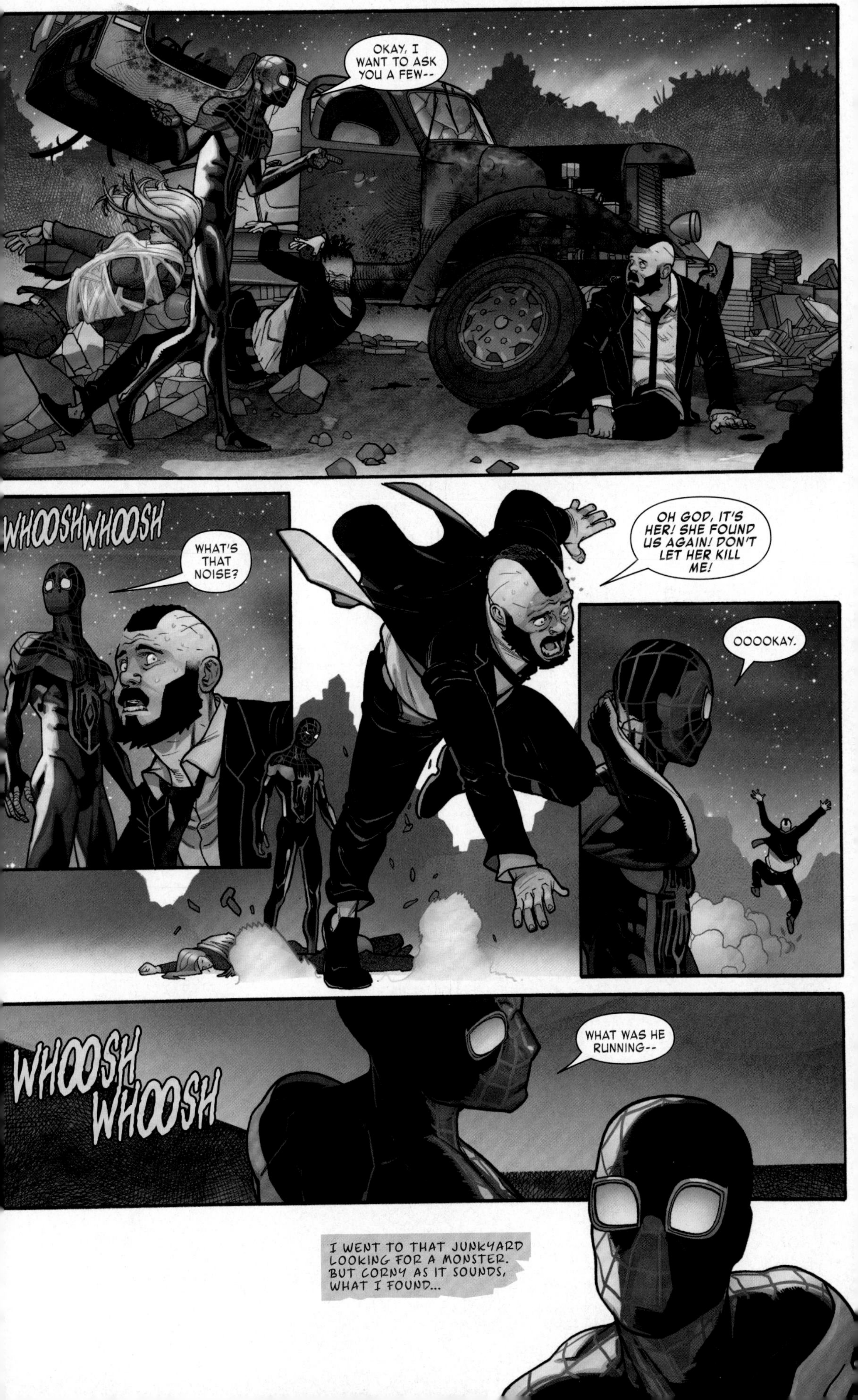
OKAY, I WANT TO ASK YOU A FEW--
WHOOSHWHOOSH
WHAT'S THAT NOISE?
OH GOD, IT'S HER! SHE FOUND US AGAIN! DON'T LET HER KILL ME!
OOOOKAY.
WHOOSH WHOOSH
WHAT WAS HE RUNNING--
I WENT TO THAT JUNKYARD LOOKING FOR A MONSTER. BUT CORNY AS IT SOUNDS, WHAT I FOUND...

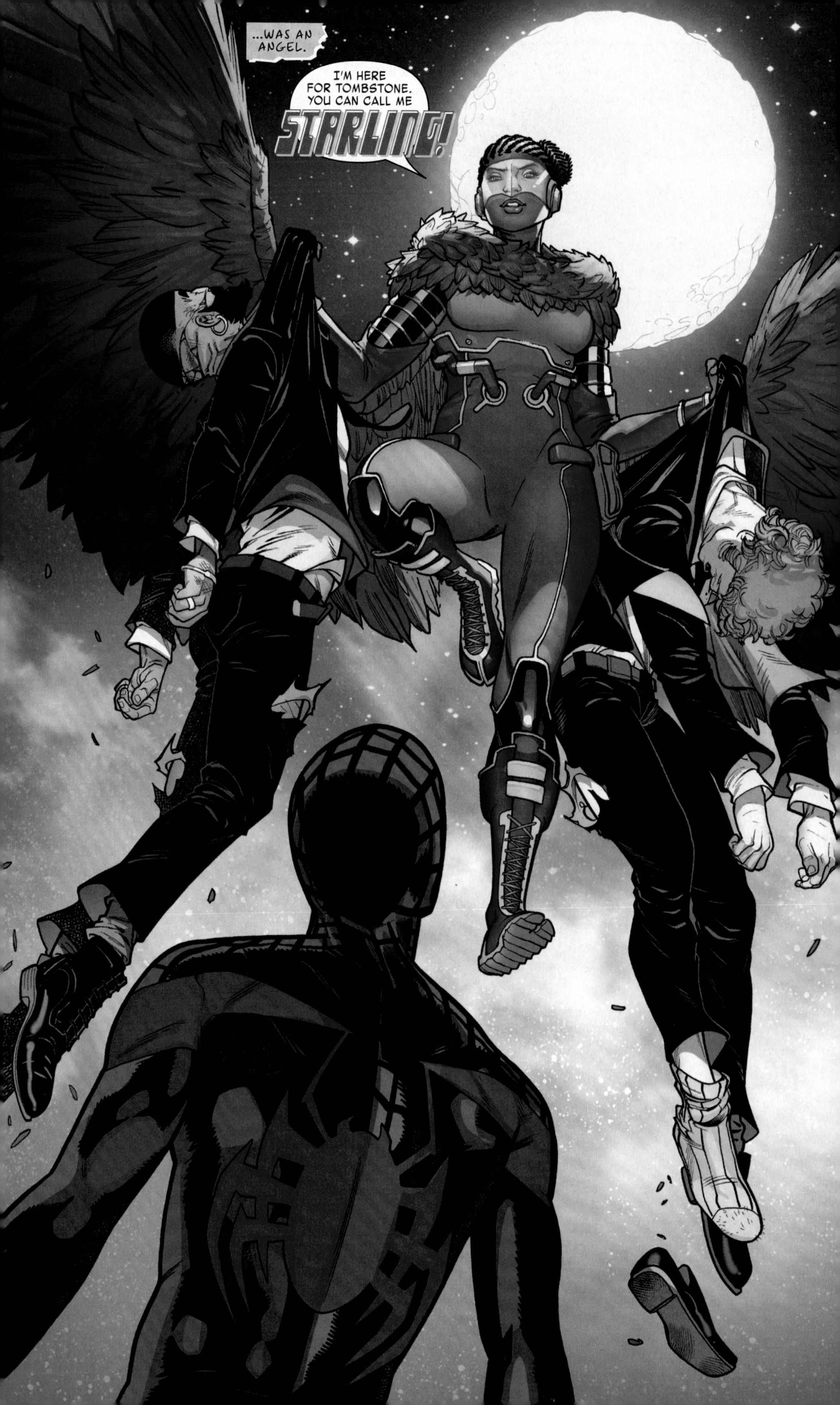
...WAS AN ANGEL.
I'M HERE FOR TOMBSTONE. YOU CAN CALL ME STARLING!

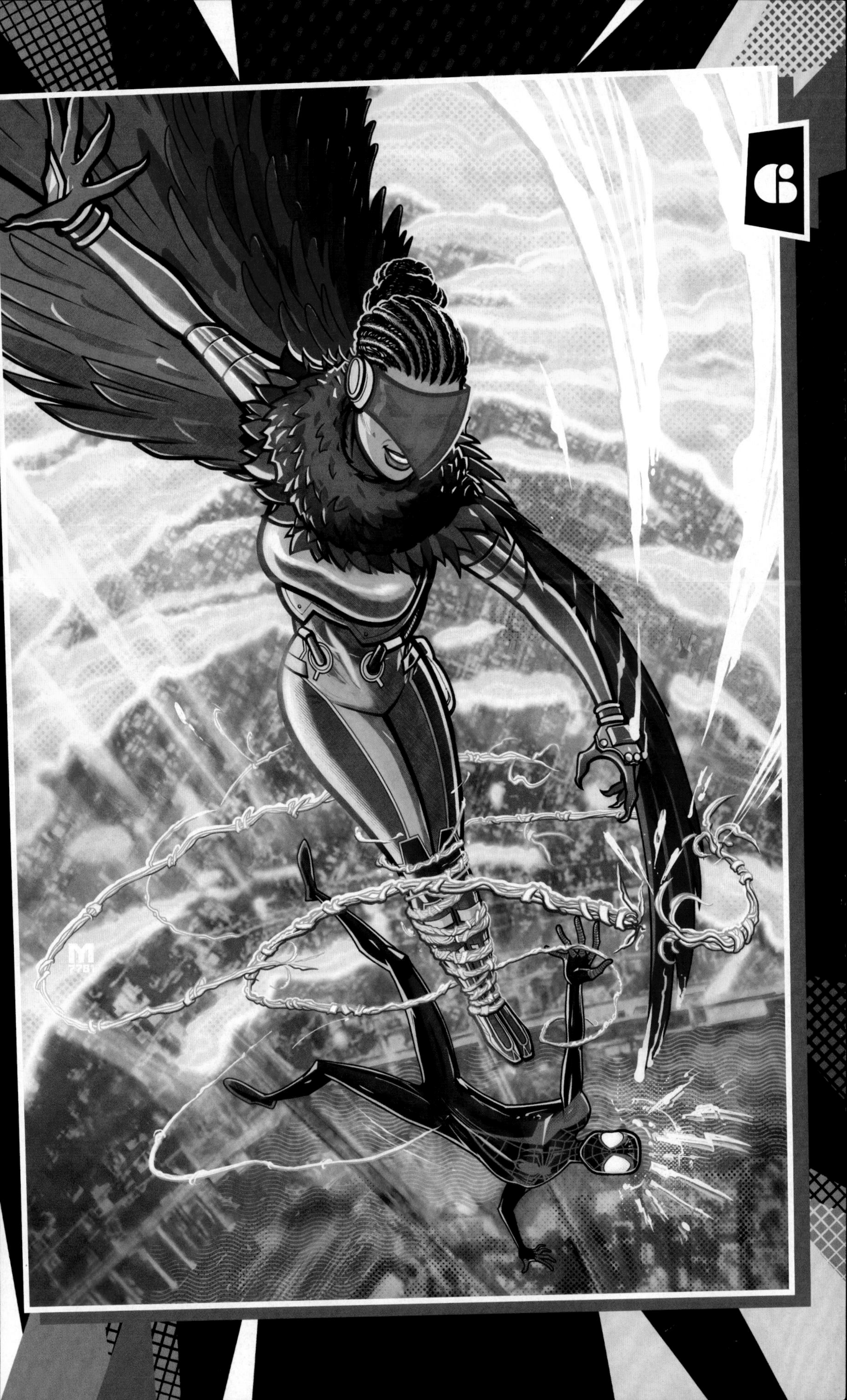
6

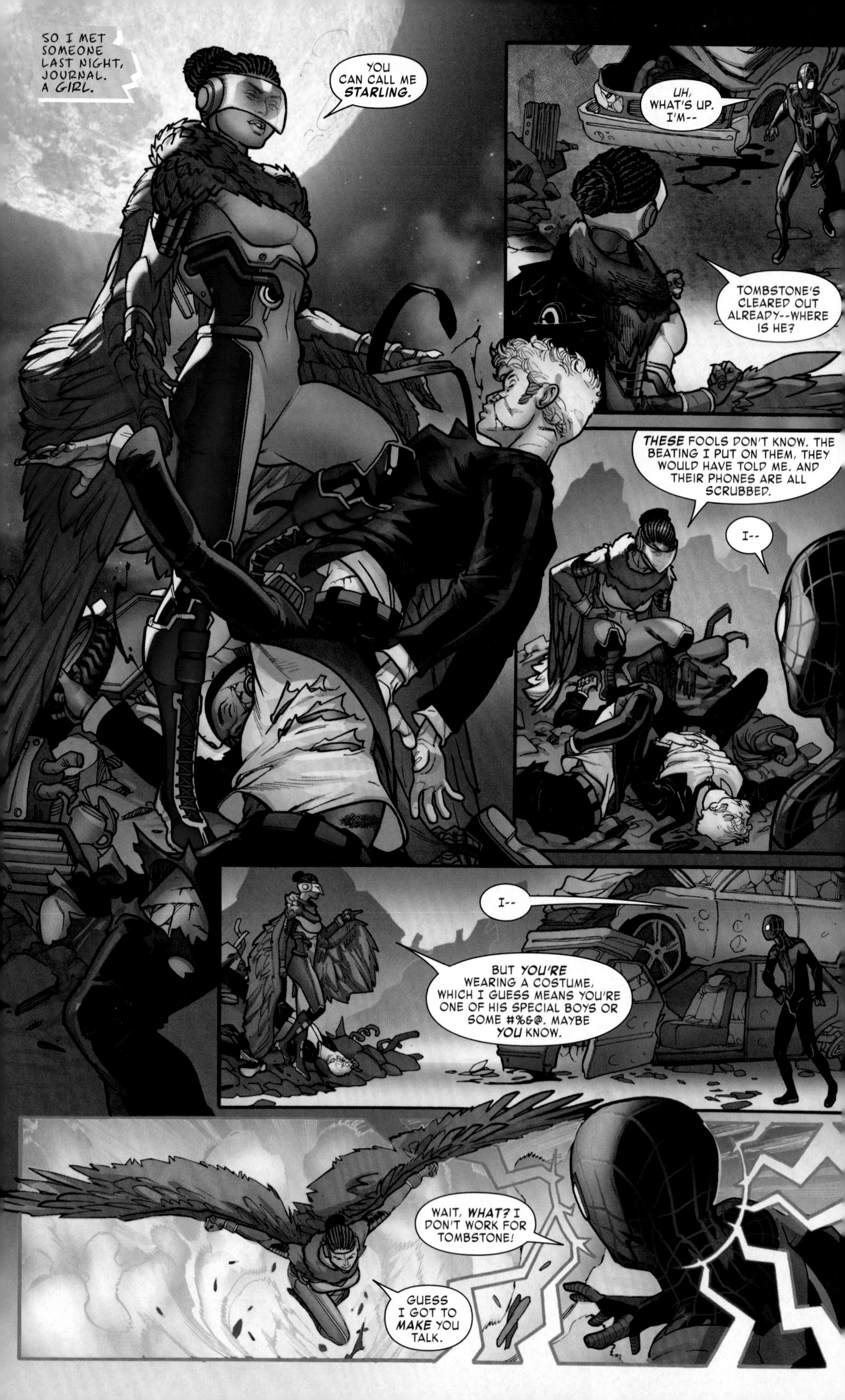

SO I MET SOMEONE LAST NIGHT, JOURNAL. A GIRL.
YOU CAN CALL ME STARLING.
UH, WHAT'S UP. I'M--
TOMBSTONE'S CLEARED OUT ALREADY--WHERE IS HE?
THESE FOOLS DON'T KNOW. THE BEATING I PUT ON THEM, THEY WOULD HAVE TOLD ME. AND THEIR PHONES ARE ALL SCRUBBED.
I--
I--
BUT YOU'RE WEARING A COSTUME, WHICH I GUESS MEANS YOU'RE ONE OF HIS SPECIAL BOYS OR SOME #%&@. MAYBE YOU KNOW.
WAIT, WHAT? I DON'T WORK FOR TOMBSTONE!
GUESS I GOT TO MAKE YOU TALK.

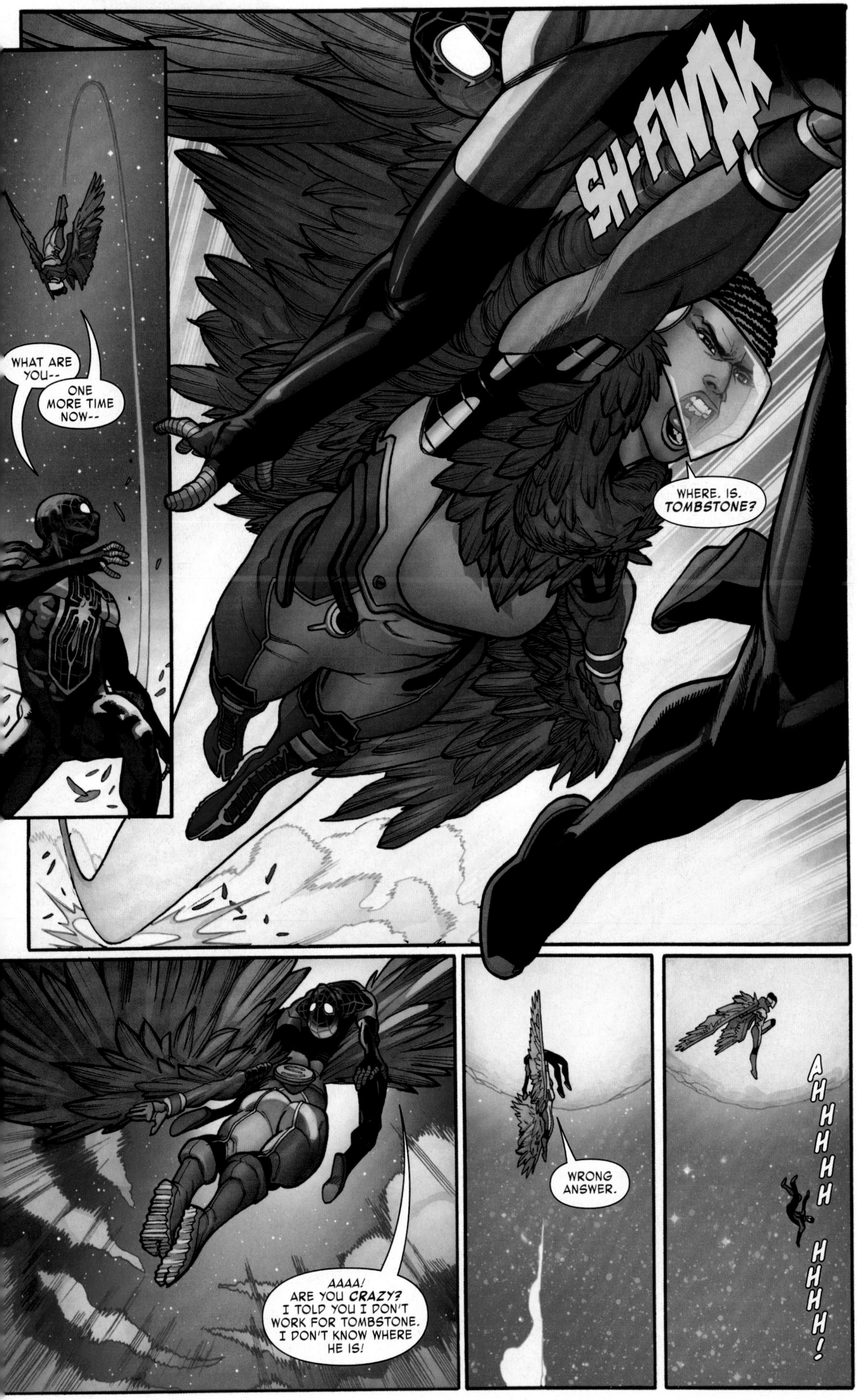
WHAT ARE YOU--
ONE MORE TIME NOW--
SH-FWAK
WHERE. IS. TOMBSTONE?
AAAA! ARE YOU CRAZY? I TOLD YOU I DON'T WORK FOR TOMBSTONE. I DON'T KNOW WHERE HE IS!
WRONG ANSWER.
AHHHHHH HHHHH!

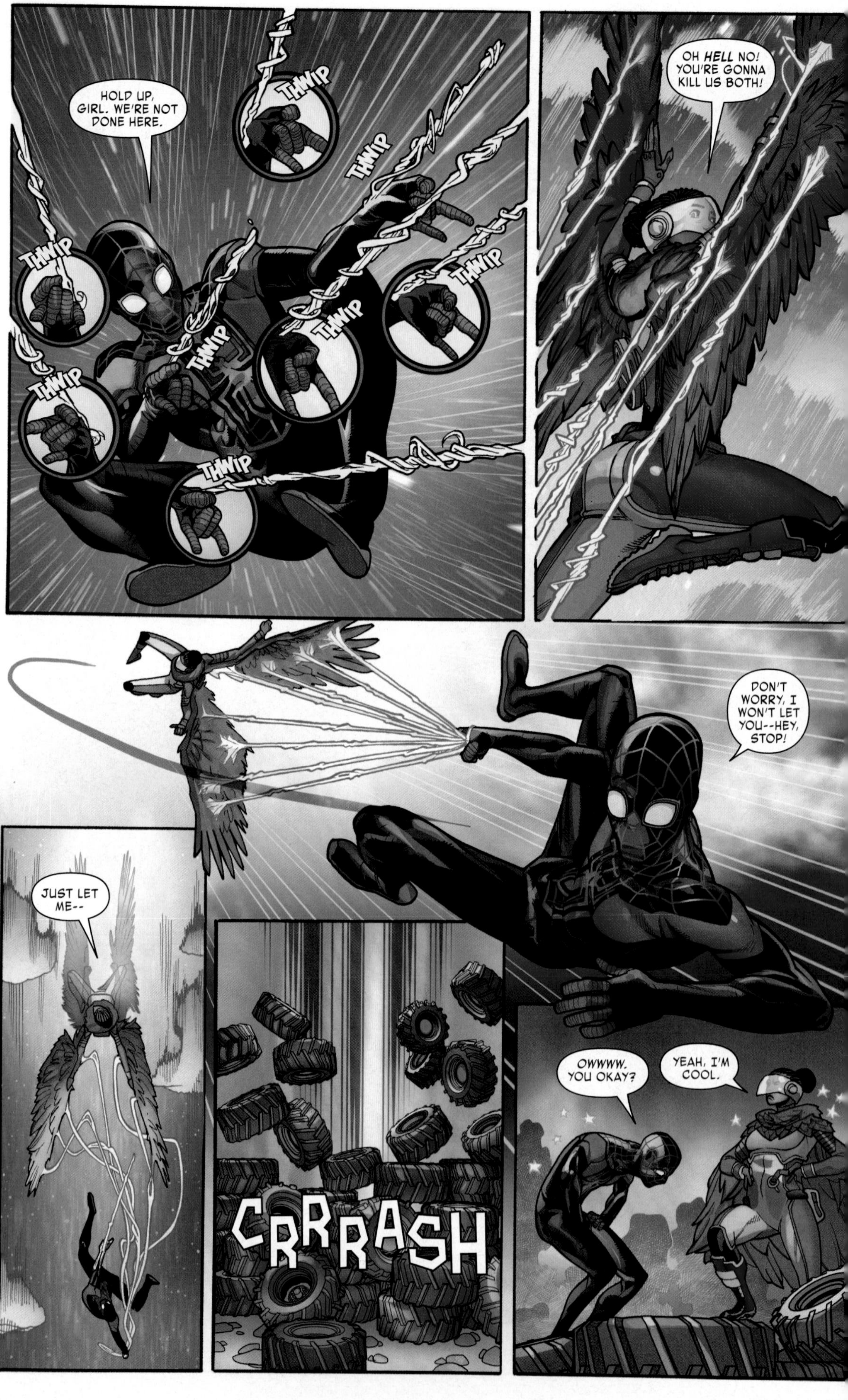
HOLD UP, GIRL. WE'RE NOT DONE HERE.
THWIP
THWIP
THWIP
THWIP
THWIP
THWIP
THWIP
THWIP
OH HELL NO! YOU'RE GONNA KILL US BOTH!
DON'T WORRY, I WON'T LET YOU--HEY, STOP!
JUST LET ME--
CRRRASH
OWWWW. YOU OKAY?
YEAH, I'M COOL.

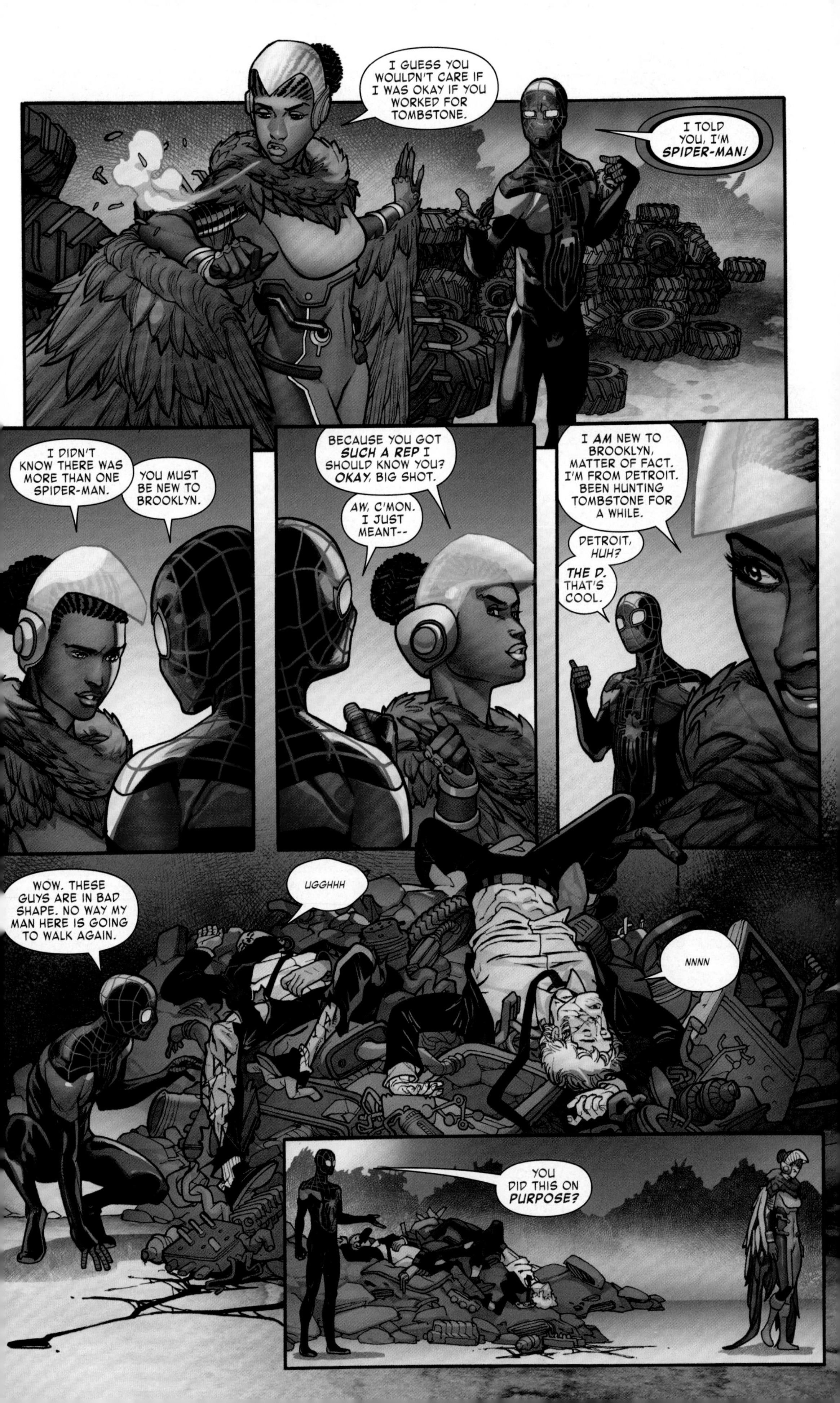

I GUESS YOU WOULDN'T CARE IF I WAS OKAY IF YOU WORKED FOR TOMBSTONE.
I TOLD YOU, I'M SPIDER-MAN!
I DIDN'T KNOW THERE WAS MORE THAN ONE SPIDER-MAN.
YOU MUST BE NEW TO BROOKLYN.
BECAUSE YOU GOT SUCH A REP I SHOULD KNOW YOU? OKAY, BIG SHOT.
AW, C'MON. I JUST MEANT--
I AM NEW TO BROOKLYN, MATTER OF FACT. I'M FROM DETROIT. BEEN HUNTING TOMBSTONE FOR A WHILE.
DETROIT, HUH?
THE D. THAT'S COOL.
WOW. THESE GUYS ARE IN BAD SHAPE. NO WAY MY MAN HERE IS GOING TO WALK AGAIN.
UGGHHH
NNNN
YOU DID THIS ON PURPOSE?

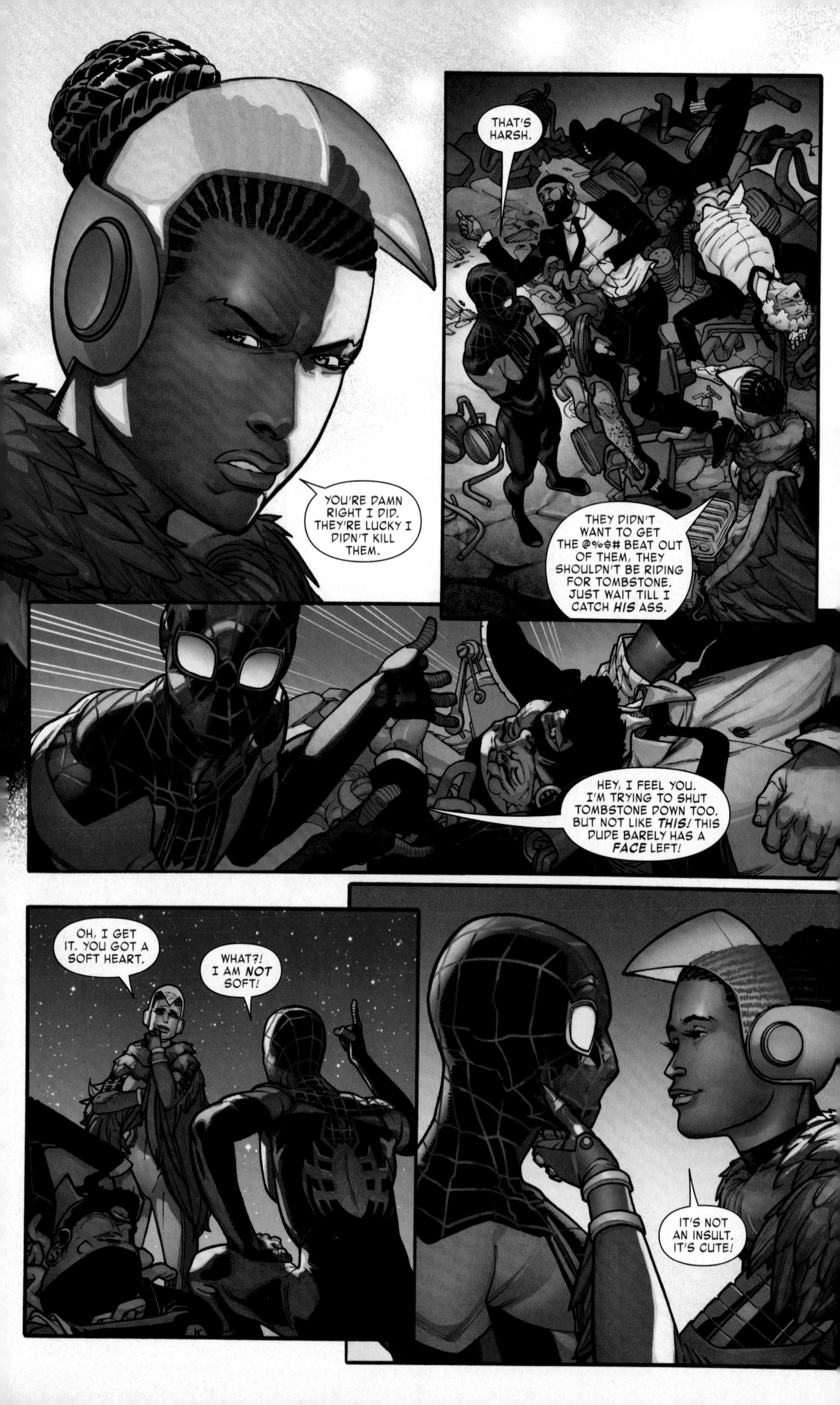
THAT'S HARSH.
YOU'RE DAMN RIGHT I DID. THEY'RE LUCKY I DIDN'T KILL THEM.
THEY DIDN'T WANT TO GET THE @%$# BEAT OUT OF THEM, THEY SHOULDN'T BE RIDING FOR TOMBSTONE. JUST WAIT TILL I CATCH HIS ASS.
HEY, I FEEL YOU. I'M TRYING TO SHUT TOMBSTONE DOWN TOO. BUT NOT LIKE THIS! THIS DUDE BARELY HAS A FACE LEFT!
OH, I GET IT. YOU GOT A SOFT HEART.
WHAT?! I AM NOT SOFT!
IT'S NOT AN INSULT. IT'S CUTE!

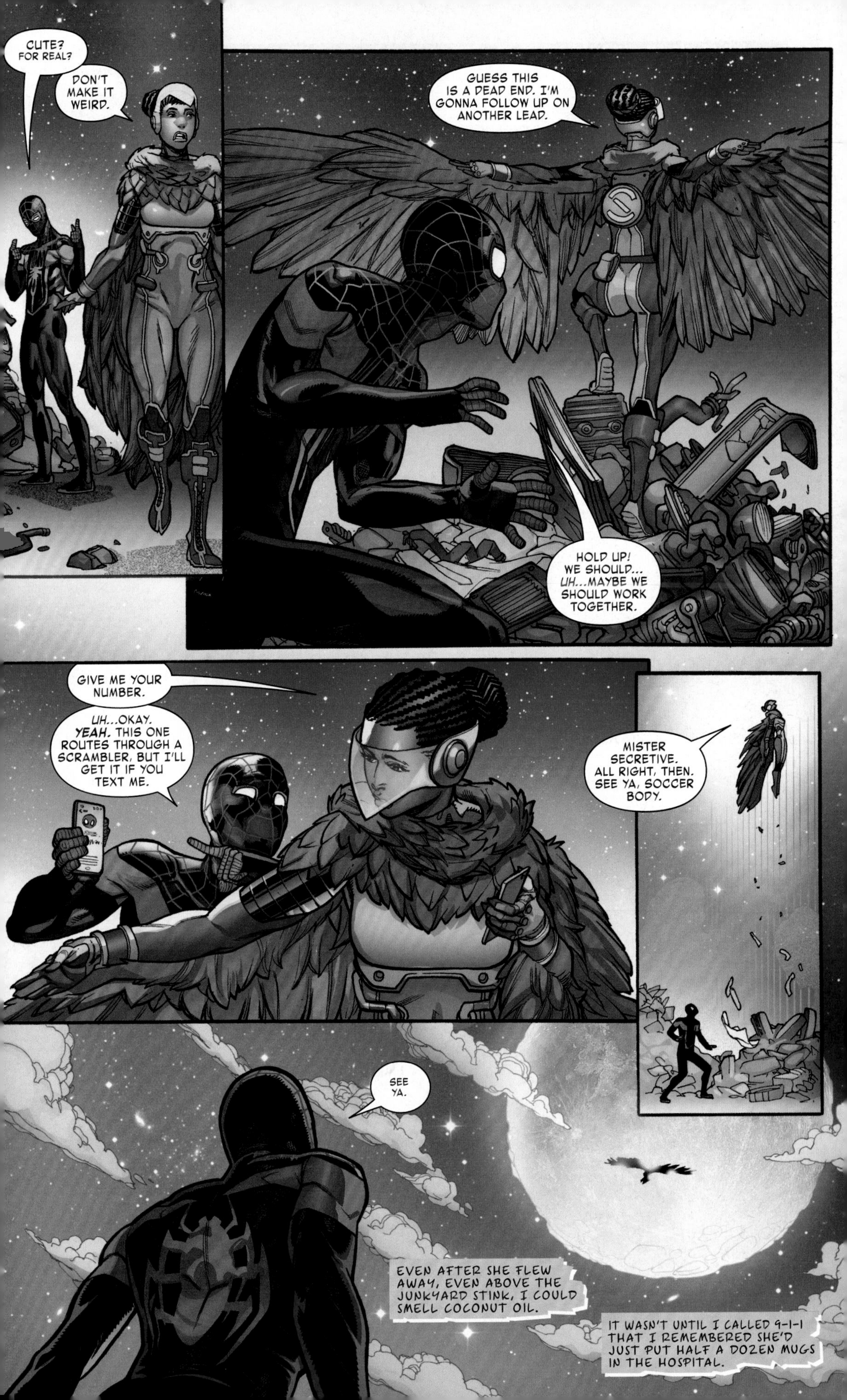
CUTE? FOR REAL?
DON'T MAKE IT WEIRD.
GUESS THIS IS A DEAD END. I'M GONNA FOLLOW UP ON ANOTHER LEAD.
HOLD UP! WE SHOULD... UH...MAYBE WE SHOULD WORK TOGETHER.
GIVE ME YOUR NUMBER.
UH...OKAY. YEAH. THIS ONE ROUTES THROUGH A SCRAMBLER, BUT I'LL GET IT IF YOU TEXT ME.
MISTER SECRETIVE. ALL RIGHT, THEN. SEE YA, SOCCER BODY.
SEE YA.
EVEN AFTER SHE FLEW AWAY, EVEN ABOVE THE JUNKYARD STINK, I COULD SMELL COCONUT OIL.
IT WASN'T UNTIL I CALLED 9-1-1 THAT I REMEMBERED SHE'D JUST PUT HALF A DOZEN MUGS IN THE HOSPITAL.

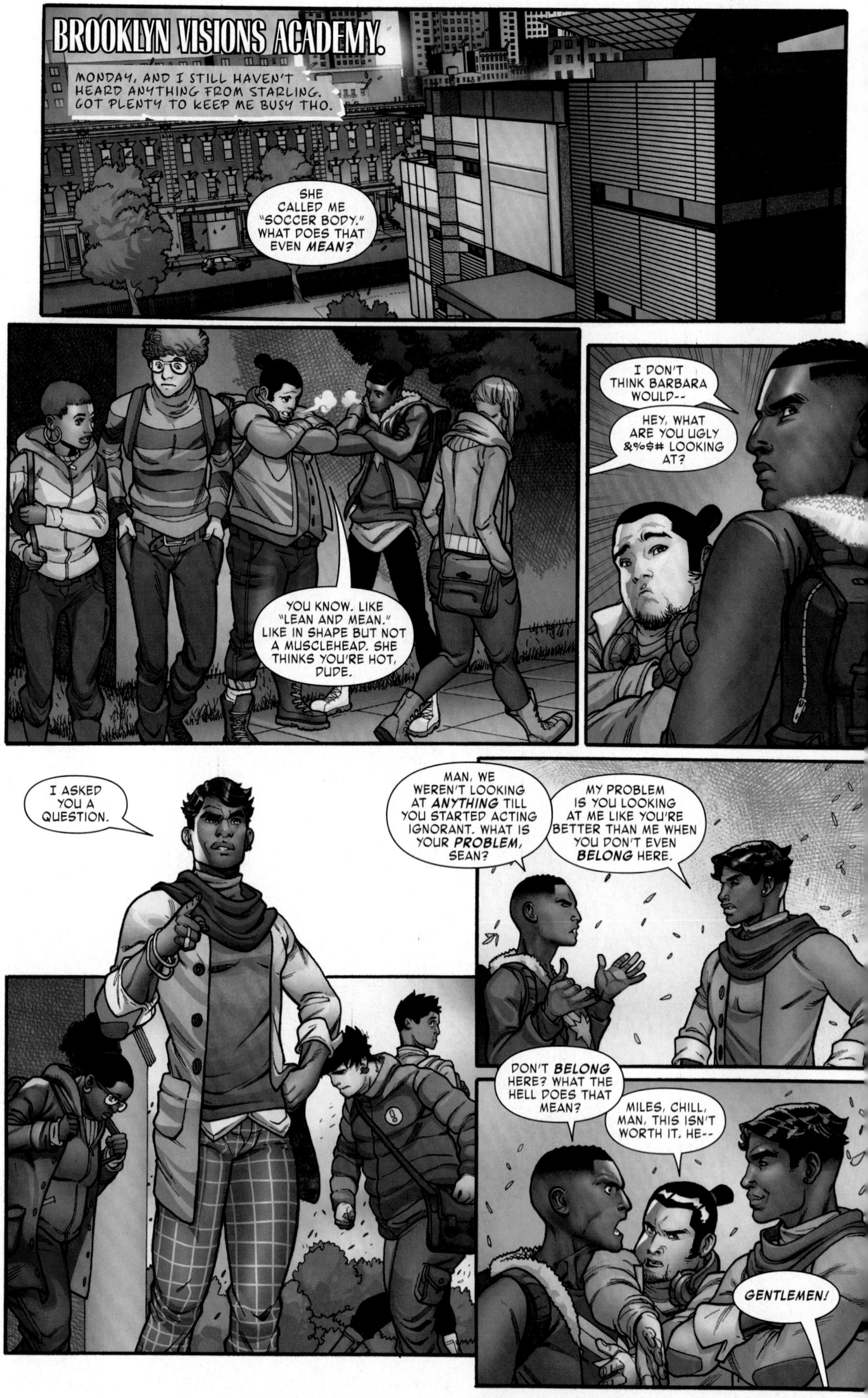
BROOKLYN VISIONS ACADEMY.
MONDAY, AND I STILL HAVEN'T HEARD ANYTHING FROM STARLING. GOT PLENTY TO KEEP ME BUSY THO.
SHE CALLED ME "SOCCER BODY." WHAT DOES THAT EVEN MEAN?
YOU KNOW. LIKE "LEAN AND MEAN." LIKE IN SHAPE BUT NOT A MUSCLEHEAD. SHE THINKS YOU'RE HOT, DUDE.
I DON'T THINK BARBARA WOULD--
HEY, WHAT ARE YOU UGLY &%$# LOOKING AT?
I ASKED YOU A QUESTION.
MAN, WE WEREN'T LOOKING AT ANYTHING TILL YOU STARTED ACTING IGNORANT. WHAT IS YOUR PROBLEM, SEAN?
MY PROBLEM IS YOU LOOKING AT ME LIKE YOU'RE BETTER THAN ME WHEN YOU DON'T EVEN BELONG HERE.
DON'T BELONG HERE? WHAT THE HELL DOES THAT MEAN?
MILES, CHILL, MAN, THIS ISN'T WORTH IT. HE--
GENTLEMEN!

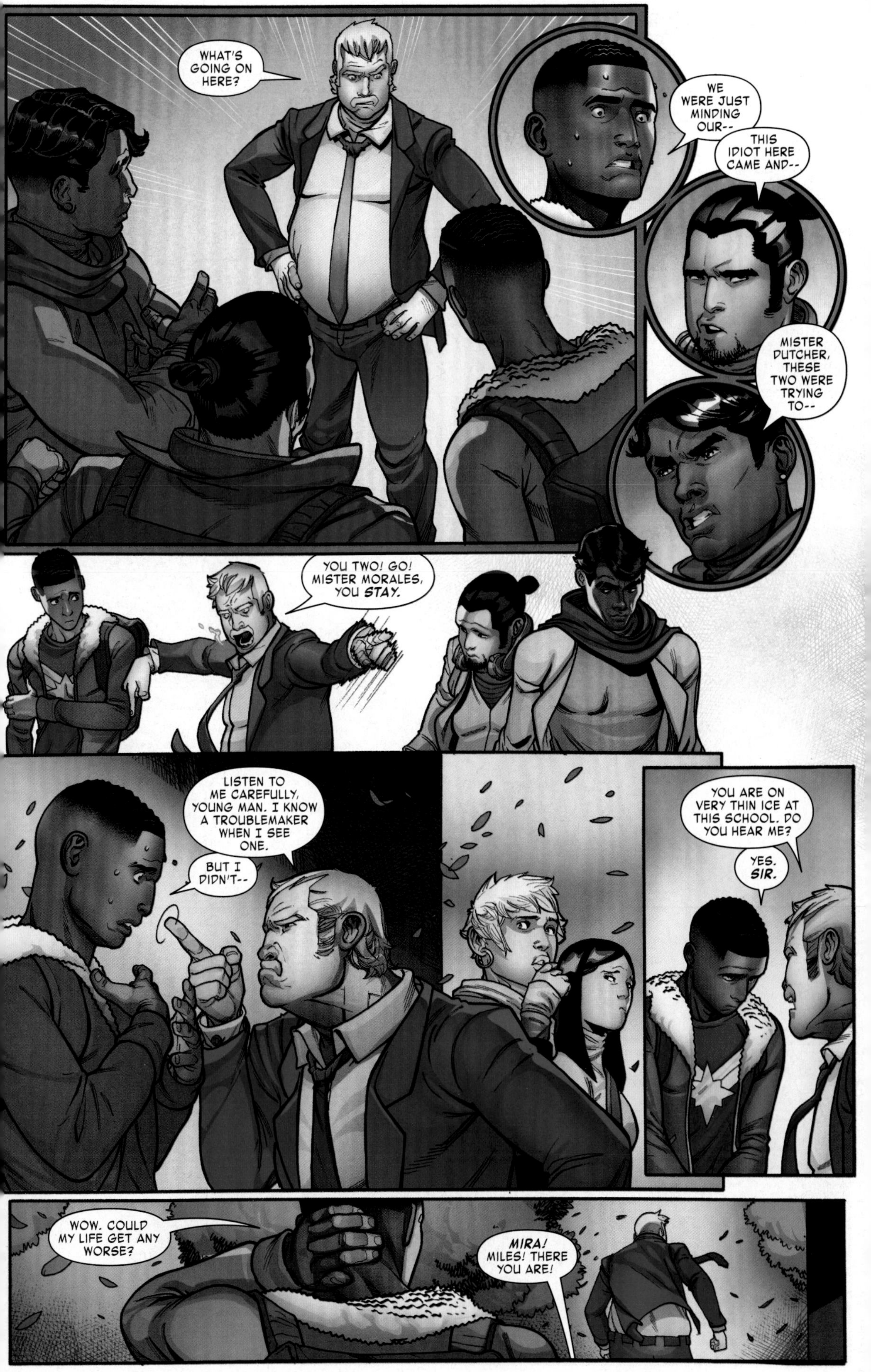
WHAT'S GOING ON HERE?
WE WERE JUST MINDING OUR--
THIS IDIOT HERE CAME AND--
MISTER DUTCHER, THESE TWO WERE TRYING TO--
YOU TWO! GO! MISTER MORALES, YOU STAY.
LISTEN TO ME CAREFULLY, YOUNG MAN. I KNOW A TROUBLEMAKER WHEN I SEE ONE.
BUT I DIDN'T--
YOU ARE ON VERY THIN ICE AT THIS SCHOOL. DO YOU HEAR ME?
YES. SIR.
WOW. COULD MY LIFE GET ANY WORSE?
MIRA! MILES! THERE YOU ARE!

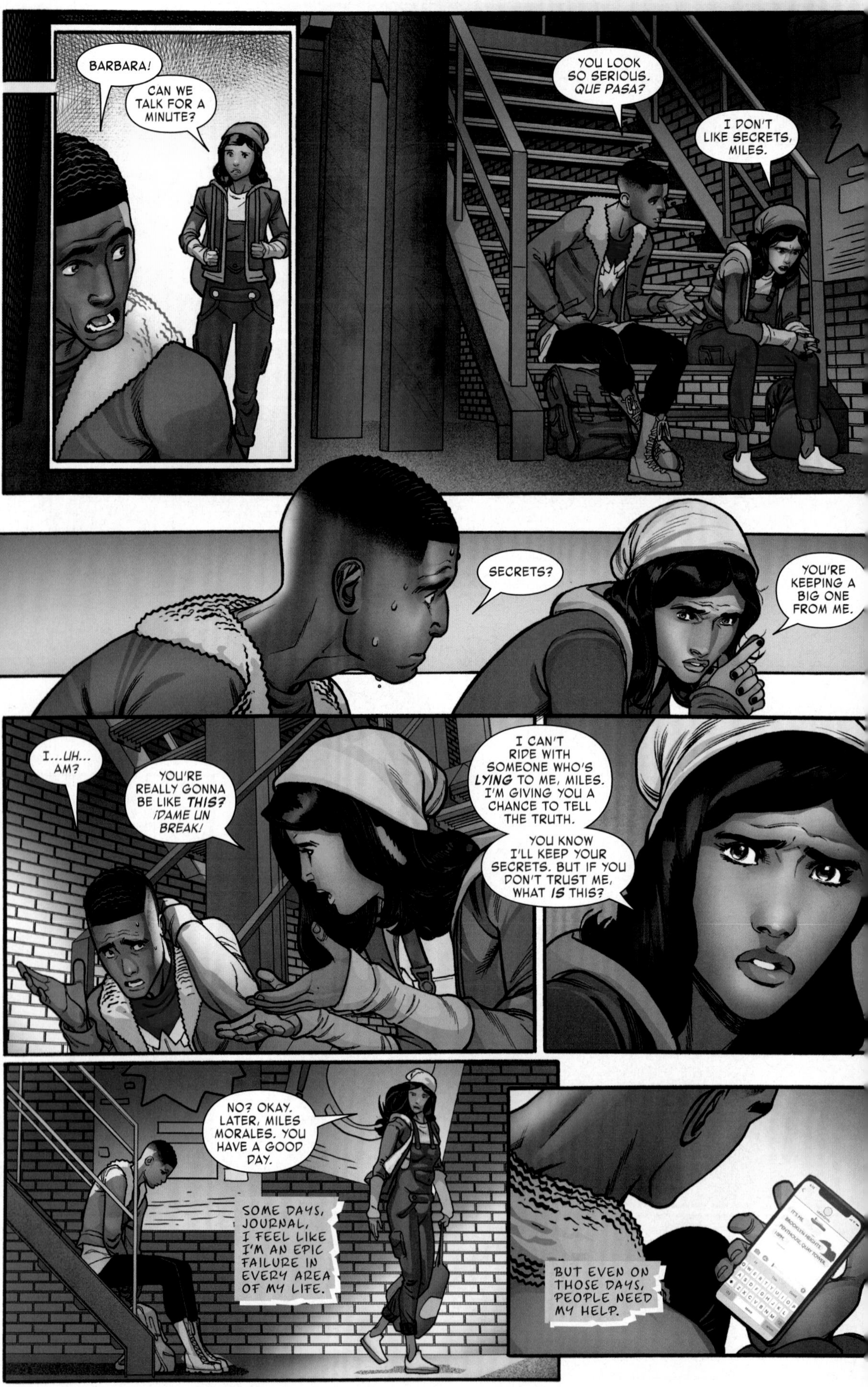
BARBARA!
CAN WE TALK FOR A MINUTE?
YOU LOOK SO SERIOUS. *QUE PASA?*
I DON'T LIKE SECRETS, MILES.
SECRETS?
YOU'RE KEEPING A BIG ONE FROM ME.
I...UH... AM?
YOU'RE REALLY GONNA BE LIKE *THIS?* *¡DAME UN BREAK!*
I CAN'T RIDE WITH SOMEONE WHO'S *LYING* TO ME, MILES. I'M GIVING YOU A CHANCE TO TELL THE TRUTH.
YOU KNOW I'LL KEEP YOUR SECRETS. BUT IF YOU DON'T TRUST ME, WHAT *IS* THIS?
NO? OKAY. LATER, MILES MORALES. YOU HAVE A GOOD DAY.
SOME DAYS, JOURNAL, I FEEL LIKE I'M AN EPIC FAILURE IN EVERY AREA OF MY LIFE.
BUT EVEN ON THOSE DAYS, PEOPLE NEED MY HELP.

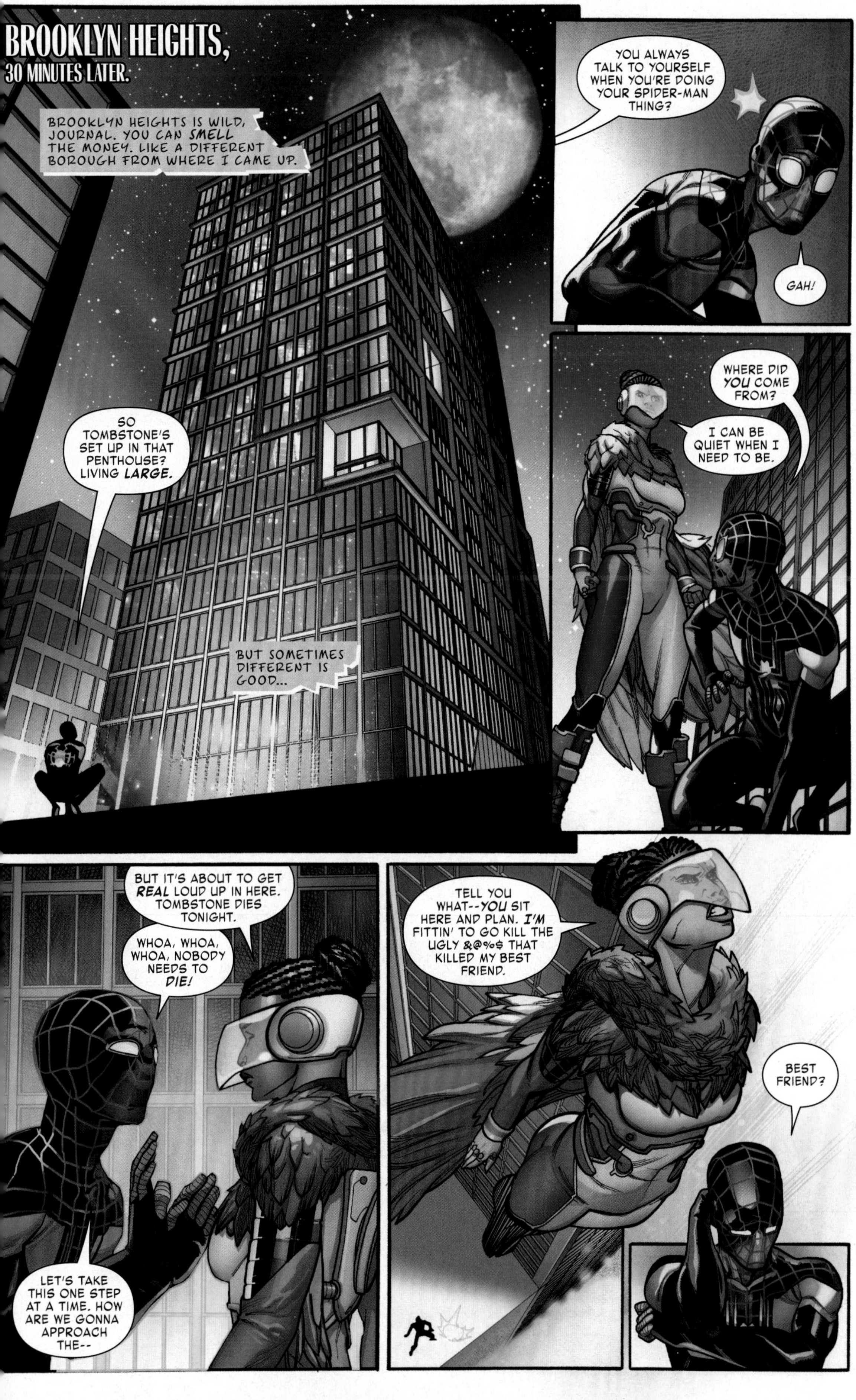
BROOKLYN HEIGHTS,
30 MINUTES LATER.
BROOKLYN HEIGHTS IS WILD, JOURNAL. YOU CAN SMELL THE MONEY. LIKE A DIFFERENT BOROUGH FROM WHERE I CAME UP.
SO TOMBSTONE'S SET UP IN THAT PENTHOUSE? LIVING LARGE.
BUT SOMETIMES DIFFERENT IS GOOD...
YOU ALWAYS TALK TO YOURSELF WHEN YOU'RE DOING YOUR SPIDER-MAN THING?
GAH!
WHERE DID YOU COME FROM?
I CAN BE QUIET WHEN I NEED TO BE.
BUT IT'S ABOUT TO GET REAL LOUD UP IN HERE. TOMBSTONE DIES TONIGHT.
WHOA, WHOA, WHOA, NOBODY NEEDS TO DIE!
LET'S TAKE THIS ONE STEP AT A TIME. HOW ARE WE GONNA APPROACH THE--
TELL YOU WHAT--YOU SIT HERE AND PLAN. I'M FITTIN' TO GO KILL THE UGLY &@%$ THAT KILLED MY BEST FRIEND.
BEST FRIEND?

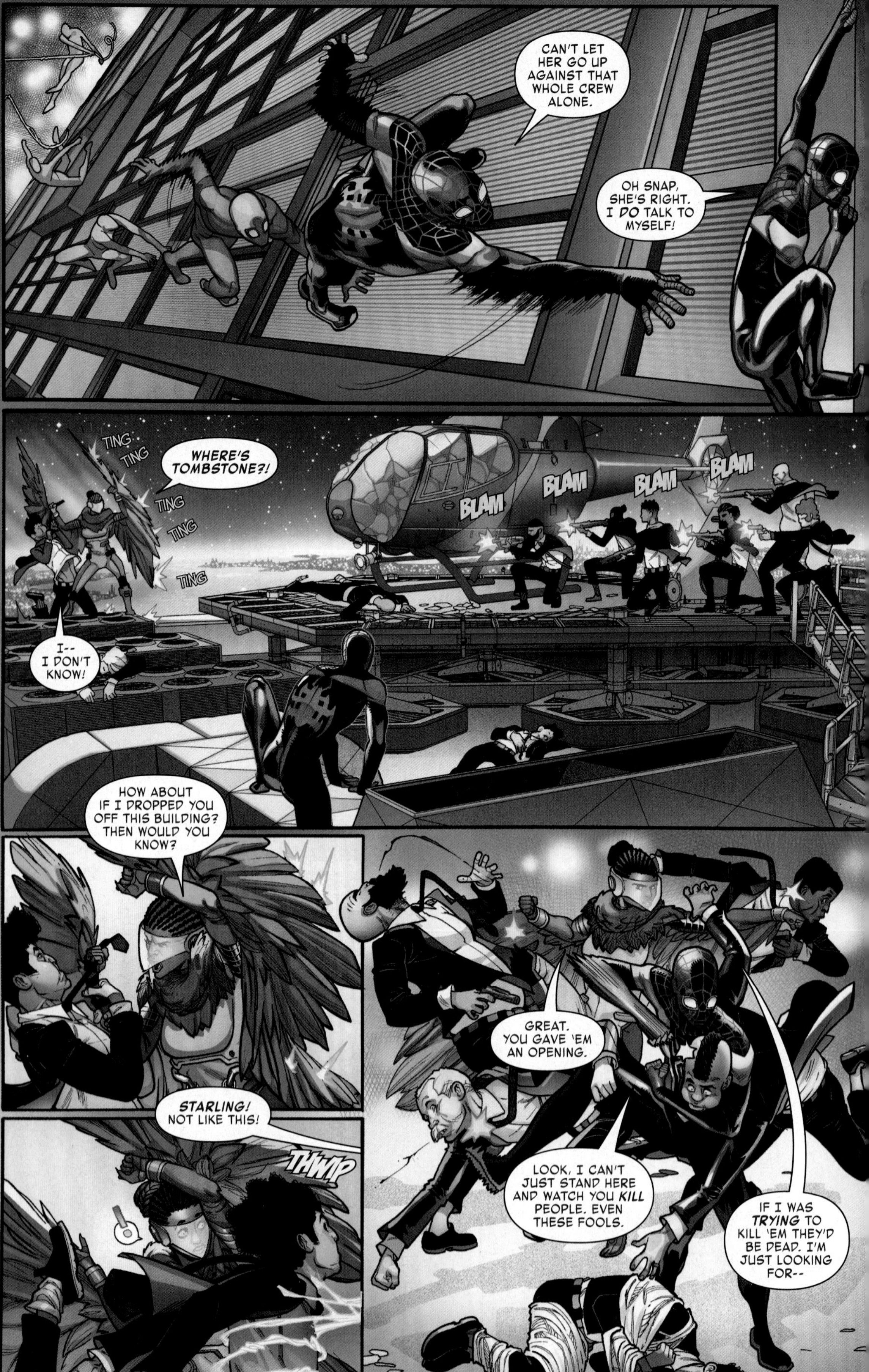
CAN'T LET HER GO UP AGAINST THAT WHOLE CREW ALONE.
OH SNAP, SHE'S RIGHT. I *DO* TALK TO MYSELF!
TING
TING
WHERE'S TOMBSTONE?!
TING
TING
TING
BLAM
BLAM
BLAM
BLAM
I-- I DON'T KNOW!
HOW ABOUT IF I DROPPED YOU OFF THIS BUILDING? THEN WOULD YOU KNOW?
GREAT. YOU GAVE 'EM AN OPENING.
STARLING! NOT LIKE THIS!
THWIP
LOOK, I CAN'T JUST STAND HERE AND WATCH YOU *KILL* PEOPLE. EVEN THESE FOOLS.
IF I WAS *TRYING* TO KILL 'EM THEY'D BE DEAD. I'M JUST LOOKING FOR--

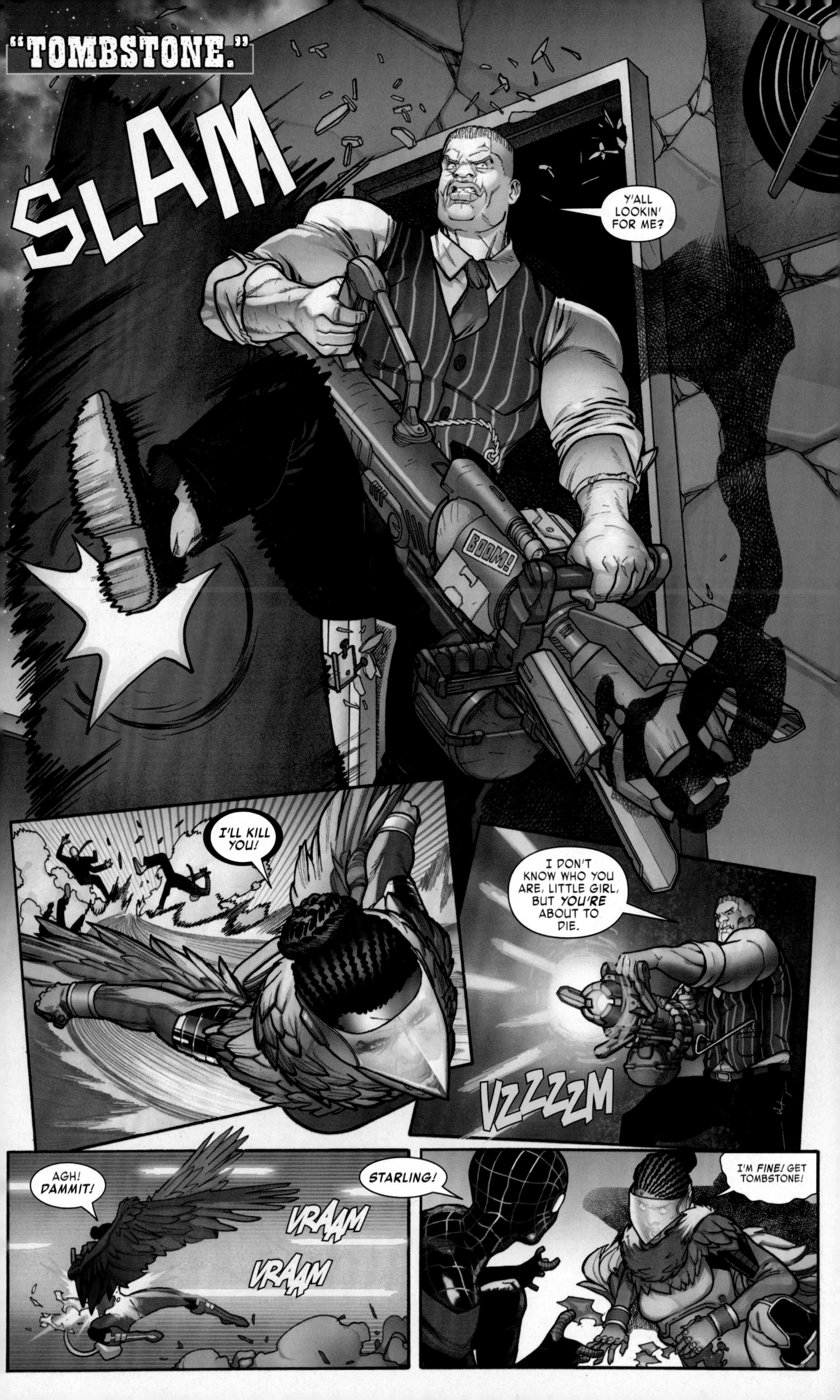
"TOMBSTONE."
SLAM
Y'ALL LOOKIN' FOR ME?
BOOM!
I'LL KILL YOU!
I DON'T KNOW WHO YOU ARE, LITTLE GIRL, BUT *YOU'RE* ABOUT TO DIE.
VZZZZM
AGH! *DAMMIT!*
VRAAM
VRAAM
STARLING!
I'M *FINE!* GET TOMBSTONE!

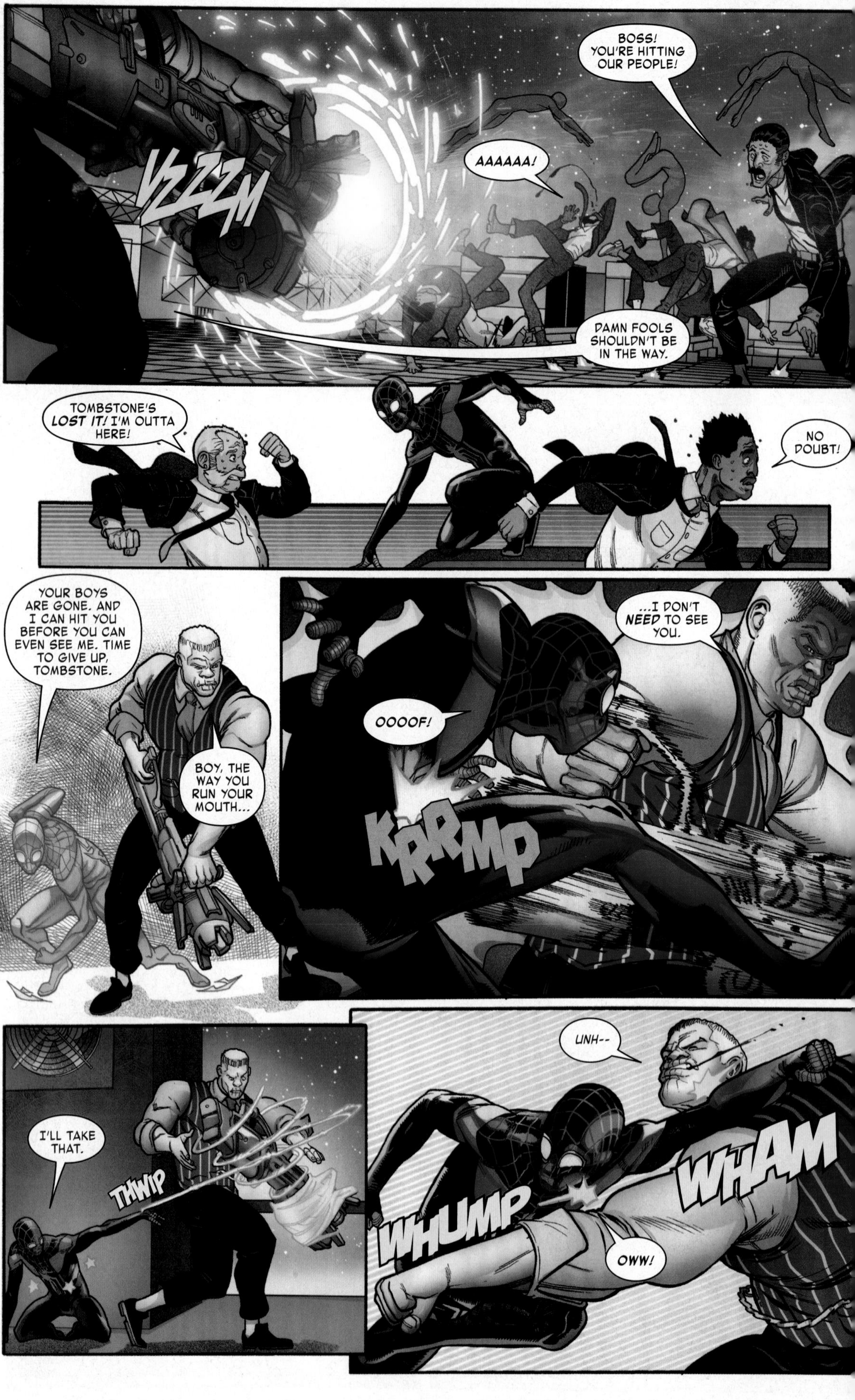
BOSS! YOU'RE HITTING OUR PEOPLE!
AAAAAA!
VZZZM
DAMN FOOLS SHOULDN'T BE IN THE WAY.
TOMBSTONE'S LOST IT! I'M OUTTA HERE!
NO DOUBT!
YOUR BOYS ARE GONE. AND I CAN HIT YOU BEFORE YOU CAN EVEN SEE ME. TIME TO GIVE UP, TOMBSTONE.
BOY, THE WAY YOU RUN YOUR MOUTH...
...I DON'T NEED TO SEE YOU.
OOOOF!
KRRMP
I'LL TAKE THAT.
THWIP
UNH--
WHAM
WHUMP
OWW!

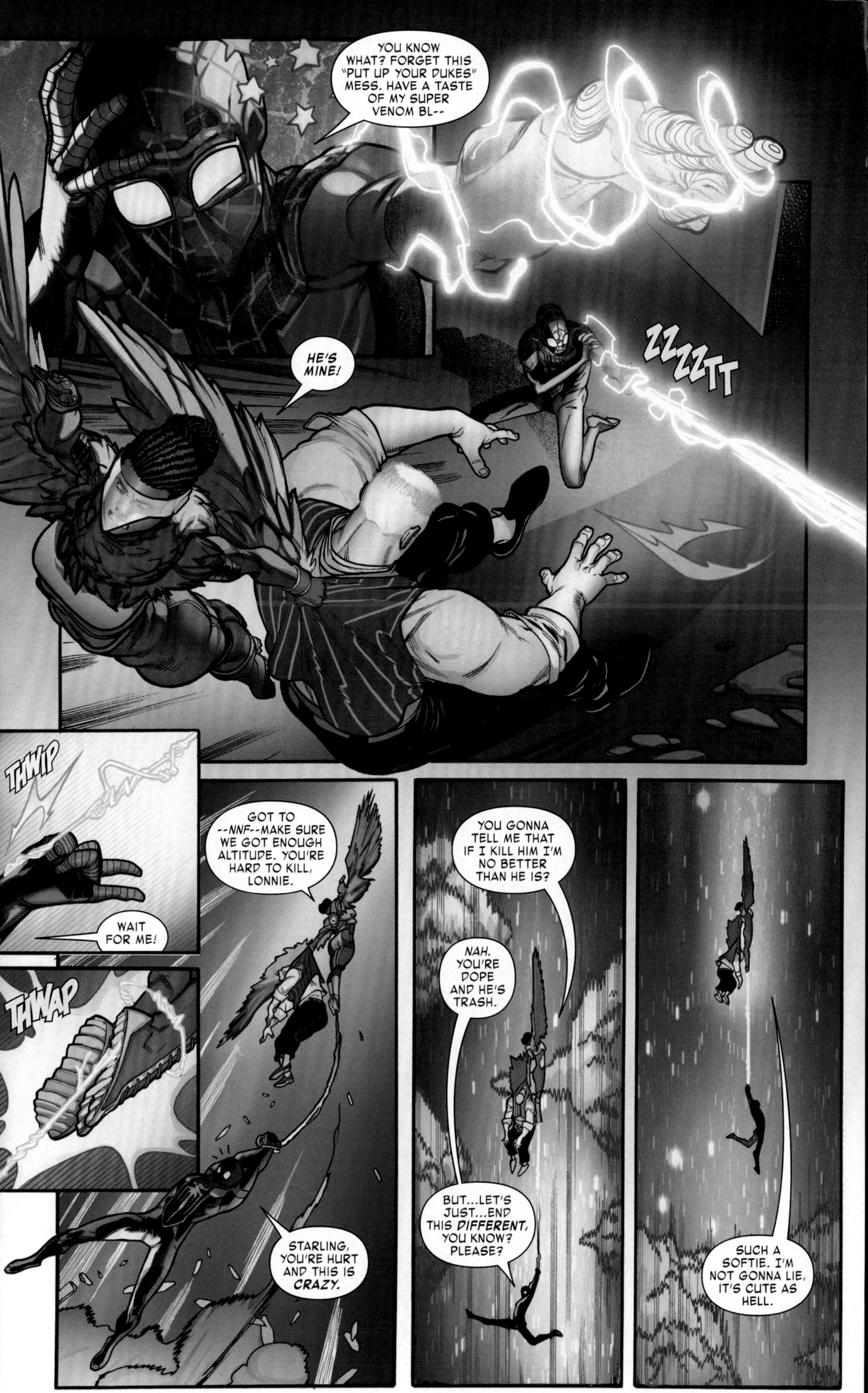

YOU KNOW WHAT? FORGET THIS "PUT UP YOUR DUKES" MESS. HAVE A TASTE OF MY SUPER VENOM BL--
ZZZZTT
HE'S MINE!
THWIP
WAIT FOR ME!
THWAP
GOT TO --NNF--MAKE SURE WE GOT ENOUGH ALTITUDE. YOU'RE HARD TO KILL, LONNIE.
STARLING, YOU'RE HURT AND THIS IS CRAZY.
YOU GONNA TELL ME THAT IF I KILL HIM I'M NO BETTER THAN HE IS?
NAH. YOU'RE DOPE AND HE'S TRASH.
BUT...LET'S JUST...END THIS DIFFERENT, YOU KNOW? PLEASE?
SUCH A SOFTIE. I'M NOT GONNA LIE, IT'S CUTE AS HELL.

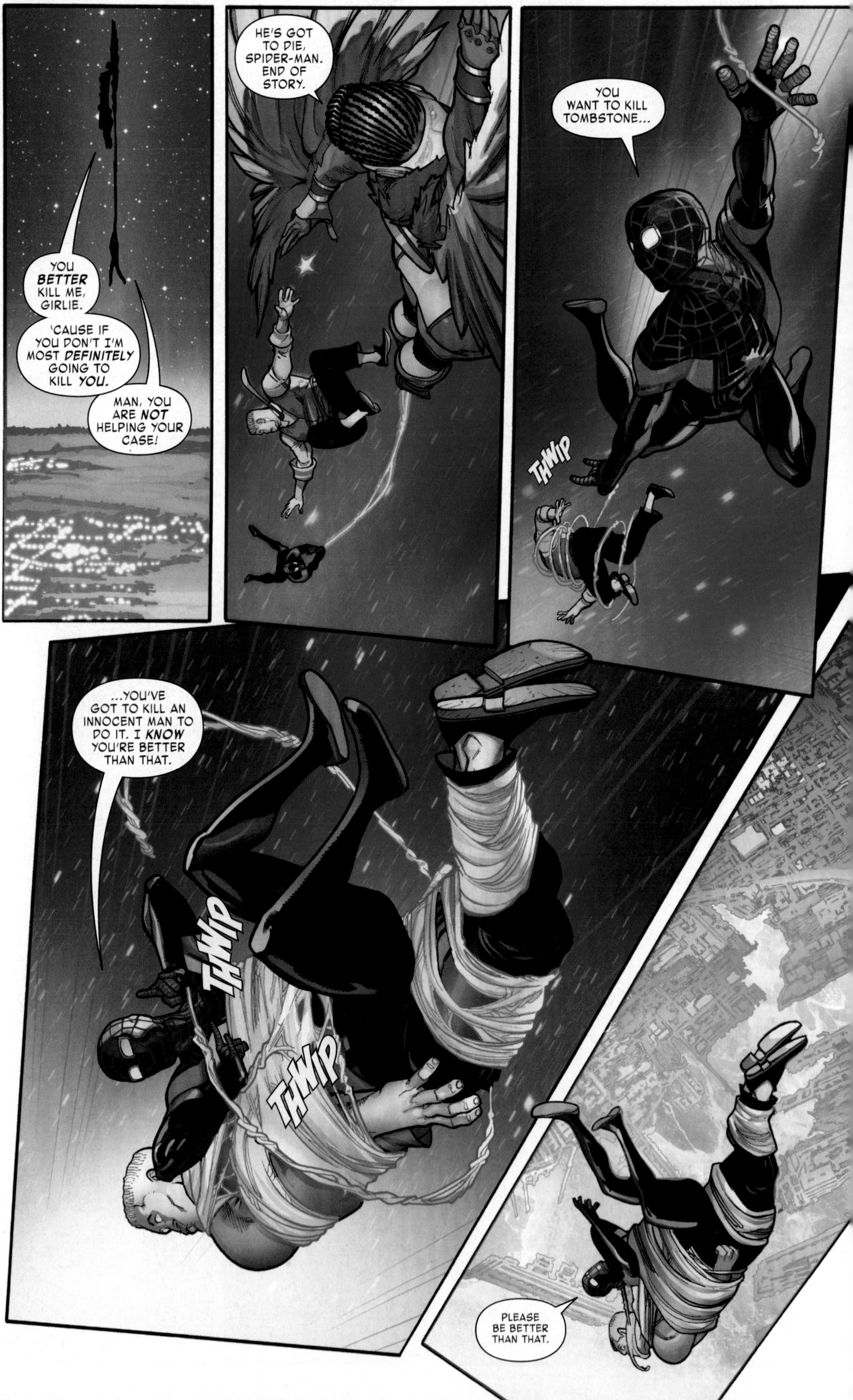

YOU BETTER KILL ME, GIRLIE.
'CAUSE IF YOU DON'T I'M MOST DEFINITELY GOING TO KILL YOU.
MAN, YOU ARE NOT HELPING YOUR CASE!
HE'S GOT TO DIE, SPIDER-MAN. END OF STORY.
YOU WANT TO KILL TOMBSTONE...
THWIP
...YOU'VE GOT TO KILL AN INNOCENT MAN TO DO IT. I KNOW YOU'RE BETTER THAN THAT.
THWIP
THWIP
PLEASE BE BETTER THAN THAT.

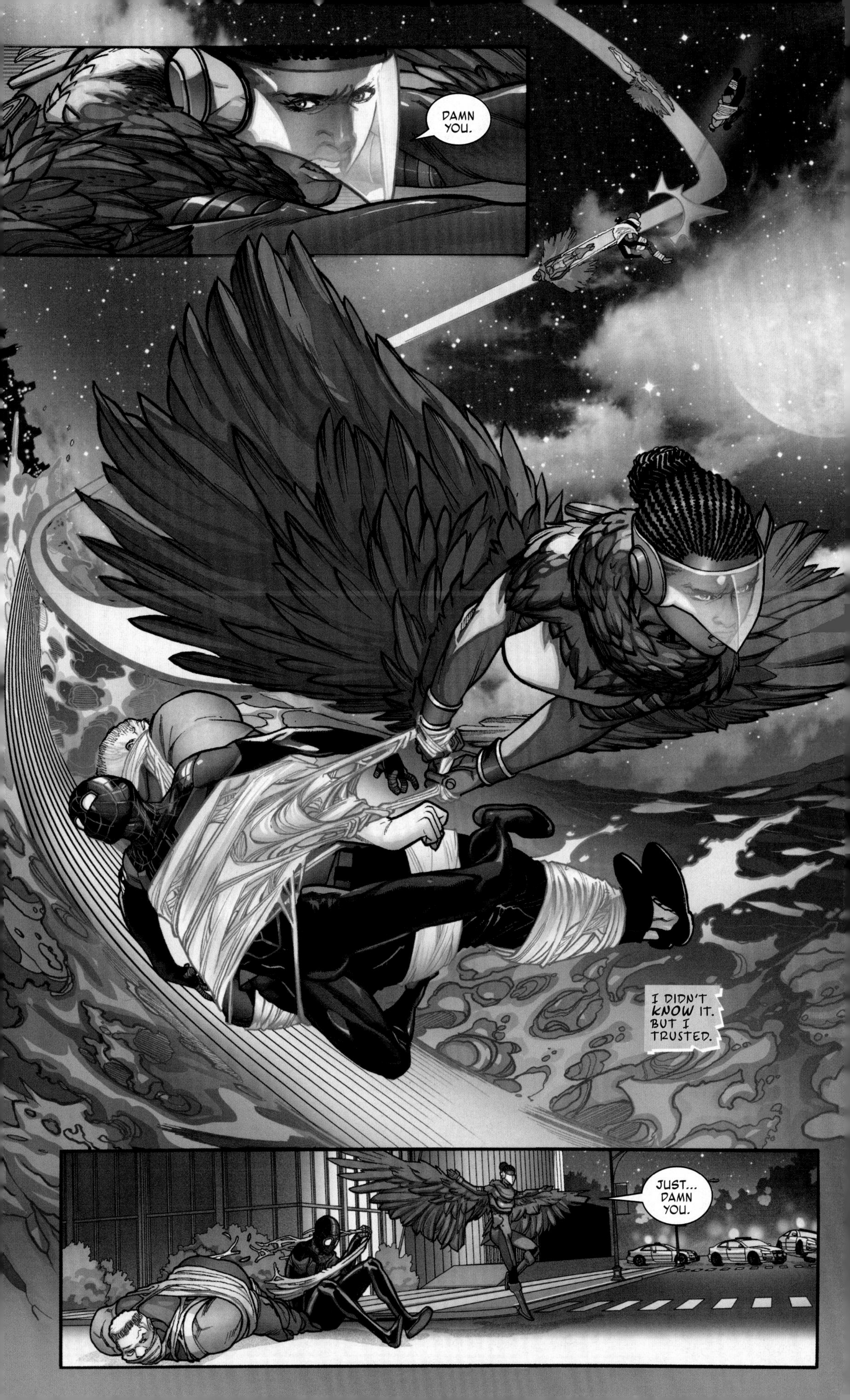
DAMN YOU.
I DIDN'T KNOW IT. BUT I TRUSTED.
JUST... DAMN YOU.

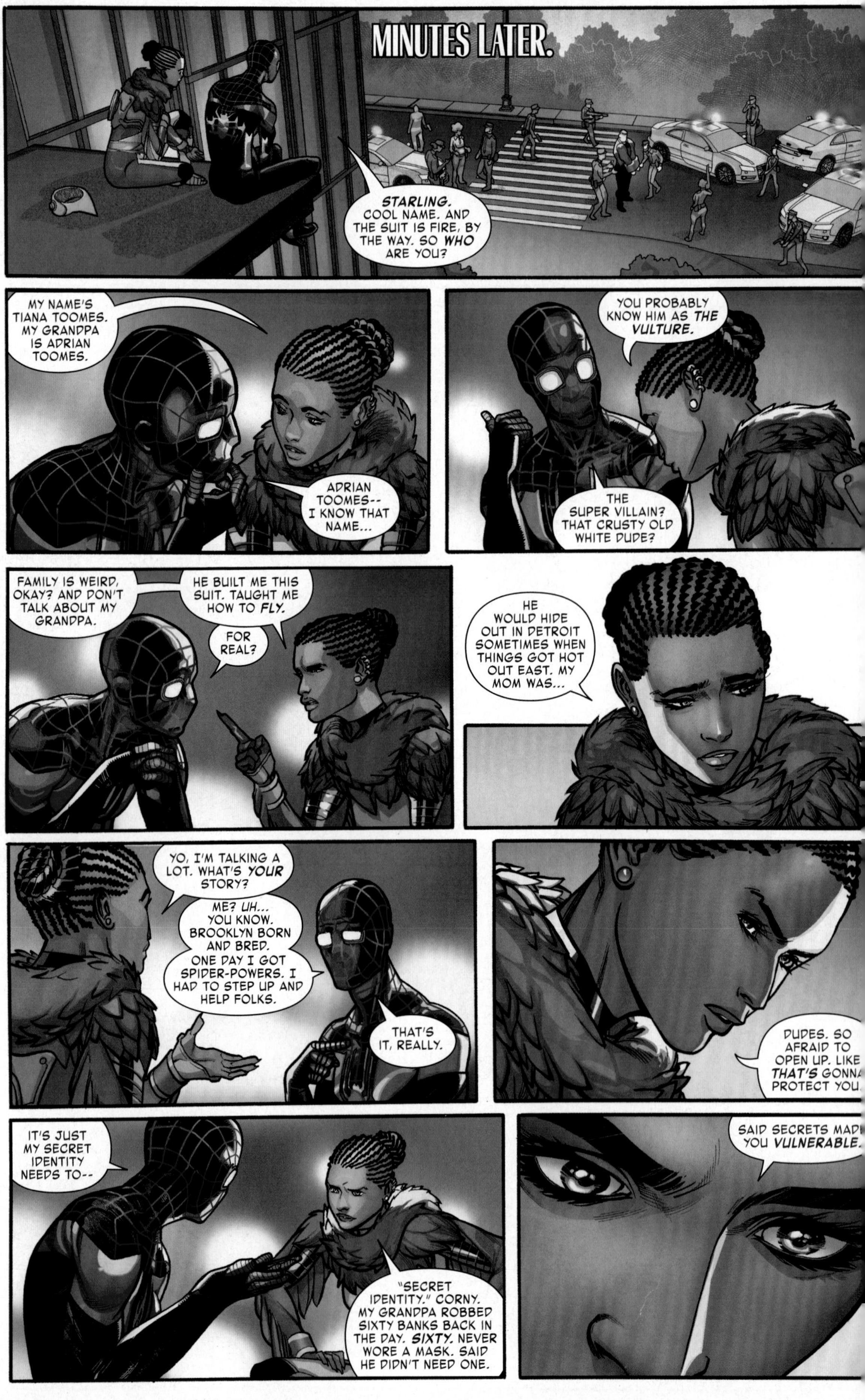
MINUTES LATER.
STARLING. COOL NAME. AND THE SUIT IS FIRE, BY THE WAY. SO WHO ARE YOU?
MY NAME'S TIANA TOOMES. MY GRANDPA IS ADRIAN TOOMES.
ADRIAN TOOMES-- I KNOW THAT NAME...
YOU PROBABLY KNOW HIM AS THE VULTURE.
THE SUPER VILLAIN? THAT CRUSTY OLD WHITE DUDE?
FAMILY IS WEIRD, OKAY? AND DON'T TALK ABOUT MY GRANDPA.
HE BUILT ME THIS SUIT. TAUGHT ME HOW TO FLY.
FOR REAL?
HE WOULD HIDE OUT IN DETROIT SOMETIMES WHEN THINGS GOT HOT OUT EAST. MY MOM WAS...
YO, I'M TALKING A LOT. WHAT'S YOUR STORY?
ME? UH... YOU KNOW. BROOKLYN BORN AND BRED. ONE DAY I GOT SPIDER-POWERS. I HAD TO STEP UP AND HELP FOLKS.
THAT'S IT, REALLY.
DUDES. SO AFRAID TO OPEN UP. LIKE THAT'S GONNA PROTECT YOU.
IT'S JUST MY SECRET IDENTITY NEEDS TO--
"SECRET IDENTITY." CORNY. MY GRANDPA ROBBED SIXTY BANKS BACK IN THE DAY. SIXTY. NEVER WORE A MASK. SAID HE DIDN'T NEED ONE.
SAID SECRETS MADE YOU VULNERABLE.

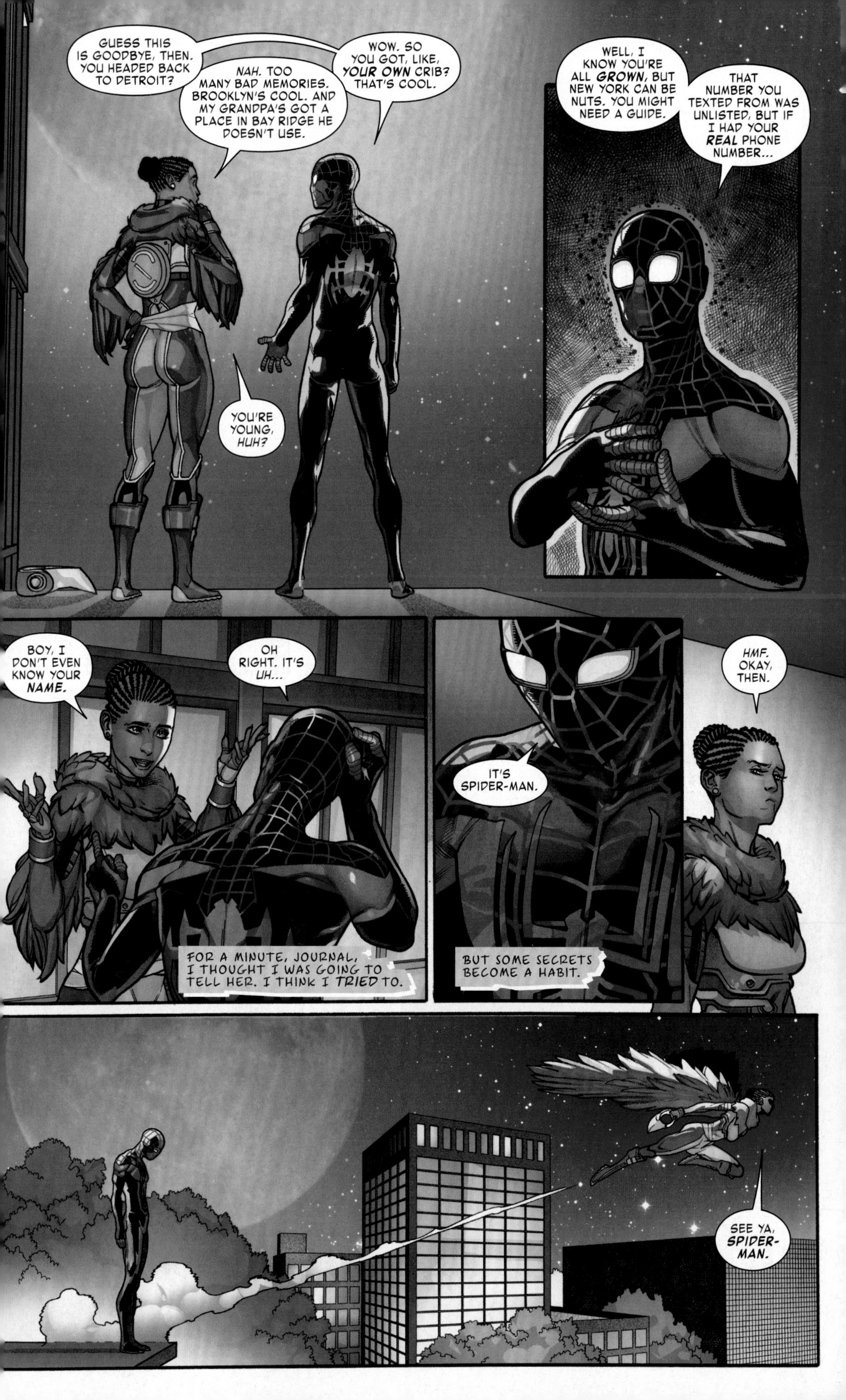
GUESS THIS IS GOODBYE, THEN. YOU HEADED BACK TO DETROIT?
NAH. TOO MANY BAD MEMORIES. BROOKLYN'S COOL. AND MY GRANDPA'S GOT A PLACE IN BAY RIDGE HE DOESN'T USE.
WOW. SO YOU GOT, LIKE, YOUR OWN CRIB? THAT'S COOL.
YOU'RE YOUNG, HUH?
WELL, I KNOW YOU'RE ALL GROWN, BUT NEW YORK CAN BE NUTS. YOU MIGHT NEED A GUIDE.
THAT NUMBER YOU TEXTED FROM WAS UNLISTED, BUT IF I HAD YOUR REAL PHONE NUMBER...
BOY, I DON'T EVEN KNOW YOUR NAME.
OH RIGHT. IT'S UH...
FOR A MINUTE, JOURNAL, I THOUGHT I WAS GOING TO TELL HER. I THINK I TRIED TO.
IT'S SPIDER-MAN.
HMF. OKAY, THEN.
BUT SOME SECRETS BECOME A HABIT.
SEE YA, SPIDER-MAN.

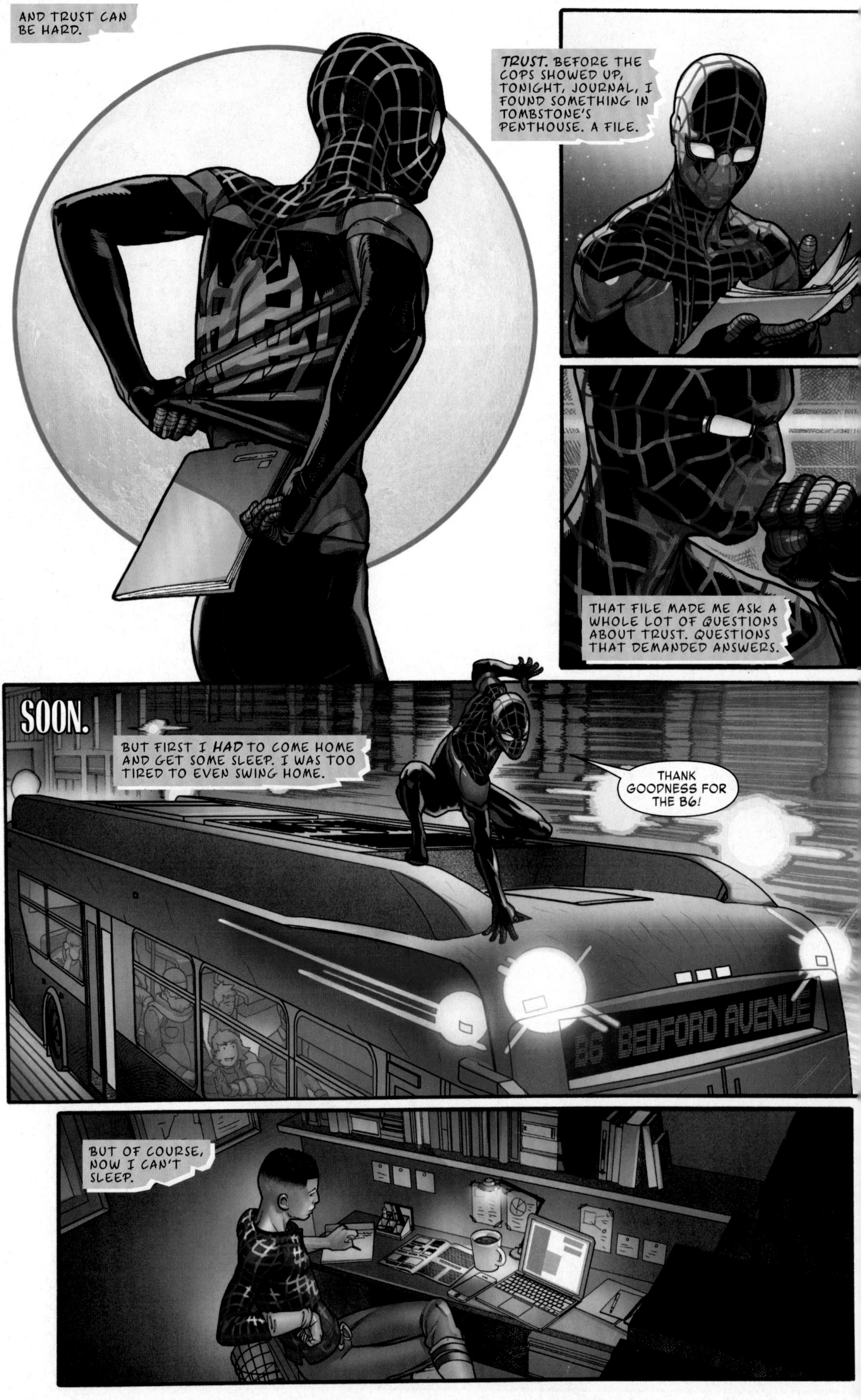
AND TRUST CAN BE HARD.
TRUST. BEFORE THE COPS SHOWED UP, TONIGHT, JOURNAL, I FOUND SOMETHING IN TOMBSTONE'S PENTHOUSE. A FILE.
THAT FILE MADE ME ASK A WHOLE LOT OF QUESTIONS ABOUT TRUST. QUESTIONS THAT DEMANDED ANSWERS.
SOON.
BUT FIRST I HAD TO COME HOME AND GET SOME SLEEP. I WAS TOO TIRED TO EVEN SWING HOME.
THANK GOODNESS FOR THE B6!
B6 BEDFORD AVENUE
BUT OF COURSE, NOW I CAN'T SLEEP.

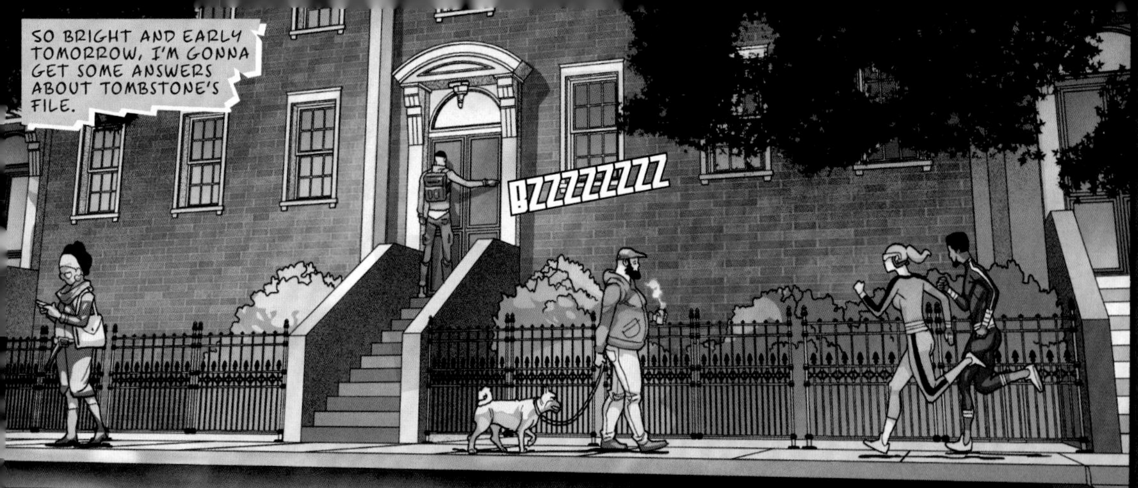
SO BRIGHT AND EARLY TOMORROW, I'M GONNA GET SOME ANSWERS ABOUT TOMBSTONE'S FILE.
BZZZZZZZZ

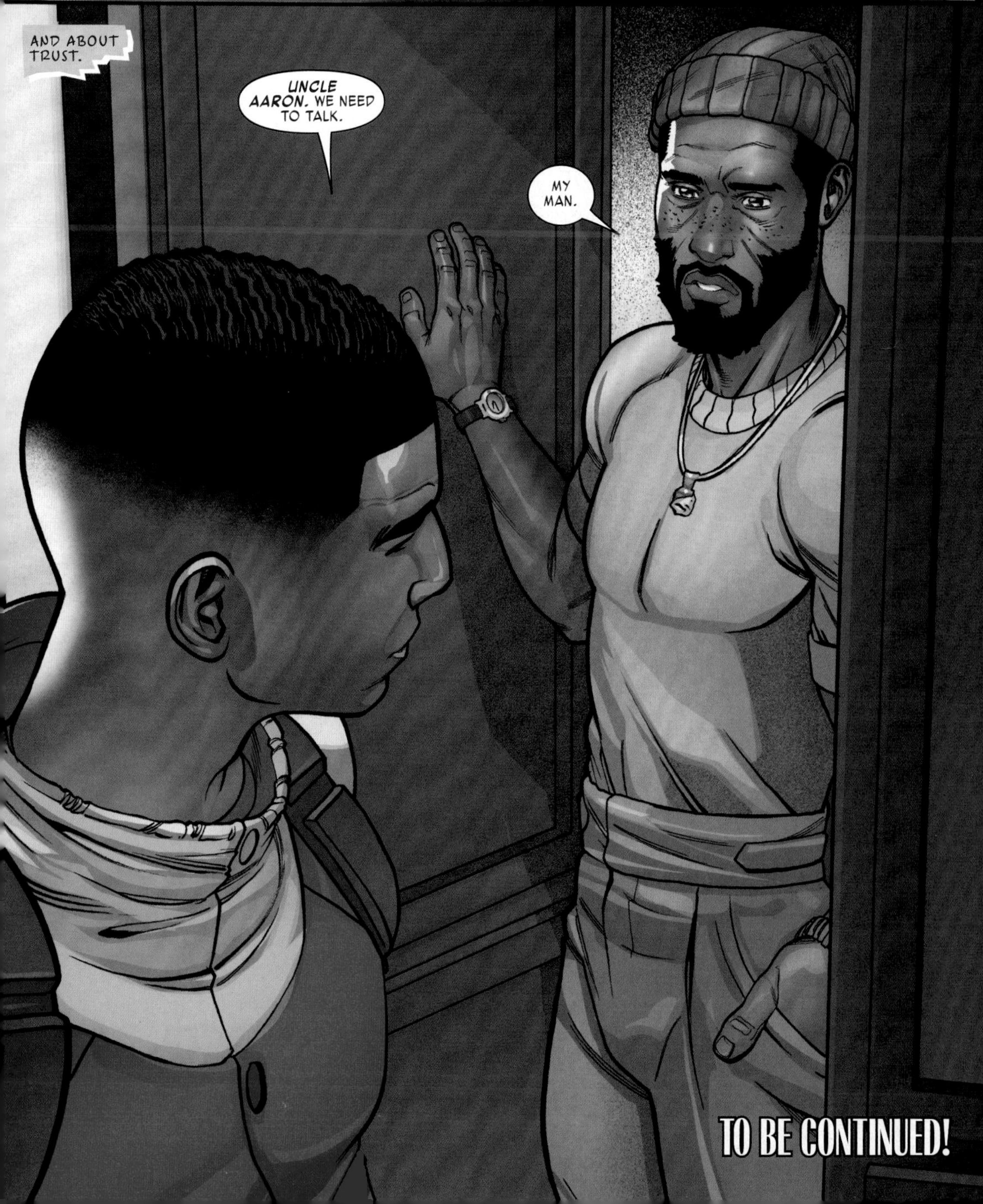
AND ABOUT TRUST.
UNCLE AARON. WE NEED TO TALK.
MY MAN.
TO BE CONTINUED!

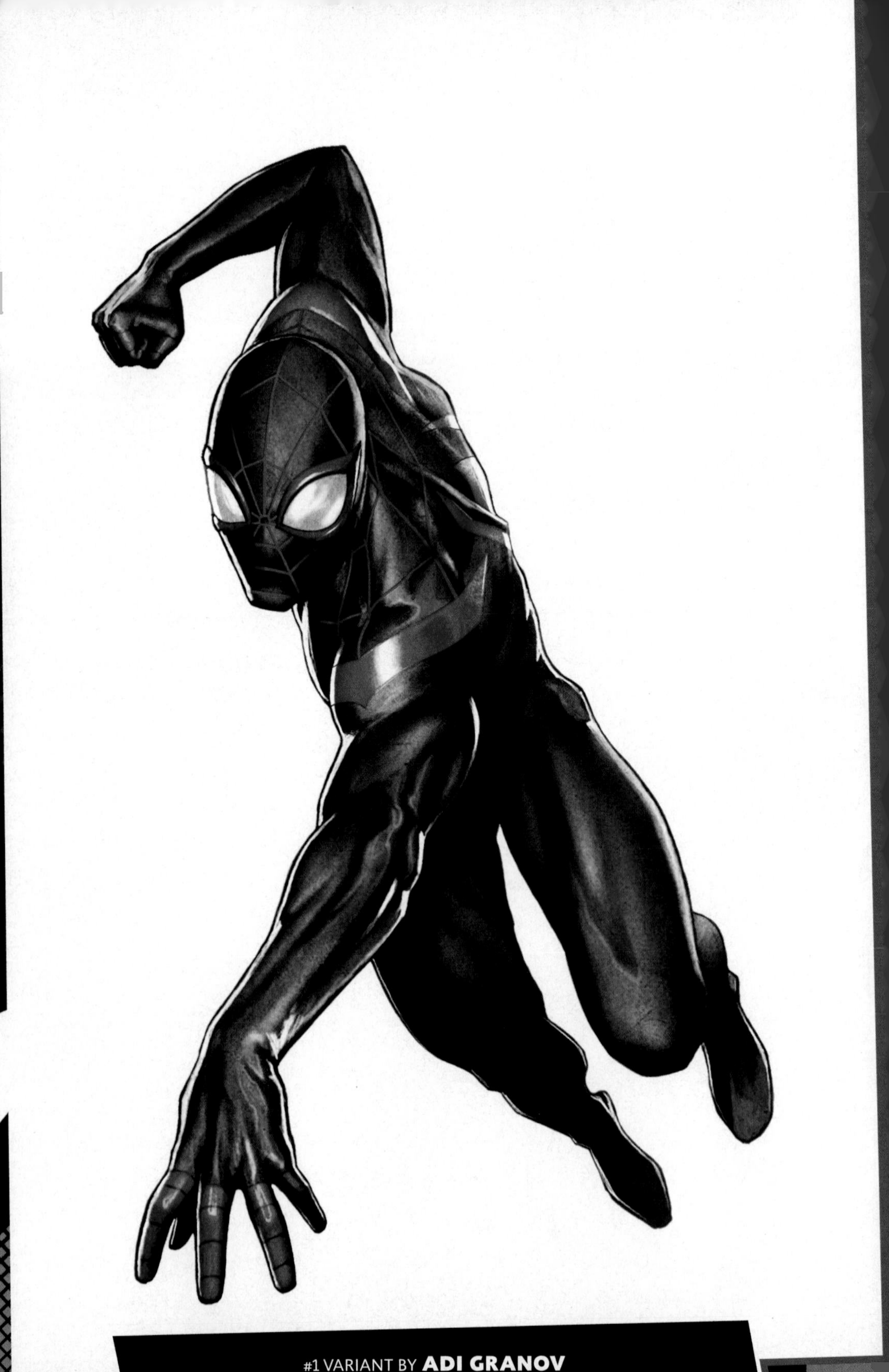

#1 VARIANT BY **ADI GRANOV**

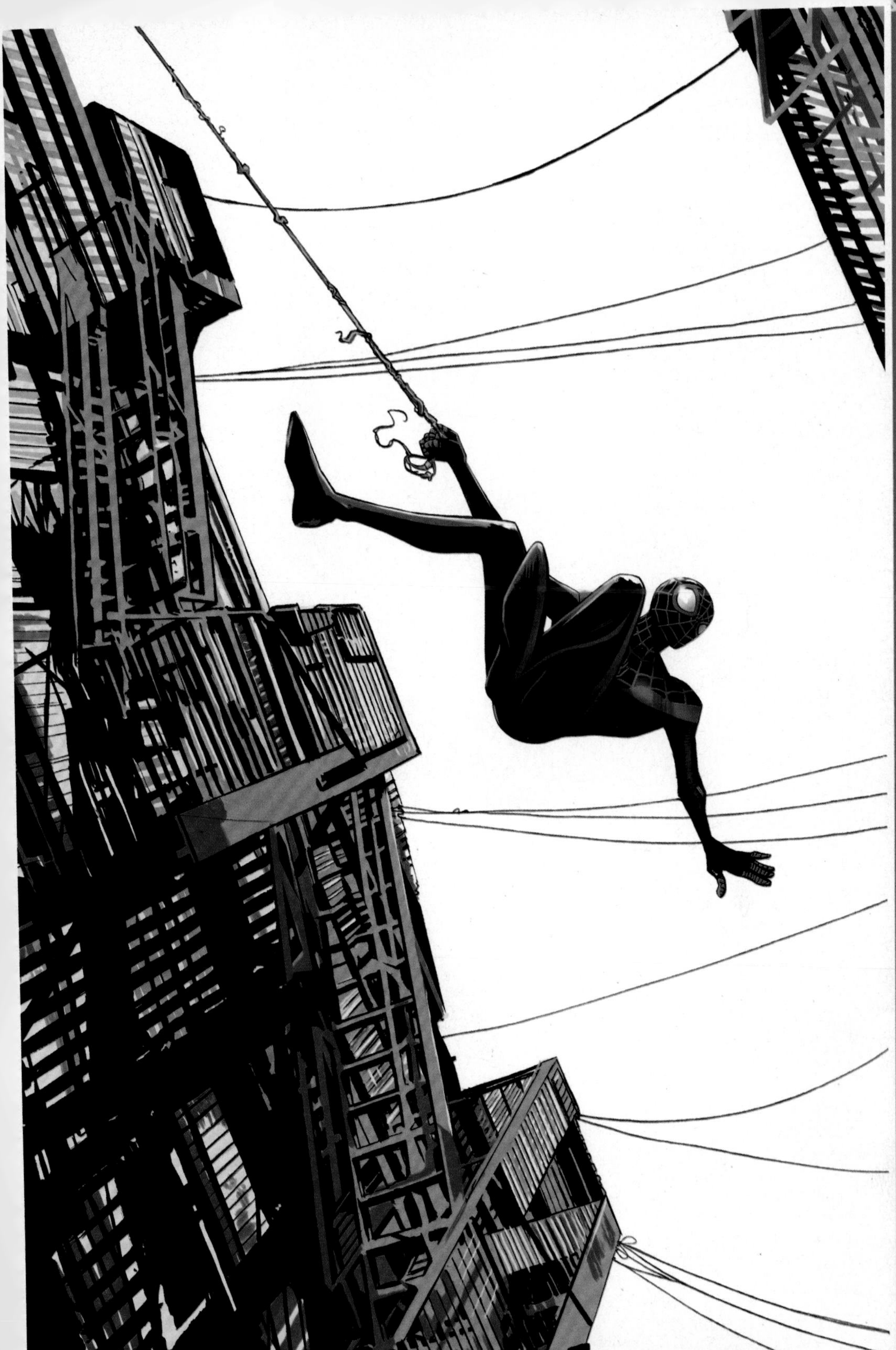

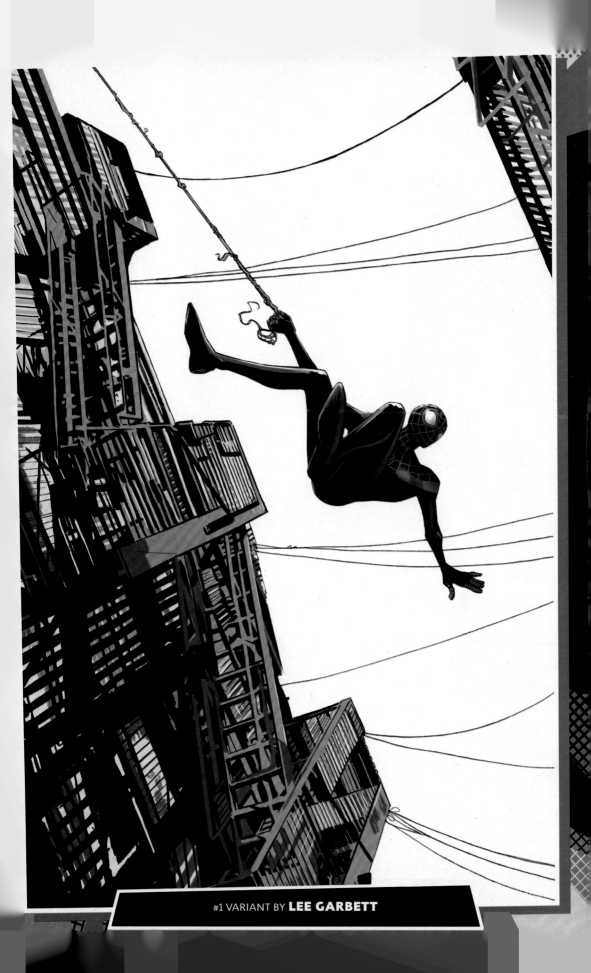

#1 VARIANT BY **LEE GARBETT**

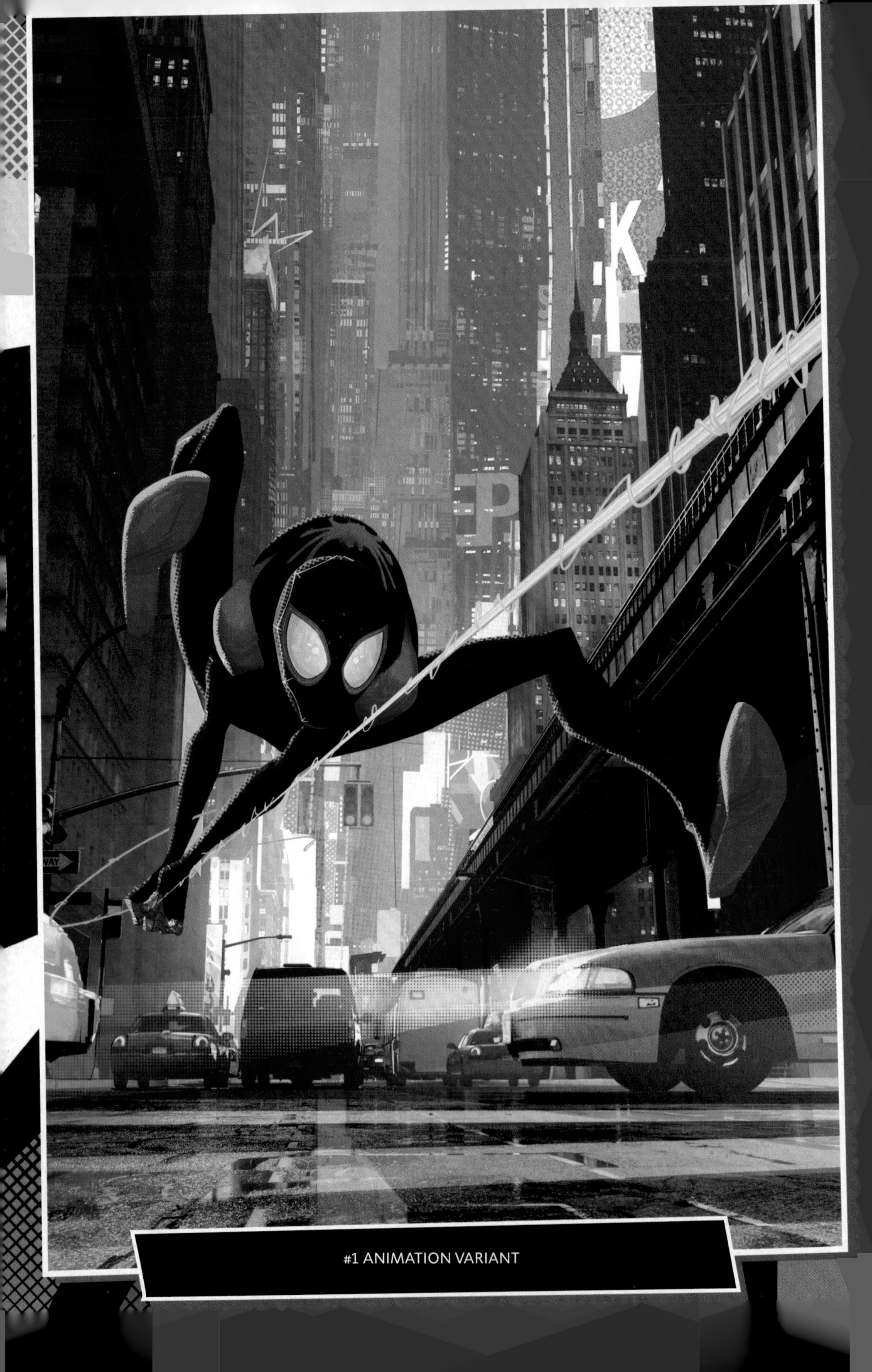
K
P
ONE WAY

#1 ANIMATION VARIANT

#2 VARIANT BY **SANA TAKEDA**

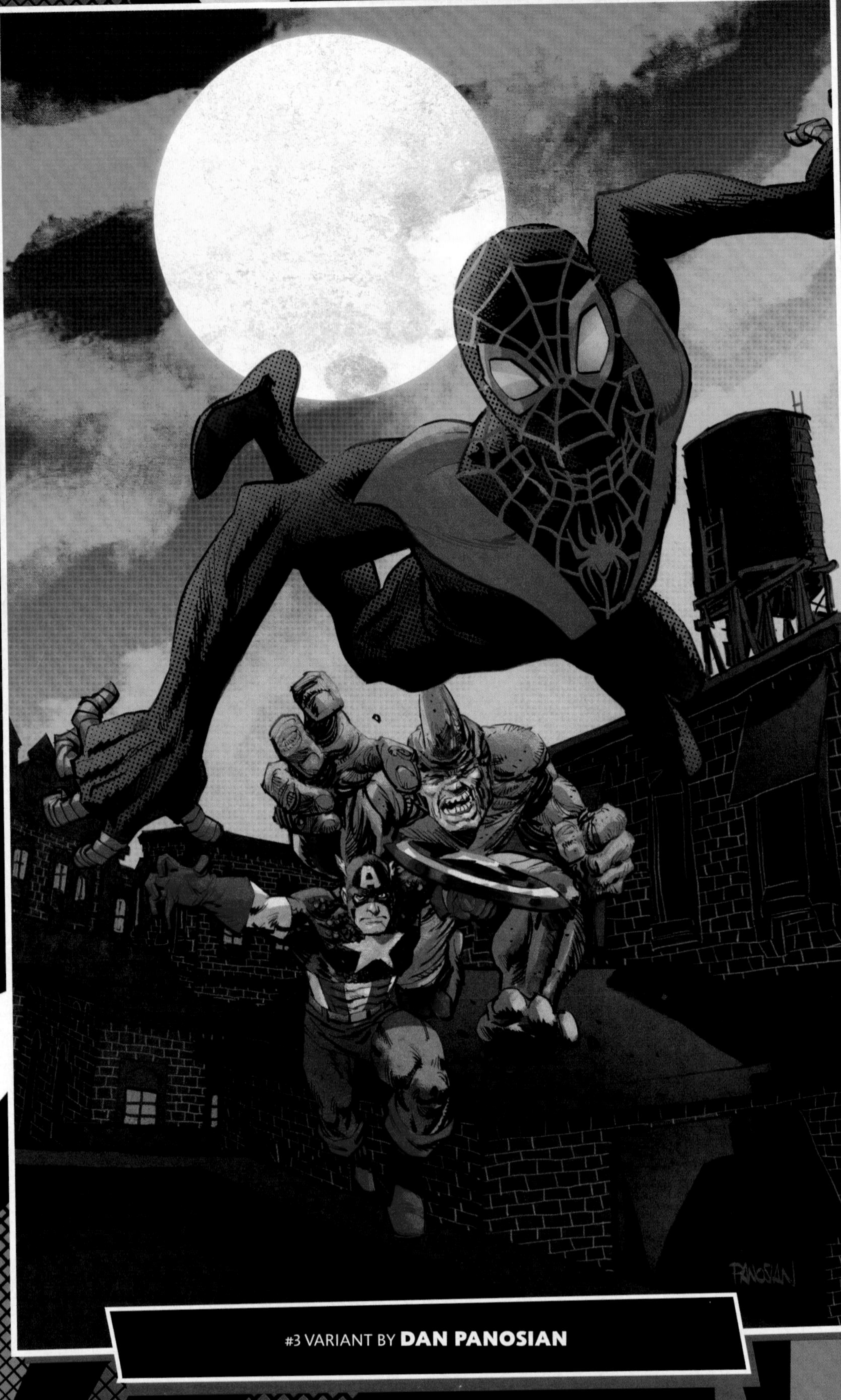
PANOSIAN

#3 VARIANT BY **DAN PANOSIAN**

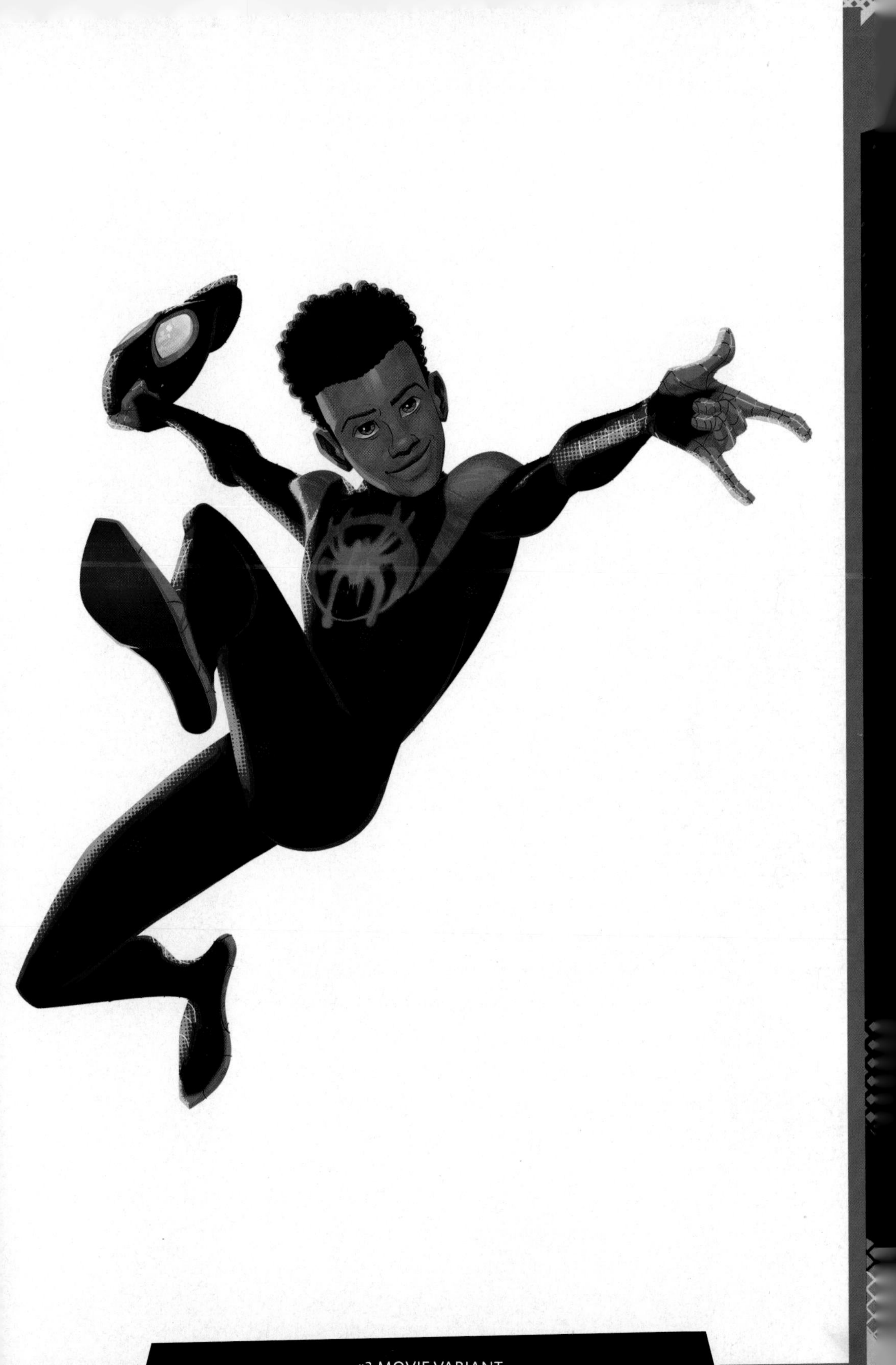

#3 MOVIE VARIANT

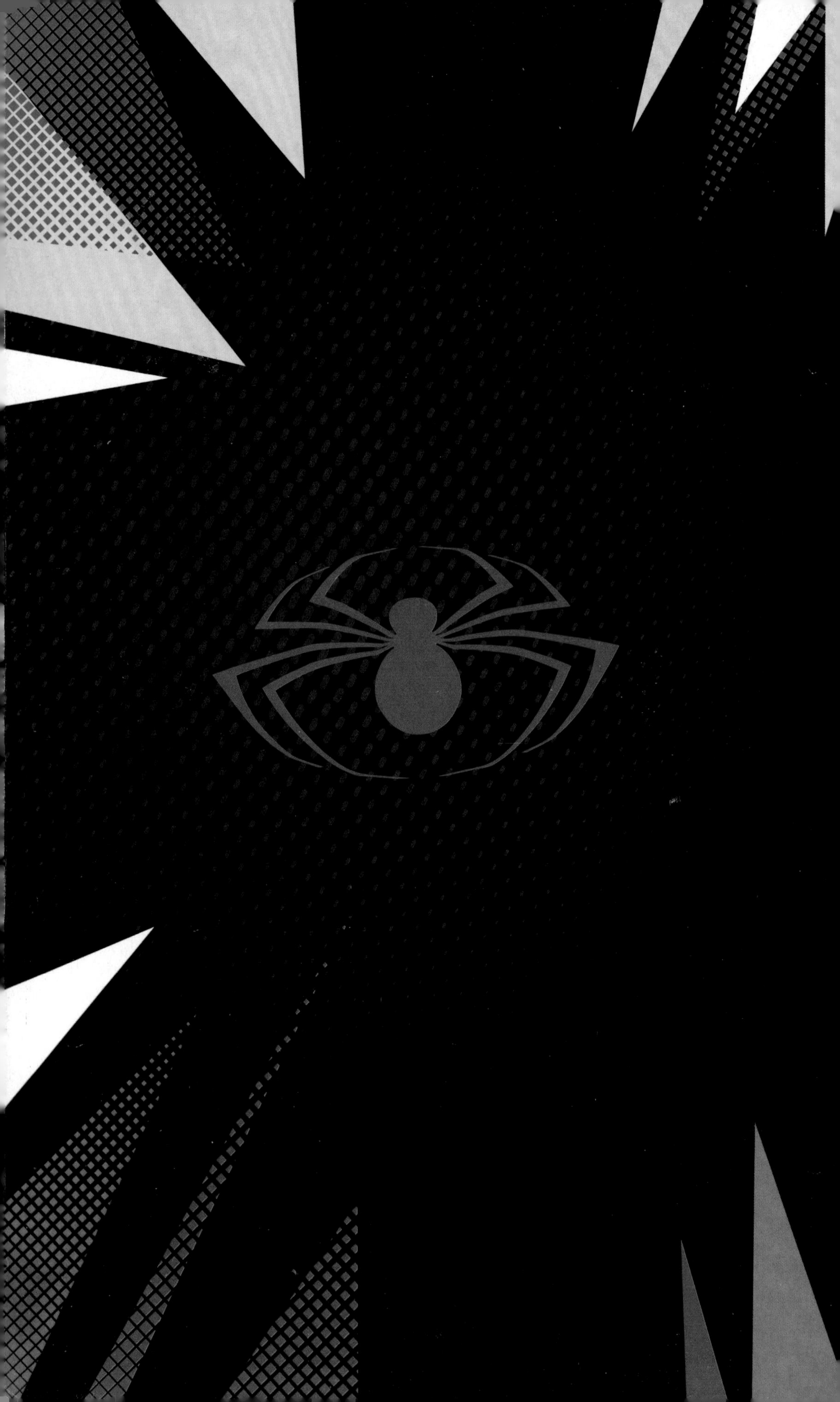